I0975158

Duecento

THE LATE MIDDLE AGES
IN ITALY

HÉLÈNE NOLTHENIUS

Duecento

THE LATE MIDDLE AGES
IN ITALY

WITH FORTY-EIGHT
MONOCHROME PLATES

NEW YORK
McGRAW-HILL BOOK COMPANY
MCMLXVIII

All Rights Reserved.

No part of this publication may be reproduced, stored in a retrieval system, or trans-
mitted, in any form or by any means,
electronic, mechanical, photocopying, re-
cording, or otherwise, without the prior
written permission of McGraw-Hill, Inc.

Library of Congress Catalog Card Number
66–28077

First Edition. 46875

This book was published in Dutch under the
title *D UECENTO, Zwerftocht door Italië's
late middeleeuwen* by Het Spectrum (Utrecht
and Antwerp), and in German under the
title *D UECENTO, hohes Mittelalter in
Italien* by Werkbund-Verlag (Würzburg).
The present translation was made from the
German edition, with reference to the Dutch;
the poems were translated from the Italian.

This translation © Darton, Longman &
Todd Ltd, 1968.

Printed in Great Britain.

Contents

Foreword

THIS IS the story of an age: an age that was a strange mixture of heaven and hell and which combined so characteristically the grace of youth with its boisterousness. Ideas old and new were fighting it out together. Popes and emperors were at war, cities and nations struggled with one another, ravaging tyrants roared through the land from north to south—and amid all the clash of arms there was the gentle music of the troubadours. Returning crusaders were begging their way home, lepers and prisoners and prophets went crying of their woes from one town to another—yet all the while the painters were covering the walls of chapels with their astonishing pictures. Here was the noise of battle, and there were the quiet songs, but everywhere was the memory of the smile of the beggar-saint.

This is Italy: Italy full of blood and blossom, as portrayed in the old chronicles, the frescoes and the songs of seven hundred years ago; Italy as she still is today, with her bare mountains and her sweltering plains, with her olive trees and oxen, and her little grey towns on the hilltops, Orvieto and Cortona, Spello, Todi and Assisi. Untouched by the changing centuries her walls and towers stand, the same bells still summon the people through the narrow streets. The *podestà* still rides amid the fluttering flags, and it seems as if it were still the barefoot Francis who is preaching in the piazza by the fountain.

How shall we evoke this living past? Mere facts and figures from the chronicles are not enough: they are but the materials for an epic. Many learned books have been written, and were it not for the researches of the historians, none of us could discover the treasures of the past. But once we have been led to them, we find that they are alive: songs never die, and the lilt of their words and melodies live with us today as do the silent witnesses of stones and paint.

List of Plates

Introduction

Abbrevio mei ditta,
Longhezza breve scritta.

Now brief be my reciting,
And short my longest writing.

Jacopone da Todi.[1]

LONG AGO, the Latins had become the lords of Italy. They had defeated the Samnites and the Etruscans and had begun to build up Rome, the *Urbs*. They had driven out the Gauls and Carthaginians and had brought the Teutons to their knees. Gradually they had conquered the world, but gradually their character had changed: security and ease had altered them: their rulers now were not consuls but emperors, it was no longer the soldier and worker who were important, but the politicians, no longer the hard-working peasant, but the corrupt tradesman. But then the Empire, with all its power and glory, collapsed: the barbarians of the north were no longer to be held. Yet beneath the ruins of that first Rome, in crypts and catacombs, lay the seed of another Rome, whose spiritual lordship within a thousand years was to wield a power from the Lateran and Vatican as great as the power of arms from the Capitol and Palatine. And thus Christian Rome grew out of the soil of Italy: Italy, with all her wars and trafficking, was to have the privilege of bearing the Easter light of Rome and to shed much blood to defend it. Vandals, Huns, Goths and Lombards came in successive waves to attack her; her own lords and knights fought one another to gain control; and all the time the popes and 'Fathers of the Church' were quietly writing down their wisdom for posterity. Rome remains, though churches and palaces rise and fall within her walls, and saints and sinners go their way. St Benedict planted his monasteries like seeds throughout Italy and they became the focus of many wonders. Four hundred years later his monks were marrying and wasting monastic property. Bishops in Oriental festive garb caroused through the nights with their feasting; by day they went hunting with falcons upon their anointed hands. No wonder, for their popes had become the plaything of the nobility and the prize of worldly business. Legend, with its unique woman pope, Joan, is more moderate than the facts: the mothers, nieces and mistresses who pressed in around the Holy See like hyenas upon their prey.

Finally in the eleventh century healing came from Cluny: at last a real ruler mounted St Peter's Chair: Hildebrand the monk. He could be stern with others, because he was stern with himself. But he came at a moment when a new struggle was just beginning: two great powers, Church and State, were both claiming sovereignty, and this began to eclipse all other problems in Church and State alike. As the struggle approached its climax a new century dawned that was destined to be a period both of glory and corruption, the period we know as the *Duecento*, the thirteenth century.

This century is like a gryphon with both wings and claws, like a mythical creature half saint and half beast, and it is only gradually that we are beginning to see both sides of the picture. The Middle Ages are now no longer dismissed as dark and ignorant, nor yet exalted as if peopled only by saints.[2] For it is the two qualities together that provide the power of the Pre-Renaissance.

One of the last sayings of the great Huizinga was the assertion that the medieval achievement of the West, in all that is great and beautiful, must be seen as a whole and the contribution of each land examined in turn.[3]

What was this achievement? It would seem that Art, Reason and Holiness preside like three graces over this century, and their light still shines today. But there were horrors also: the three furies of Injustice, Cruelty and Hatred have their part and damaged the foundations of that century as much as the three graces adorned it. Yet history brings us consolation, for surely the three graces prevailed. So much of our vision we owe to Dante, our thought is still being trained by Aquinas, and Francis still warms our hearts today, while the nameless terrors of that violent age only reach us now like the faint echo of a storm long past.

In spite of the advice of the learned historian from Leiden, we will here confine our attention to Italy. Certainly alongside Francis from Umbria there was Dominic from Spain, Anthony from Portugal and St Louis of France; unquestionably the learning of Oxford or of the Sorbonne was not inferior to that of Bologna, and cathedrals were rising throughout Christendom at the same time as the basilica on the hillside of Assisi; the minstrels were at home in France long before they ever were in Sicily or in Tuscany. But in no other land, we think, was the thirteenth century so important, or its effect so startling, as in Italy. Nowhere else was the thirteenth century the meeting point of two worlds, the interregnum between the Middle Ages and the Renaissance; for here not only historical events but the characters of men look both ways: the Emperor Frederick, St Francis, and almost all the poets and painters of Tuscany. Nowhere else did so distinctive a culture rise out of this collision of two worlds as here in the small independent communities, each of which began to weave together the elements of the past and of the future into a new pattern. On the one hand they clung to their old traditions, their ancient symbols and legends, while on the other hand they were full of the new spirit of adventure, enquiry and criticism, which was coming into conflict with the piety of the past. Their rulers were at once tyrants and philosophers, now consulting their magicians in matters of government, now uttering hard and realistic theories, which though presented in solemn manifestoes in antique style were more influenced by Arabic rationalism than by the traditions of the West. Many of the painters, though still professing allegiance to the principles of the Byzantines, were abandoning the anonymity of the Middle Ages, and next to the traditional Madonnas and angels, with large tranquil eyes, they were painting modern saints in the new individual style. The poets still wrote allegories and learned disputations as before, but they were beginning to use the vernacular instead of Latin and to leave the impress of their own personality upon their work in a way that no Italian writer had dared or been able to do before. This was the milieu in which the poet grew up who, on the model of the Latin Aeneid but now in his own Tuscan tongue, wrote his account of his journey through the nether world, and who when describing the mystical joy of Paradise did not hesitate to invoke Apollo.

But what of the other lands? The balance of the opposing forces is in no way so marked. Northern Germany was still buried in its forests, and emperors and spiritual lords were powerless before their vassals and the robber-knights. Even where the land was no longer pagan, where the Cistercians fought and began to settle, the inhabitants were still barbarians. In south Germany the first minstrels had appeared, and their songs have an irresistible charm: the charm of the childlike, embarrassed, a little uncouth; but what else could be expected from a vernacular so recently come into being. For even Dante describes his own learned and rich idiom as a language of mere children, 'who are able to say no more than Mama and Papa'.[4]

England could in some places look back to a richer past, but on the throne were ne'er-do-wells or adventurers: Richard, in whose lion-heart there was more room for poetry than for politics, and his brother John, lacking in understanding and honour as he was lacking in land. Later came the more energetic Edward I, with his strong sense of legislation, but although the schools of Oxford were renowned and many monasteries were centres of great learning, it would be another hundred years before the humanism of the Continent could reach English shores.

Spain is too much soaked in Arabic culture to count as a European type of the medieval mind—with all due respect for the brilliant achievements of the court of Alphonso the Wise. The same applies to the vestiges of Latin culture on the Bosphorus.

But then there is France. Wherever Italy outstrips the others, France is there before her. France had a start of many years over the rest of Europe, and she was already looking back over a rich cultural tradition when the newcomers around her had as yet no past behind them. She was well acquainted with war: a large area was under English rule and Provence was crippled by the Albigensian struggle. But the businesslike Blanche was able to present her saintly son Louis with a well-organised state, and the *esprit gaulois* began to extend its influence on every side. Paris was a centre of theology long before Rome and indulged a passion for philosophical speculation with a kind of precocious maturity that characterises the whole period. The art of miniature had spent itself and the refinement of romanesque was fading before a bored public, and both poetry and song show traces of decadence. The seed of 'the great' and 'the beautiful' had been sown in France long ago and the harvest was now home. In these things the twelfth century was for France as revolutionary as the thirteenth was for Italy. But on the other hand the classical renaissance never overtook the Franks as quickly as it overtook the successors of Cicero and Virgil south of the Alps. In fact, it hardly reached France until the fourteenth century, by which time the new age was fully established in Italy. In the thirteenth century the culture of France was altogether more settled and mature than was that of Italy, and for this very reason lacks the enthusiasm and drive which came to the fore so rapidly in the Italian *Duecento* and gave it so capital an importance.

The children of the European family made up a restless household, so different were their origins and background. The core of their world was still small. Hungary, Scandinavia and Pomerania were recently converted, suspect, and scarcely counted; in Swabia, Brandenburg and Prussia there were still heathens; and of Africa and Asia beyond the Mediterranean hardly anything was known in 1200. But the spirit of adventure and discovery was beginning: travellers returned from Tartary and China, missionaries were converting the Wends and the

Balts, business deals were being done everywhere between Scotland and Asia Minor; and then there was always the crusading adventure. But by the thirteenth century that high ideal of former days, when France was leading that first real Christian international movement with the cry *Deus le volt*, had become almost meaningless. Only with the greatest difficulty did the papal emissaries get a handful of crusaders from the cities, and they often had to be tempted by indulgences.[5] The utter failure of the organisation, when pilgrims got lost or fell among robbers or succumbed to the plague by the thousands, is not to be explained merely by the ignorance or foolish confidence of the people, but, in fact, by lack of interest in the thing on the part of the management. So little had been gained in the Holy Land, and anyway the crusades had long ago lost their novelty. 'This passion, at once chivalrous and devout, had by now become something quite unpractical in Europe', says Gregorovius.[6] Jerusalem was no longer seen as the object of heroic conquest, but as an occasion for negotiating with the formerly terrible Saracens. The leader of the crusade was excommunicated, and the Church was working against him. The Holy City itself, moreover, did not stay long in Western hands, and when at the end of the century Acre fell, the glorious age of the crusades was finished for ever. Pilgrimage had become piracy, the Templars and the Order of St John had grown weak, and with the culture of the Levant many diseases of the Levant were also brought home. Henceforth anyone who wanted to fight the Muslims could do so more effectively, and much nearer home, in Spain, where the saintly Ferdinand of Castile was spending his whole life trying to drive out the Moors from Cordova and Seville. Here at least there were some results to show: in 1236 Christendom rejoiced to see the bells carried on Moorish shoulders from the mosque of Cordova to Santiago de Compostela, whence two and a half centuries before they had been stolen by Almanzor. Finally, the hatred of the Saracens had become meaningless, since no immediate danger threatened from that quarter. Instead it was the Mongols who were the real danger, and all the forces of Europe were called out against them. But 'Holy Wars' no longer held any appeal: there had been too many of them, they had been preached too often, now against heretics, now against rebels, and most attractively against the Holy Roman Emperor. Since the time of Charlemagne the lords of the north had been coming south with their armies and bringing back culture and an imperial crown. Whatever the intentions of the Ottos of Saxony or the Henrys of Swabia, when they came to Rome with outstretched hands, be it to beg or to threaten, they were seldom strong enough to get their way: the time had not come for the struggle to become international. This first happened when the Hohenstaufen Frederick came on the scene: Barbarossa roared through the land, and both his military power and his devotion to the crusade reduced Christ's Vicar to silence. A quarter-century later a second Frederick brought Rome still nearer the danger zone: for he was not only German Emperor but also ruler of the Two Sicilies; thus gradually the struggle between Church and State began to involve everyone. Although the battles were fought in Italy and Germany, the other countries soon became heavily committed. It was a matter of balance of power: the lords of France, Spain, Holland and Sweden were placed in the field for this or that party alternately, and the Germans temporarily checked, then their old adversaries—the French—appeared on the scene in order to take their place as leaders of the opposition. There were innumerable facets to this conflict: an awakening nationalism played its part, as did also commercial interests and not least personal enmities, as in the time of that fierce old man Gregory IX. It cannot be denied that the struggle has all the appearances of a very earthly struggle for power, in which neither side had more spiritual motives than the other. Yet there is something of heaven and earth on both sides. The German quarrels about investiture were only a pretext: the true conflict lay much deeper. It is nearly as old as sin itself, it is the conflict between nature and supernature, carried through into the conflict between Church and State with all its consequences. Which power is supreme? For a long time the two swords in Luke 22 had been seen as symbols of the two powers, and for that reason, when both swords came to be wielded, there was seldom agreement. On the one hand, the papacy was called the sun, which gives light to the moon that is the Empire, since God's representative has the right to dispense power on earth. On the other hand, the Emperor Frederick II with equal passion represented the free and divine origin of the secular State, in virtue of which he could free the Church, which is a purely spiritual power, from all earthly possessions and political concern, and set himself upon the throne as the secular counterpart of the Pope. Thus it was that the age-old dispute became for the first time an open conflict between two carefully thought out ideas, of which one belongs mainly to the world of the Middle Ages, while the other belongs to the Renaissance. It was this deep division that caused the conflict to assume forms of an intensity and complexity that have no parallel outside thirteenth-century Italy, where the two ages meet.

Salute manda, lo tu' buon Martini,
Berto Rinier, de la putente Mangna.
Sacci, ch'i' ò cambiati i grechi fini
al la cervugia fracida bevangna,

e le gran sale e' nobili giardini
a mosche, a neve e al loto di montangna,
la buona usança de li panni lini
ch' usar solea chon voi e la champangna.

Ben puo' far beffe di mia vita fella,
che spesse volte siem sença tovagla;
sette siem che mangiam per iscodella

e non avem manti per asciugagla,
asciughiamci al gheron de la gonella
quando no' siam ben unti di sevagla.

Berto Rinier, Martini sends you greeting,
   Your good friend writes from Germany which stinks.
D'you know, there's no more good Greek food for eating,
   And all they have is rotten beer for drinks.

Just think of our big rooms and gardens, seating
   Full company of friends for our high jinks,
With neat white tablecloths at every meeting—
   While here of flies, mud, snow is all one thinks.

Laugh, if you will; for my good living flatter
   Me; tablecloths are rare enough out here,
There's seven of us feeding at one platter,

   And napkins? Oh, no need for that, my dear,
We wipe our fingers on our clothes, no matter,
   They're stiff with grease and won't mind one more smear.

Cecco Angiolieri of Siena[1]

1

The Teutons

EVERY NORTHERN traveller approaching Italy should pause when he comes to the Alps. Millions of them have done so before. Here the northern pilgrim looked forward past the snowclad mountains to the magic of the south, and here he looked back at the last traces of the familiar northern things. It might be one of those little towns on the banks of the infant Rhine. This is a river he knows. The roofs are still high-pitched as in the north, and the churches still have their little steeples. This is the land where he still hears a northern dialect, the language of Notker of St Gallen. And here are the great south German abbeys: Reichenau, for instance, still there on its midstream island in the Rhine for the traveller of today to see, if he has time to pause.

Reichenau was a centre of Christian culture in the tenth century. This was the home of the learned Strabo and of Berno the musician, here the library had gathered all the wisdom of the world. Here Hermann the Lame wrote the *Salve Regina*. Here in the abbey church the 'Sequences' were heard at Mass—so shocking to the traditionalists of the chant. It was also here, amid the surrounding hills, that Caesarius of Heisterbach was born.

After this pause let the traveller take the road to Rome. He has for company the crowds of northern pilgrims, the groups of solemn German lords on their way to an emperor's coronation, the scattered hungry scholars; they have all come this way. They have all had the experience of the impact of the classical land upon their simple northern minds. Now they may speed over the passes or dive through the tunnels, and no longer need they beg their board at the hospices along the way; but the impact is the same. The northerner often looks patronisingly on these carefree sons of the south; but the road to Rome always goes past Canossa. . . . Here and there are remains of heavy German castles, built to subjugate the land, but now they lie in ruins while the graceful Roman buildings stand. Tanks and jeeps may roar along the Via Appia, but eventually the northerners have always humbly had to bow.

It was not only a desire for conquest that brought the Teutons south; nor it was merely a genuine veneration for the Pope of Rome. Yet every northern visitor has somewhere hidden away a feeling of inferiority, a curious mixture of love and resentment towards that land which, even if they sacked it and left hardly a stone standing in many villages, still reminded them they were barbarians. In a world which glories in its broken pillars and ruined palaces, one more ruin, caused by the invaders of the Middle Ages or of today, is of small consequence.

The northern visitor, pilgrim or warrior, from the time of Alaric the Destroyer, has always come to Italy agog for the wonders he has heard of from visitors who were before him. He has always somehow felt that he must go there. After all, were not the German Kaisers the legitimate successors of the Roman Caesars? By the end of the twelfth century there had emerged two focal points, belonging to two different worlds: the one in Rome where the Pope was, and the other in the remote and mysterious island of Sicily. Bishop Conrad of Hildesheim wrote home about it.[2] Beyond Naples, the bewitched city, impregnable since Virgil the Magician had bewitched it, lies the great kingdom, the navel of the world. Beyond Scylla and Charybdis, still viciously alive, is the mighty Trinacria. Here the terrible Cyclops as of old spews out his fury through the mouth of Etna, and Arethusa never ceases to moan about the rape of Proserpine. There is gold here, as much as anyone desires; and silken cloth and precious stones—did they not once bring a hundred and fifty mule-loads of these back to Germany? And this was but a minute fraction of the treasure of the palace of Palermo. There beggars could live like princes and people

learned the black arts effortlessly: for everywhere it was possible
to find Arabs who were skilled in these things. Small wonder,
then, that Wolfram of Eschenbach's *Parzifal* found his magic
castle in Sicily, or that the royal child of Sicily and Germany,
born in 1194, was surrounded by legends from the day of his
birth: Frederick II of Hohenstaufen, '*das chint von Pulle*' (the
child of Apulia).

A century and a half before his birth twelve bold knights
knocked at the door of a Sicilian palace and offered their
services to the local lord, who was a Greek. The knights were
brothers, sons of Count Tancred the Norman, who had sent
them out to find their fortunes. And this indeed they did;
before long they had driven out the Saracens and then, having
fallen out with their Greek friend and driven him out too, they
took possession of the whole of South Italy: Sicily itself as well
as Apulia and Calabria. The first duke was Robert Guiscard
'the cunning', a broad-shouldered blond warrior, whose war
cry alone (so a Byzantine princess tells us, with a mixture of
admiration and fear)[3] could put to flight an army of sixty
thousand men. He was a skilful ruler and remained on good
terms with the Pope, his overlord. But when his great-niece,
Princess Constanza, married a German prince, the whole of
Europe was startled and there were many furrowed brows at
the papal court, for the union of the German Empire with the
Sicilian lands (that is, everything south of the papal states)
meant that the Pope in his *patrimonium* was completely surrounded. As it happened, Constanza's young husband, Henry,
died suddenly, but the union of north and south had been
effected. For Germany itself there followed an unhappy period
of internal strife: the Saxons and the Hohenstaufen struggled
for the leadership, to which neither had any serious claim.
Princes and bishops fought one another, and war, plague and
interdict brought misery to the land. There were those who
had visions of Dietrich of Bern rising from his grave and,
mounting a ghostly horse, riding through the Mosel valley,
bewailing the fate of Germany.[4]

In far-off Palermo, however, a fatherless child was growing

up, the orphan son of Henry and Constanza. His names were prophetic: Frederick after his grandfather Barbarossa, and Roger after the wild Norman who subjugated the south. The mass of legends which surrounded his birth at least show how he was regarded by the rest of Europe. As ruler of the united Empire, the biggest state in the West, for some he was the Lord's Anointed, while for others none other than Antichrist. One story was that his mother was a nun, who had been released from her vows in order to contract that disastrous German marriage.[5] According to another story she was not a nun, but a sour old maid, whose brothers were glad to get rid of her to Prince Henry. But her father had desired otherwise, for he had seen prophetically the misery she would bring to Italy, and on his deathbed he had bound them by oath not to let her marry; but they forgot their oath in their eagerness to get rid of this tiresome creature.[6] Yet another story tells that she was already advanced in years when she married: at least thirty, and forty when Frederick was born, and everyone thought she was past child-bearing, and consequently doubts were raised about whether he was really her child at all, although she had proposed (the story continues) to silence evil tongues by giving birth to him publicly in the market place at Melfi[7]—a feature that reappears in the later mystery plays about the mother of Antichrist. There was also a story about his father, that Frederick was not the child of Henry but of a certain butcher of Jesi, but Frederick always refused to give an answer when questioned about it, and this evidence of silence was taken by some as certain proof.[8] But at the same time Frederick grew up to be such a typical Hohenstaufen and such a born ruler that the truth about his origins seems plain enough.

This extraordinary man completely overshadows the other leaders of his time, and his contemporaries did not have the means at our disposal today of assessing his character: they simply called him Antichrist, when we should see him as a realist. Perhaps a person of such a sceptical turn of mind would have fitted more easily into almost any period of history than into the romantic *Duecento*. But since men make history, and history also makes men, it is possible to attempt to explain the 'phenomenon of Frederick' by reference to his German, Norman and Italian descent and to the situation of the country in which he was brought up. Both elements represent a highly international background, where a mixture of races and cultures readily give birth to a character of remarkable originality and genius.

One only has to go south of Naples off the main roads to find oneself outside Europe: cave dwellings and the characteristic *trulli*, half Moorish square white houses, complete with animals and ragged children, with the tall palms rising into the merciless blue sky with its burning sun, women as shy as they are in the East, and dialects that have scarcely anything in common with Italian. But this same land, once fabulously wealthy, was for centuries sought out by foreigners as a paradise. In Frederick's time it was a wooded land, with streams and fertile fields, and palm trees shading the mosques and palaces. The women went veiled, and the population was a mixture of Arabs, Jews, Negroes, Greeks, Germans, Normans, Spaniards, and of course, Italians.

The many races which came to Sicily, like the sailors on the lotus isle, seemed soon to forget their wars and their homeland, be it as far as Byzantium or Normandy, and settled here, peopling the pleasant coastland which surrounds the rugged interior and developing the towns: Palermo with its natural harbour, Syracuse with its natural fortress on the peninsula, long claimed by Pisa, and Monreale with its hill sanctuary which grew up in Arab, Norman and Byzantine styles. Every culture could find a home here, and still in 1270 municipal decrees were published in four languages: Latin, Greek, Arabic and Hebrew—not yet in Italian.[9]

This was the background of Frederick's childhood, and his guardians, sometimes a German and sometimes a pope, apparently gave him little attention, for no one seemed seriously to think of him as an heir to the throne. There was little comfort or even adequate provision for him in the tumbledown castle, so that (if we are to believe the chronicles) some kind-hearted citizens took it in turn to look after the boy, and the future 'Stupor Mundi' spent most of his childhood on the streets. Doubtless it was there that he began to learn the nine languages which it was later said that he knew.[10] At the age of thirteen he was a mature, cynical and rather unruly young man, Western by education and by faith, Western in his ambition to occupy his father's throne, but Oriental in his love of the wisdom and realism of the East and his admiration of the spirit of the Quran. These Eastern influences were powerful factors in the formation of his character, and even later of his political outlook. In his last years he looked forward to a peaceful end in *felix Asia*.[11]

These elements of two worlds in his character must have contributed much to the undoubted enchantment of his personality, which apparently owed little to his external appearance, for he was slender, red haired and beardless, unprepossessing compared to his forebear Robert Guiscard, and according to one contemporary he had a slight cast in one eye.[12] The Arabs used to say that he would not have fetched two hundred drachmas in the slave market.[13] But beneath this unathletic and unmilitary appearance lay great powers of endurance and considerable strategical skill. Above all he had a brilliant intelligence and a wide knowledge of the scholarship and achievements of his time, as well as of the literatures of both East and West. Not far from his residence at Foggia he allowed the Saracens to build a city of their own, named Lucera, and here the muezzins chanted from the minarets and decrees were issued in the name of 'our Sultan Frederick'. Nowhere did he feel so secure and at home as in this town, and his personal bodyguard was drawn from here. But these were not the only Easterners at his court: among his favourite companions were philosophers and astrologers from the Levant, whom he would exchange with those of other princes, and the sometimes slightly disrespectful way in which the learned Arabs occasionally answered his innumerable questions he always took in good part.[14] There is a legend that the great Averroes paid a visit to his court,[15] but Averroes died when Frederick was still a child; yet the legend

is a meaningful symbol, for the thought of that philosopher
may often be detected in Frederick's decrees, and in his jokes
and conversations with his friends. There is perhaps a wayward
humour in the way he addressed his enemy in Palestine, the
Sultan Al-Kamil, as 'his best friend', but there is also a symbol
here, for with Frederick his cultural affinity with the Sultan
weighed much more than mere political opposition. The
Saracens had never seen a crusading leader like this young
Kaiser, when in 1229 he came to Jerusalem seeking absolution
from his excommunication. He conversed in fluent Arabic with
their envoys and had discussions with their savants. He was
greatly interested in the culture of Islam; he had no objection
to the anti-Christian prayers of the muezzins, and at midday
half his court rose to say the Mohammedan prayers.

But there is a sad side to all this friendliness, for when he
had attained his object through negotiation with the Sultan
and had been the first Westerner to enter the Holy City after so
many years, no bells were rung and no Mass was celebrated.
The Emperor himself was still under Pope Gregory's ban, and
so he placed the crown of the King of Jerusalem on his own
head—an action that makes us think of Napoleon centuries
later. Thousands of pilgrims had followed him and had fulfilled
their heart's desire of visiting the holy places, but the Patriarch
of Jerusalem had insulted him, and he seemed more at home
with the infidels. An English crusader wrote home: 'He has
married the Sultan's daughter, and fifty more Saracen maidens
as well',[16] and it was later said that the women of the south
wore black veils in mourning at the departure of the Christian
Prince.[17] It was also said that he had an imperial harem, and
for one so steeped in Eastern ways it is not impossible; but it
would seem that women played a relatively minor part in his
life. He had four legitimate wives, who all died young after
leading lonely lives, and he had several mistresses, but his
court was an entirely male society, and apart from intellectual
debates his passion was for animals. He regarded as his greatest
treasure—apart from his son Conrad—the astrolabe or plane-
tarium which the Sultan Al-Kamil sent him,[18] and then his

horse Draco and the famous elephant which caused such a stir in Italy. In addition to his household which consisted largely of Turks and Negroes, he never travelled without taking with him his menagerie: camels, leopards, monkeys, bears, lions, exotic birds and a giraffe. This made such an impression in Europe that we even read of an impostor in Germany many years after the Emperor's death claiming to be Frederick and proving it by showing his mules and three Moors in his service;[19] but this was a far cry from the Kaiser's neat black pages, the *servitelli nigri* Musca and Marzuch.[20]

He had a special love for his falcons, which he trained and looked after himself. But it was a dispassionate kind of love, which did not prevent him from killing one of them in cold blood for having attacked an eagle: a falcon must not attack the king of its own race.[21] In his later years he wrote a book about this love of his, *The Art of hunting with birds*.[22] It is a remarkable book, written in careful but unadorned Latin, which shows us the real man through his hobby, much more graphically than his resounding official manifestoes. It is also characteristic of him in its minutely logical treatment of the subject. Laying aside the traditional superstitions which surrounded it, he begins by declaring that he will present things as they are: *manifestare ea quae sunt sicut sunt*[23]—an unusual approach at the period, because natural history in his time was so intimately bound up with legends and fables. He had specimens brought from afar, sending men for the purpose as far as Lübeck and Persia; on one occasion he sent a man who had been condemned to death to go instead down a dangerous cliff and fetch back the nest of a rare white falcon.[24] In the same way it is said that he sent the famous swimmer of Messina, Nicholas Piscis— Schiller's 'Diver'—to dive into Charybdis and find out what was there.[25] Legends were investigated, and sometimes after carefully quoting the story, as that of Pliny about the phoenix, he soberly adds: 'This, however, we cannot believe.'[26] Even Aristotle, that great investigator, does not escape criticism: 'What Aristotle says in his *Liber Animalium*, that all birds with curved claws are birds of prey, is not so.'[27]

It is understandable that this man was not always welcome in the world of the West: 'Faith cometh by hearing' had been the rule, and here was a man who wanted to investigate. Averroes had indeed gone before him, but few Europeans had rejected authority as readily as Frederick was doing. Perhaps he shared the view of the more advanced scholastics that the verification of the perceptible world was as legitimate as the acceptance of the world of revelation; but it may be doubted whether he ever made this distinction himself. That he rejected Pliny would have caused no concern; that he accused the Stagyrite of lying would have been no sacrilege before the days of Aquinas; but if this cynical layman should invade the field of theology, it would be another matter. It would only be the next step to deny the Virgin Birth as being against the laws of nature, *quae sunt sicut sunt*—and this indeed was whispered of him. His characteristically dry humour readily played on sacred matters, as when on the way back from the Crusade he said: 'If Jehovah had known about Sicily, he would not have made such a fuss about Palestine.'[28] Still more significant was his remark in later years, when he passed a cornfield: 'How many gods are ripening here!'[29] Did his jokes turn to blasphemy because of the fact that he was separated from the Church, however much he had tried to reconcile his notions of empire with hers? Or did they betray an underlying disbelief? And then there was the story of the dying man whom he had nailed up in a box, in order to demonstrate that the soul died with the body, since it could not get away.[30] His general scepticism showed itself also in the series of questions he put to his court astronomer Scotus: Where is hell, relative to the earth? And what about heaven? How far apart are they? What is beyond the last heaven, if there are several? What do the angels and saints do there, in the presence of God? How many hells are there? What are the names of the devils who live there?[31] It was beyond the limited intelligence of a Michael Scotus to satisfy so much materialistic curiosity. In this respect it was necessary to wait for Dante with his exactitude for detail to create a cosmogony including the revealed truth of faith and symbolic constructions of the under-

standing. This scepticism of the Emperor in regard to trans-
cendental reality characterises also his attitude in the conflict
with the Church: it assigns to him the role of a Renaissance-
man as opposed to the papal theory which was developing more
and more towards the late medieval doctrine of the *plenitudo
potestatis*. Clergy were tolerated at court more in spite of than
because of their office, but they must remember they are only
court officials and there would be trouble if they sided with the
Church over the excommunication or interdict and went so
far as to refuse the sacraments. Then there would be confiscation of property and imprisonment, but always, of course, with
the protestation that there was no curtailment of their freedom.[32] It is apparently untrue that Frederick turned churches
into latrines,[33] but all the same it is significant that among his
numerous building works there is only one church, and a
rather unimportant one at that.[34]

Nevertheless this royal agnostic learned very much from the
Church and from Christian culture, and most particularly from
Pope Innocent III. Without his doctrine of the spiritual
supremacy of the Holy See, Frederick's doctrine of the
sovereignty of the State could never have been conceived, at
any rate in that form. In this matter he was a forerunner of
Hegel: in the course of his practice of government he evolved
theories which were the more remarkable for being entirely
opposed to the whole medieval system. There is an indication of
this in the half-mocking use of biblical terms at the Sicilian
court. The Emperor would refer to his birthplace as 'the New
Bethlehem',[35] a knight could write to him: 'For your sake we
undergo these trials, as the martyrs did for the sake of Christ',[36]
or even: 'The Fathers awaited the coming of Christ no more
eagerly than we awaited yours.'[37] Peter de Vinea, the Emperor's
right-hand man, when Dante meets him in hell, is made by
the poet to speak like another Peter: 'I am he who held both
the keys to Frederick's heart.'[38] Is this a suggestion that Peter
de Vinea saw himself as the heir of the keys of the kingdom—
the sacred kingdom of Sicily? 'Sicily, the apple of our eye, shall
be a mirror of perfection for all who look therein, the envy of

every prince, the model for every kingdom'[39]—these are
Frederick's words introducing his *Liber Augustalis*, the famous
Constitutions of Melfi of 1231. Here was the first authoritarian
state, built upon the laws of the Romans, Normans and
Hohenstaufen, but so thoroughly centralised that it had something of the police state about it, so that one pope remarked:
'Without his commandment no man shall move hand or foot
in all the land.'[40] For Frederick this was a compliment, and
with satisfaction he called Sicily the 'Mother of tyrants'[41] just
as he called Milan the 'Mother of heretics and rebels'. But it is
sinister to reflect that the term *Mater Tyrannorum* comes from
Augustine's friend Orosius, who was referring to Satan. Here
we have the ingenious inversion of Christian ideas and doctrines
with which the Emperor justified the right of his state to exist;
it is really more important than all the laws derived from this
political theory:[42]

> As Almighty God reveals himself to the faithful in the
> Trinity of Persons, so he reveals himself to the statesman as
> Absolute Justice.
> As God the Father is manifested through Christ, so is Justice
> manifested through the Emperor.
> As Christ has founded his Church, so the Emperor has
> founded his State.
> As the Church is necessary for the salvation of souls, so is the
> State necessary for material salvation. The State has not been
> imposed upon mankind because of original sin, as the Fathers of
> the Church have taught; on the contrary, the Prince and the
> State are the only salvation for helpless creatures, who without
> their laws would go to perdition. Nature itself called the State
> into being; Providence only created the State in so far as it
> created the forces of natural circumstances.

In this shifting of emphasis we can distinguish the beginnings of Frederick's theories. He only brought Providence into
the process of creation of the State because in 1230 he was still
very anxious to avoid conflict with the Church, and, in fact, in
his *Liber Augustalis*, as in his other writings, his *Providentia* is

very much of a lay figure. The real force, for this thirteenth-century Macchiavelli, is the *necessitas rerum*, which explains everything. Thus in his book on falconry, when asking whether birds of prey got their claws and beaks from God in order to harm other creatures, he answers: No, but because they need them.[43]

The State therefore becomes the Temple of *Justitia*, and state officials become her priests, who were trained at the state university of Naples with the strictness of a seminary. The Emperor himself is exalted as the High Priest who performs the *sacratissimum mysterium* of his office, the people are taught that he is omnipresent and infallible, and he utters his law through the mouth of his *Logotheta* ('he who places the Word'), Peter de Vinea, who in the Byzantine manner stands between the *sacra majestas* and the *profanum vulgus*. To his subjects the Emperor must have seemed almost divine, but to us how medieval it seems to romanticise his clear theories dictated by reason. It is obvious that so romantic an expression of despotism could only appeal to the un-Western taste of Sicily, where for centuries it was the custom to fall to one's knees before the ruler and to kiss his feet. Only there could a decree like that of Melfi have been made: 'Discussion of any judgement, decision or disposition of the Emperor is sacrilege.'[44] Roger the Norman had done the same thing there before, without being ridiculed, but he could not have risked it in Lombardy, and even the Germans were not prepared to accept so much Byzantinism at that time. Thus it was that Frederick of Hohenstaufen, Kaiser of the greatest Empire of the West, reigned as undisputed lord only in his south Italian native land, and even there he could only maintain his rule by stern repressive measures, so that as soon as he was dead countless people wanted to be rid of the hated *Todeschi*. He had his share of power, but he also had his share of the troubles of every tyrant. There were plots to murder him: people of his own intimate circle turned against him, relatives even, his own personal physician, his most trusted lieutenant, Peter de Vinea, the *logotheta*. . . . It must have hurt him to find that these were all southerners, since he had such a love of the southern lands. But he was surely far too intelligent not to have known that not all his opponents were evil men, nor to have realised that they had other motives beyond what he called the Judas money of the Pope.

What of the men who remained faithful to him? They did not share Frederick's idealism, which might have redeemed their selfishness, nor his brilliant genius, which might have outshone their brutality. There was Guido of Suessa, whose special delight was in executions, and who refused to his enemies on the scaffold the right to go to confession, saying: 'They're the Pope's friends, and so they go straight to heaven.'[45] He came to a grisly end himself: one dark night he was fleeing for his life, when his horse slipped into a deep sewer, and man and horse together sank into the stinking slime. Then there was the Margrave Uberto Pallavicini, who, though officially in the Emperor's service, in fact served none but himself. As he lay in his cradle, a cock had pecked out one of his eyes, but his remaining eye, raven black, 'glowed like a furnace, day and night, with evil intent', and he was even more expert than Guido in the art of torture.[46] Then there was Alberic of Romano, who, in anger over the loss of a falcon, 'pissed upon the altar', and obliged the ladies of Treviso to walk naked under the gallows where their husbands hung dying. His own end was gruesome enough: after his wife and nine children had been strangled before his eyes, he was torn to pieces by horses.[47] Lastly there was the arch-demon of them all, Ezzelino, brother of Alberic and son-in-law of Frederick, the terror of Verona and Padua. Frederick himself had set him on the path in a manner reminiscent of Herodotus, when they were walking in a garden and Frederick struck off the heads of the flowers, saying: 'That is how to treat your subjects.'[48] The advice did not fall on deaf ears: as soon as Ezzelino came to power, torture and death were the order of the day. The county of Treviso had never known such violence as that of Ezzelino in 1252, when scarcely a man escaped his frenzy.[49] He is described as covered from head to foot with curly black hair and always in armour, he was such a woman-hater 'that it was believed he had never slept with a woman',[50] and was an undoubted case of true sadism. But in the Middle Ages no one thought of distinguishing between a psychopath and simply a son of the devil. They merely saw him as the agent, and relative, of the Emperor, who was in any case the Antichrist and received the blame for it all.

Frederick's had been a life of struggle: Jerusalem had fallen into his hands and slipped away again, Germany had welcomed him and then betrayed him, Lombardy had revolted and never admitted defeat, the popes had been surrounded, but had the final victory, for in 1245 Frederick was finally deprived of his throne, excommunicated and outlawed, becoming an outcast from the whole of Christian society. At one stroke there is an end of his renaissance irony; his reasoning becomes satanic. For five years he raged up and down Italy like a madman, a lonely man amid a crowd of frightened flatterers. Pope Innocent IV had fled to Lyons for safety, and Frederick was in sole command in Italy, determined to cow the population into submission: hostages were murdered, cities burnt to the ground, the possession of papal letters meant losing hands and feet, the illegal possession of arms meant hanging without trial, the height of the gallows corresponding to the victim's rank.[51]

The people thought this must be the end of the world, and when they saw the imperial cavalcade they felt that the riders of the apocalypse had come indeed, with the almighty and mysterious prince in their midst, his face hidden by his visor. Legends about him sprang up quickly, astrologers and magicians were consulted, the Sibylline oracles scrutinised. . . . How long would the agony last? The secret books said two hundred and sixty-seven years. . . .[52] And then, in the middle of the century, he suddenly died. Rumours began at once: surely Frederick was to die in Florence—was that not the prophecy? Was that not why he had never been there for years? But then the news came through: it was not in the Tuscan Fiorenza that he had died, but in a remote hunting lodge in Apulia, called Castel Fiorentino, where he had taken refuge, shaken by fever. The prophecy was right after all, but the doubts remained: the terrors of a lifetime could not be allayed overnight at his death, and many were convinced that he had merely gone to a distant land and would return. For years the incorrigible Florentines wagered with one another about it;[53] from time to time false Fredericks appeared in Sicily and Germany and frightened people anew. The rumours were halted for a moment by the report that a pious friar had been praying near the coast of Calabria, and at the moment of Frederick's death had seen the Emperor with five thousand men at arms ride into the mouth of Etna.[54] That certainly sounded credible, and yet . . . 'He lives and he lives not', the Sybilline oracle had said. The doubts continued.[55]

When Frederick II died the imperial history of the *Duecento* declined. None of his sons could rise to his stature. Henry, as conceited as he was weak, had already committed suicide during his father's lifetime. Conrad brought more ill than good to Sicily during his four years of government. The other three had something of their father's charm, but not his personality or intelligence. Frederick of Antioch, King of Tuscany, was so handsome and attractive that people forgot that he was lame. Enzio, the 'eyas' and fair-haired poet, fell into the hands of the Bolognese. His father offered as ransom a circle of silver to go round the whole town, but they would not release him. Their only answer was: 'It does sometimes happen that a little dog catches a big boar.'[56] But they treated their captive honourably: he was free to entertain his friends when he wished and he could spend as much money as he wanted. Once he tried to escape and was to be smuggled out in a wine vat, but a lock of his hair got caught in the lid, and everyone knew what was happening—no one else in Bologna had golden hair like that. Henceforth he was kept in more careful custody, and he never saw his home again, for all his longing. He is buried at San Domenico.

Lastly there was Manfred, his father's favourite, a fine figure of a man and a keen musician. Any singer was sure of a welcome from him, and together with his Greek wife he was able to bring back something of the old Hohenstaufen glory to Apulia; for twelve years he held court there, twelve years of romantic, pagan enjoyment, hardly aware of the threats that were closing in on him. For Manfred, reckless and charming, was lacking in practical sense. He built a city near Monte Gargano, and called it after himself, Manfredonia; he had his own residence at Barletta, and would sometimes spend the night singing in the streets with two Sicilian fiddlers at his heels.[57] When we see the shabby little town today it is difficult to imagine the scene. The common people took him to their hearts, particularly when he made his courtiers marry the girls they had seduced, from which time, so the chronicler tells us with a grin, they tied their breeches on with seven knots.[58] Meanwhile the popes had come back from France, full of French ideas, and with Charles of Anjou, the King of France's brother, as their firm ally. Charles came to Italy with his troops, and his ambitious wife pawned her jewels to pay them. . . . That was the end of the Germans in Italy, and the pilgrims and scholars from the north, who had hoped to find their paradise.

The French were different; they did not come to Italy to learn or to find a paradise. Their own culture was older, their Provence offset Sicily, their Sorbonne all Bologna. And Rome? Seven hills by a narrow river! The Rhone was broader and Avignon far better fortified. No, Charles of Anjou never came under the spell of the south, nor did he come only as the Pope's vassal, even if his brother was a saint. The people of Italy meant nothing to him and he did not spend a penny when he arrived in Rome.[59] He came to Italy for only one thing: to become king, and his wife to become the queen. He therefore saw no reason for negotiating with Manfred; there was no room now for a Hohenstaufen, and he sent him a curt message: 'Say to the Sultan of Lucera that today either I will send him to hell, or he will send me to heaven.'[60] In 1266 he defeated and killed Manfred at Benevento, and put his wife and children into prison for life. The former Saracen town of Lucera he turned into a colony of Provencal craftsmen. The last Hohenstaufen, Conradin, son of Conrad, was a boy of only sixteen when he was publicly executed in the piazza at Naples, calling for his mother in terror when he saw the executioner's sword.

The century ended, as it had begun, in fire and blood. The Sicilians, accustomed for centuries to passive resistance to foreign rulers, hated the French even more than they had hated the Greeks, Arabs, Normans and Germans. The Frenchman who on Easter Monday 1282 laid hands on a pretty girl of Palermo was seen as a symbol of their subjection, and when he was instantly stabbed to death the action was symbolic, too. It was the signal for a bloodbath for the Angevins: the bells of the little Moorish church of San Giovanni degli Eremiti declared a desperate revolution, in which even women took part—to the horror of the Italian mainland;[61] and the Sicilians had the last word: for all the wrath of the French and the threats of the Pope, the intruders never regained their power in the island. Yet somehow Sicily could not live without foreigners, and before long they had summoned Peter of Aragon, who was related to the Hohenstaufen, and had welcomed him with their semi-Oriental festivities.[62]

Once more there were foreign troops in Italy, but that is the story of another century, when another world began. The *Duecento* closes and the Teutons are no more than a memory, but the memory of a dream of power that never quite came true.

2

The Popes

O Roma nobilis orbis et domina

cunctarum urbium excellentissima

salutem dicimus tibi per omnia——

Te benedicimus salve per saecula

O noble Rome, thou mistress of the earth,
  More excellent than any city thou.
We greet thee, we proclaim thy every worth,
  We bless thee always, evermore and now.[1]

THIS WAS the song of the pilgrims as they came over the last hill on the path to Rome and suddenly the distant city came into view. They had done this for centuries, kneeling down on the road, tired and dusty, for their journey's end was now in sight.

For many of them it had been a long journey from the north, and they had seen many strange things on the way: the Alps with their everlasting snow, the grim passes through the mountains, now the vineclad slopes of Italy, the rows of cypresses, the little fortress towns upon the hilltops, and here, farther south, the heat and the bare, sunbaked hills. They had heard strange tongues and had watched the sunburnt people go about their farming in a different way from theirs. There had been perils also: sometimes they had found a war in progress, always they had been ready for robbers. But what matter? Here at last was Rome.

When the modern traveller approaches Rome the first thing he sees from afar is the cupola of St Peter's. But in the Middle Ages it was different: the distant view must have been more like that of an industrial town of today with its factory chimneys; the medieval skyline of Rome was a mass of slender towers and heavy ramparts. Already in the tenth century we hear of 381 towers and 46 bastions; in the thirteenth century over 200 campanili joined them, together with 300 fortified towers of the various noble families, who would sometimes throw down a neighbour's tower one evening, only to find it rebuilt by next morning. Frangipani, Pierleoni, Annibaldi, Savelli, Conti, Orsini, Capocci and the dreaded Colonna—these were the elements of the deadly rivalry. In turn they would storm and capture the ancient monuments, which in turn they would fortify, sniping at one another from the Colosseum or the Arch of Constantine, or from this or that temple or aqueduct. The Gaetani controlled the Via Appia from their fort on the mausoleum of Cecilia Metella, known at the time as 'the Oxhead'. The Colonna fortified the Augusteum, the mausoleum which the people called 'Lagusta', and from here and the near-by Montecitorio (near the present Piazza Colonna) they defended the rights of the Emperor against those of the Pope. Rome does not change much: Italy is still governed from the Montecitorio, where the present Parliament sits.[2]

The great buildings stood out among the little streets: the Quirinal, heavily fortified, and the Lateran, where the papal curia still held state. But evidences of ancient Rome for the most part lay neglected and overgrown: the Baths of Caracalla were surrounded by swamps, there were struggling vegetable

plots on the sunny side of the Seven Hills and around the
Pantheon, and cattle grazed in the Forum. But the Capitol
remained the political centre; assemblies and elections were held
in Piazza Aracoeli; here the proud initials S.P.Q.R. were
added to statues, frontier stones and manifestos, here were
Rome's trophies of war, the municipal bell of one city, the bars
from the gates of another, the wheel of a Lombard chariot
. . . Miserable booty in the eyes of those who remembered
the triumphant processions of Antiquity . . . But did the
medieval Romans think in these terms? Had they any feeling
for the glories of the past?

In the south the people were the offspring of East and West
together, and their characters had been inevitably moulded
by the Normans and Germans who had ruled there; but Rome
still maintained the imperial inflexibility. Yet it was an unconscious heritage, for in medieval Rome no one's heart thrilled
at the thought of the marching legions, no one blushed at the
sight of the statues of the mighty on the Via Appia surrounded
by hovels and pigsties, or paused to think as they tore down the
temples to build themselves stables. But they were probably the
same in the time of Augustus; it must have been few who
realised what was afoot. Here in medieval Rome, when
foreigners came to rule, the people were only remotely conscious
of their past and were absorbed in the petty quarrels between
Pope and Emperor, ready to accept a bribe from the highest
bidder. Small wonder that their foreign masters despised them.
'If you want to manage these people,' said a cardinal who afterwards became Pope Clement IV, 'you have to meet them with
a haughty air, then frighten them with threats, and add a little
violence.'[3] And this from a Frenchman. It was the foreigners
who tried to remind them of their heritage. It was Frederick,
the German, who realised that the dream of the new Roman
Empire must have Rome as its capital. *Quirites*, he called the
rascals in the passionate letters in which he tried to arouse in
them an awareness of their old imperial dignity and an understanding of the new, and to enlist their support against the
Lombards. 'Behold, those who once were your subjects and

paid tribute to you, are now offering you insults instead of gold!
O how you are fallen away from the mighty works of your forefathers, how you have abandoned the valour of the ancients,
whose rule no city dared resist! They, not content with subject-
ing their neighbours, had extended their power abroad, with
Spain as a distant province, while Carthage they cut off in full
bloom.'4

The *Quirites* on their Capitol were flattered indeed, rejoiced
and no doubt wept; but in the end they felt that all this was
after all the Kaiser's Empire and not their own; and therefore
Frederick for all his eloquence had no more than their nominal
adherence.

Another foreigner who tried to appeal to Rome's past greatness was Brancaleone degli Andalò from Bologna. In 1252, in
the general chaos that followed the death of the Emperor and
the prolonged absence of the Pope, he was invited to Rome as
senator. He saw the solution plainly enough, as might be
expected from one trained in the law schools of Bologna. Within
three years he had turned the republic into a city-state on the
pattern of the free cities of Tuscany and Romagna. Of course,
the Romans did not like this and soon they had him in prison.
They would have killed him, if he had not taken the wise pre-
caution of sending some of their notable men as hostages to his
native city. This made them change their mind and they
restored him to all his honourable offices; and when, shortly
afterwards, he died, they placed his head in a magnificent
shrine for the people's veneration on the Capitol. It is less
trouble to venerate a dead man than it is to obey him when he
is alive. They were not great men who lived among the ruins
of Rome.

What is humanly speaking difficult to understand is how
this city of ruins ever succeeded in laying claim to the leadership of the world. It was an anonymous cleric of 1240 who wrote
this warning to the prelates of Europe who had been invited to
the Council: 'Do not venture into Rome. How can you entrust
yourselves to a city where the clergy and citizens are permanently at war on the side of the pope or the emperor? The heat

is unbearable, the water is foul, the food is disgustingly bad. You can cut the air with a knife, for the whole place swarms with gnats and scorpions. The people are dirty and disagreeable, spiteful and unfriendly. The whole city in fact is undermined by the catacombs, which are full of snakes and all the time emit poisonous fumes.'5 But in spite of this, the cardinals, bishops and abbots of Christendom took ship at Genoa, though more than a hundred of them fell into the hands of the imperial fleet. In spite of this, the stream of pilgrims never ceased, nor the cry *O Roma nobilis* from the hills. For all these people the material conditions of the *Urbs* were unimportant: they came to greet the representative of the Carpenter and to visit the Fisherman's tomb. And if distress happened to come to their notice—as far as possible the destitute and sick *peregrini et Romipetae* were kept away from the centre of the city—they praised God for the city which had room for the great and the lowly together. They had no eyes for those princes who saw themselves marching in the footsteps of the legions, but only for those princes who saw the heirloom of Rome carried over to a spiritual plane, the heirloom of the Caesars which had become Christ's and the basis of Christian culture. Often these princes had been obliged to take flight, to Rieti, Orvieto, Perugia, Anagni, and once even to Lyons, but they always returned. *Roma nobilis* owed her nobility to the popes, and no amount of ruins, swamps or street fighting could make her *Roma deplorabilis*: this could only happen when the popes disowned their own nobility.

'*O Roma deplorabilis*—O sorry Rome,' cried Bishop Arnulf of Orleans in the tenth century, 'a light to the world in the days of our fathers, but now a bearer of darkness so black that coming generations shall shudder to speak of it. Where shall our city of refuge be now? For the mistress of the nations has lost her strength, her power both divine and human is gone.'6

In comparison with those bad times of Marozia and Luitprand, Rome of 300 years later was not in such poor shape. Yet the old bitter satires on the avarice and corruption, nepotism and simony of the papal court were still in circulation. A grammarian's joke of the time reminds those who come to plead a case in Rome to be sure to use the dative case before they start work on the accusative. The theologians also had their joke about the all-important relics of the martyrs Albinus and Ruffinus (silver and gold) without which there was no entrance. Another acute parody was the *Evangelium secundum Marcam*: the 'Gospel of the Reichsmark'. Dante met many a pope in Hell who had even sold away his eternal happiness by his simony; full of bitterness, he asks one of them what price the Lord had demanded from St Peter for the keys of heaven.[8]

Whatever the reasons for it, the fact is that the people of Rome lived in fear of the papal court and held it at arm's length as far as possible. To a man, they would rise in protest the moment the Father of Christendom took any part in municipal affairs—something that was to some extent within his rights.[9] But whenever they drove the Pope and curia out of Rome they realised that they had lost their only title to respect and, in fact, also their only support, and they were quick to remember how devoted they really were to Christ's Vicar. Of course, none were so papal as the Romans, when the popes distributed bread and wine and bounty in times of need, or when they provided a free spectacle at a coronation or a council. The Council of the Lateran of 1215 was a glorious occasion, with every nation represented in the processions— almost like an imperial triumph. The Romans were filled with pride when they saw the whole of Western Christendom coming humbly to their city: ambassadors of every prince were there, with the patriarchs, bishops and abbots from Jerusalem to England and from Hungary to Aragon, all come to honour the real sovereign of Europe. All the languages of the world were mixed with their own Italian Latin, all nations bowed before the supremacy of Rome. This was even better than a mere three kings at Bethlehem! These were times when the Romans forgot their own quarrels and rivalries. But in their own affairs there were certain regular patterns: the citizens would choose their leader from anti-clerical circles; before long he would be excommunicated by his spiritual sovereign (a power exercised only too freely); the people would then take his side and without more ado plunder the Lateran; the Pope would withdraw to one of the neighbouring towns, and that was the end of law and order; robbery and murder took over, and often innocent pilgrims fell victims. Eventually things would calm down; the Pope would return and express his preference in the choice of a new mayor; and so the show would start again. It was not until the later years of the century, when there were no more Hohenstaufen in the background, that the people began to choose their senator from the papal curia.

The brief pontificate of Honorius IV (1285–7) was remarkable for the achievement of real peace within the city for two years. This was due to two very old men, both crippled with gout, brothers of the house of the Savelli, Giacopo and Pandolfo. Giacopo was a cardinal and was so paralysed that he had to use a mechanical contrivance to enable him to perform the elevation at Mass, but he was elected Pope and took the name of Honorius IV. Pandolfo, who was so stiff that he had to be carried about on a chair, was appointed senator of the city. While these two brothers ruled weapons were put away and life and limb were safe, the nobility were silenced and criminals were hanged.

The thirteenth century was spanned by eighteen popes, from Innocent III to Boniface VIII. Not without reason it is regarded as the period marking the zenith of papal power; but its decline during the century is very plain, and at the end it was almost a shadow of what it had been at the beginning. The battle which Innocent seemed to have won so gloriously against the German Emperor, Boniface lost forever against the French. Yet it seems to have little to do with the personalities of the successive pontiffs. It was not entirely owing to Innocent III, diplomatic genius though he was, that the whole of Europe lay at his feet; there were also the political circumstances of the time. Everyone from Norway to Armenia recognised his authority, both England and Aragon were regarded as papal fiefs, the King of France by personal temperament was ready to obey the Holy See, in Germany Otto the Guelph deliberately made himself his subject, and in Sicily the boy Frederick was made a papal ward. The Council of the Lateran of 1215, when all the nations of Europe came to pray together, was his last and greatest triumph. But in the latter part of the century, the Pope's lamentations about these same countries is in striking contrast: 'A glance at our unhappy world will show you at once why our treasury is so empty: England has risen against us, Germany will not obey, France is groaning and grumbling, Spain has her own troubles, Italy pays us nothing and costs us much. How can a pope, without recourse to unholy means, provide money or troops for himself or anyone else? Never before, in any undertaking, have we found ourselves in such straits.'[10]

The opening of the pontificate of Boniface VIII in 1295 was an occasion for unparalleled pomp and splendour in Rome, and in 1300 he declared the first Holy Year. Hundreds of thousands answered his invitation and the city was crowded as never before: to ease the congestion of traffic the Ponte Sant' Angelo was rebuilt as a dual carriageway. And yet, in spite of the esteem in which he was held and the wealth which he had amassed, the chains were slowly being forged which soon would render him helpless and bring about his tragic downfall.

The eighteen popes of the century were of many different temperaments: some were saints, while others were certainly not. Several of them were already too old, and reigned for but a few days or weeks: the cardinals were mostly aged and Rome was not a healthy place at the time. Celestine IV reigned for seventeen days, and in 1276 there were three successive reigns, the last being that of John XXI, a Portuguese, whom some accused of practising magic, but who was certainly a skilled physician and apparently endowed with second sight. Sometimes a pope is in marked contrast with his predecessor or successor: between the brilliant Innocent and the energetic Gregory stands the gentle Honorius; and near the end of the century, after an anxious interregnum, the unworldly Celestine V was fetched from his hermitage, to be succeeded by the autocratic Boniface VIII.

Five or six conspicuous figures stand out in the series. In 1198 they elected the thirty-seven-year-old Lotario, of the house of Segni, who had studied theology in Paris and law at Bologna. He entered the city riding on a scarlet-decked horse, under a white canopy, with princes holding the stirrups and an endless procession of standard-bearers, singers, bishops and cardinals; then came the abbots of the twenty Roman abbeys, patriarchs from the Levant, the magistrates, prefects and senators of the city, the judges with their attendants, and the noble families each with their own banner.[11] The streets were decorated with flowers and triumphal arches (each costing £35), carpets and hangings. At one point he received deputations, at another an address of welcome; in one piazza bounty was thrown to the singing and dancing crowds. When he reached the Lateran he followed the ancient custom of a public profession of humility by sitting briefly on the marble *sella stercoraria*, to show himself to be 'the servant of the servants', and then went to a table to be waited upon by kings. And he took the name of Innocent III. For the next eighteen years he was the one 'from whom the kings held their kingship and the princes their princedom'; he was an aristocrat, a philosopher and a lawyer, who used all his brilliant gifts in the service of an ideal, which the popes of the previous 300 years had sought in vain to realise. It is only the fullness of power, given by Christ to his Vicar, that can grant authority to a prince of this world; only thus is Christ's command fulfilled; only thus can peace come to mankind. (Whether the prince then possesses as his own the right to rule, or whether he only holds it in trust, was a subject of discussion at the beginning of the century.) It might be argued that this theory overstepped the frontiers between the spiritual and the political, but to apply that distinction at that time would be an anachronism, and in the discussions of the *plenitudo potestatis* the frontiers were well within the realm of theology.

It is easy to think of Innocent in a leading role against Frederick of Hohenstaufen, and indeed he was the only person sufficiently gifted to play such a part; but one has to remember that at the time of Innocent's death Frederick was only twenty. Had they been more exact contemporaries, their respective theories of political power would have doubtless both been modified. Innocent saw himself as the priest-king Melchisedech, an important symbol in his theory of the single power in the world.[12] But it was left to Frederick subsequently so sharply to divide these two offices of Melchisedech that for him the king was as priestly a figure as ever the priest had been kingly.[13] Indeed, for him the monarch was as much God's representative as ever the Pope was for Innocent, for the monarch was the embodiment on earth of the eternal Justice of heaven. And these theories gave an entirely new turn to the rest of the *Duecento*.

But it was not Innocent III who came into conflict with the secularisation of his own system: the absolute primacy of his office went with him to the grave and its loss imposed a difficult legacy for his successors: the gentle Honorius III and the unrelenting Gregory IX.

As Innocent is interesting as a thinker, so is Gregory as a man. He was one of Innocent's cardinals and was also his nephew, though fourteen years his senior, so that he was eighty by the time he was elected. The political theory in which he had been trained was, in fact, quite contrary to his own temperament. For fourteen years there was an inner conflict between carefully weighed prudence and passion as he strove to preserve the Church's mastery in the world. As he lay dying in 1241 the excommunicated Emperor was at the gates of Rome, with a cardinal who had joined his party at his side. The Papal States were in the hands of the enemy, in Sicily many priests were in his prisons, in the Holy Land the Christian cause fared ill, and Europe lay under the threat of the Tartars. Even Gregory's beloved Order of St Francis had suffered a division, a matter in which, however, Gregory himself had not been unconcerned. Gregory had been in a sense the fate of the Franciscans, as indeed Francis had been his. He had been chosen as Protector of the young Order, when he was still Cardinal Hugolino, and St Francis was his intimate friend. He believed in Francis and his mission and hoped for much more for the Church from the *pauperi* of Umbria than from the political philosophy of his uncle, Innocent. But he was too much of a realist not to want to confine Francis's enthusiasm in more prosaic expressions, and he so modified the saint's words that they could be fitted into ordinary Christian lives. And what happened then? Before his eyes Elias, the General of the Order and formerly his friend, went over to the camp of his arch enemy Frederick, and the Franciscans, instead of bringing about a Christian renewal in the Church, spent themselves fighting on opposing sides. Gregory had done a disservice to the saint, though his motives were merciful, but basically emotional.

Gregory was basically an emotional man, in spite of his legal learning, his academic eloquence and his elegant letters. Much of his fighting with Frederick was conducted on an emotional rather than on a political level: there was anger in his excommunication, there was apocalyptic passion in his denunciations of him: 'The Beast is rising from the sea, whose name is infamous, whose claws are of a raging bear, and teeth as of a lion; he is cunning as a panther, and never opens his lips but to curse the name of God.'[14] He mounted the tribunal on the steps of St Mary Major's, and smoke was rising from the stakes in the piazza—the first of their grim kind. Rich and poor, religious and layfolk alike heard judgement given: branding, excommunication and death. But the people of Rome, who had just survived both flood and plague, determined to prevent the execution of these sentences and rose in revolt, driving the Pope out to Rieti. They had no time for this apocalyptic vengeance, and gradually began to feel an increasing sympathy with the excommunicated Emperor.

The conflict sharpened and Frederick marched on Rome. His fifth column had done good work there: the people scoffed at Gregory and were ready to open the gates. It was then that Gregory, now nearly a hundred years old, rose to the occasion. On the feast of St Peter's Chair the relics of the Apostles Peter and Paul, patrons of the city, were being carried through the streets in procession. Where the crowds were thickest Gregory halted. He took off the tiara, and holding it over the relics, cried in a quavering voice: 'O holy Saints, protect now your Rome, since the Romans will no longer defend her.'[15] It was a crowning gesture of Gregory's inner conflict of heart and head, and its theatrical appeal won the Romans back. They wept and ran to bar the gates against Frederick. The Kaiser, seeing that he had lost this round, withdrew and returned to Naples.

As soon as Gregory IX was dead both the Kaiser and the Church were hoping for peace. But there were only ten aged cardinals and so many cross-currents in the conclave that they could not reach a decision. Then the Senator, Matteo Orsini, gave them a push: if the reverend gentlemen were made a little less comfortable, they would get results more quickly. He had the ten of them taken under armed guard to the Palatine and locked in the ancient Septiconium of Severus—a building on the southern slopes of the Palatine which remained more or less intact until into the seventeenth century. In the hottest time of the year, cut off from light and air, penned up together in one room, badly fed and subjected to petty irritations from the guards—this was how the conclave had to await the Holy Spirit to indicate Gregory's successor and thus restore their freedom. The aged cardinals were all sick men and one died. A pope was indeed chosen, but within three weeks he was dead. During those three weeks, however, the cardinals had hastily dispersed, and it was nearly two years before the senator could persuade them to return. Then at last the Church received a new supreme head.

Innocent IV was the very opposite to Gregory: a cool, competent lawyer; not a dynamic personality—his motto was 'Sedens ago'—and no hero either. Shortly after his enthronement the moneylenders of Rome came to the Lateran demanding payment of 60,000 marks, but he hid himself in a remote part of the palace. Yet he had his success where others failed; for a moment, at least, he subdued Frederick. He had been a friend of the Emperor, and perhaps as a friend he had studied Frederick's methods so closely that when he became Pope and applied them, he at once became his enemy. The Genoese was a match for the Hohenstaufen in many ways. He kept the Emperor in suspense, as the Emperor had so often done to his predecessor, and when Frederick, partly to gain time and partly to get out of the excommunication, submitted to the humiliating conditions of the Pope, the Pope had copies of the provisional agreement sold all over the city for sixpence.[16] The Emperor was furious, and as for the meeting in person at Terni, where the final points would be settled, nothing could be expected except that the Emperor would guarantee safe passage to the Pope. Hence the Pope rode off the night before with a few attendants through the Maremma to Civitavecchia, where the Genoese fleet lay at anchor; he boarded a ship and sailed away to Lyons, where he could hold a council and depose the Emperor without interference. Frederick never forgot this: 'When I had almost check-mated the Pope,' he once said angrily, 'the Genoese came and kicked the whole chessboard over.'[17]

It is significant for the whole period that the experienced jurists cut the best figures on the papal throne, while in the hands of unworldly saints the affairs of the Church became hopelessly confused. This is particularly true of the holiest Pope of them all, who laid down his charge after a few months, feeling that he had been through the worst experience of his life.

This was during the last decade of the century. After a long *Sedisvacatio* the cardinals were as undecided as ever about whom to elect. The papacy was beginning to be a national concern: since Urban IV there had been several French popes— a Gallican intrusion which the Italians were eager to break, without, however, having anyone of their own to propose. Finally, Latino, Cardinal of Ostia, decided to have recourse to a miracle: he put on the list the name of the hermit Peter, who lived an ascetic life somewhere on Monte Morone. The vote was taken and Peter was elected. The emissaries of the conclave toiled up the mountain, tearing their silken shoes on the rough stones of the muletrack. Eventually they found the tumble-down hut and a frightened old man inside. Above his wild beard a pair of red-rimmed eyes, more accustomed to weeping than to reading, stared with horror at these unusual visitors. As they knelt down to do him homage, he knelt to them in respectful welcome. Not understanding what had happened, he attempted flight, and had to be pursued and forced to accept the honour.

Sick with fear, he was brought to Aquila on a donkey. Charles of Anjou, King of Naples, came out to meet him, and walked back beside him holding his stirrup. He seemed a friendly man, this King; so Peter clung to him, like a child to his protector. After his consecration he went with him to Naples. Why not? The King seemed so keen about it. The curia followed unwillingly, by now regretting their miracle, and Cardinal Latino could have been glad that he was already dead. Pope Celestine sat uneasily on the throne. Why was there nothing but mistrust and opposition all round him? He did his best, he gave away all he could, and prayed unceasingly for his flock. But by Advent he could bear it no longer, and after three and a half months of hesitant government, he resigned in December 1294.

It was whispered that it had been Cardinal Benedict Gaetani who had driven him to resign by pretending to be the voice of God speaking from a hiding place. But after he became Pope Boniface VIII he stopped playing God and put the unhappy Celestine in prison. Pope Boniface is the last medieval pope on the grand scale. He seemed to have all the peculiar defects of the century. Stiff and sullen, he sat upon the throne, just as he does in the statue over the Porta Maggiore at Orvieto. A lawyer with a ready tongue, he was a most imposing figure; an excellent diplomat but he was a nepotist like none before him, haughty and selfwilled. His mighty ideas about papal power were by now quite out of date; things had changed. The King of France mocked him, and had his bull publicly burnt in Notre-Dame, and the Roman nobility were more restless than ever. Of course, it was the Colonna who first fell out with him, declared that his election was invalid and called for a council and a new election. Boniface's reaction was rather pathetic: he declared a 'Holy War' against this handful of disgruntled nobles, and called upon 'the whole of Christendom' to join in a crusade against a few castles in the Campagna. Palestrina, their last stronghold, fell a victim to his rage: it was razed to the ground, ploughed over and sown with salt. The inhabitants were left to beg their way. The old rebel-poet Jacopone da Todi got involved in the conflict and was put in prison until released by the Pope's death.

Now the French and the Colonna were in league against him, and they besieged him in his home town of Anagni. While they stormed the palace he awaited them in full pontifical robes, with his golden cross in his hand. They did not kill him, but brought him as a prisoner to Rome. Anger and revenge haunted him and near the end he was out of his mind; as he lay in a fever he thought that every visitor to his bedside had come to murder him. After one last outburst he fell back in bed and died. It was said that the hermit Peter had once prophesied: 'He will come in like a wolf, rule like a lion and end like a dog.'[18]

But the century has closed, and with it Rome's part as the fortress of Holy Church. A few years later and the popes will have settled at Avignon. There would be no one left to care about *Roma nobilis* now. A forgotten village with overgrown ruins for many years to come, until the time arrived for her glory to return. But Rome of the *Duecento* was a symbol, for in spite of all her troubles she was the Eternal City, and remains so, come what may.

Lo nome a voi si facie, ser Pacino,
c'avete, e melgliorare nom si poria;
ché noi vedemo il mondo andare al chino,
perchè la pace non à sengnoria.

In gran bocie venuto è 'l ghebellino
onde la terra nabissare dovria;
chè morto e divorato ànno il giardino
da poi che venne ne la loro ballia.

Colte ne sono le rose e le viuole,
ed è vi nata cota e coregiuola:
cierto bene credo vi paja pecato.

Maravilglia mi fo se non vi duole
di quelli che vivono d'imbolio di suola
ed ànno fatto ciascuno di sé casato.

Your name, Sir *Friedrich*, cannot bear improving,
    Since *Friede*, 'peace', is what it ought to mean;
And now the world to utter ruin is moving,
    Because in this land peace is never seen.

To hell with all the earth is what's behoving,
    When noisily arrives the Ghibelline;
Our gardens they are eating up and proving
    That they're the only masters on the scene.

Unpicked remain the violets and roses,
    Our land is turning into grass and weed:
        You must be rather sad at that, I fear.

You ought to find it hurtful, one supposes,
    That people come to satisfy their greed
        And make themselves so much at home, just here?

Anonymus florentinus[1]

3

The Cities

HERE WE are, over the Abruzzi, and we have passed the northern frontier of the kingdom of Sicily without being searched, fined, locked up or hanged by the Emperor's officials. The road goes on through the Papal States, and we have not been excommunicated or robbed. We have skirted the Lazio, where the barons terrorise the people from their castles, and we are entering Lombardy in the district of the Romagna or the Tuscan League, and no one can harm us now. Not that anyone is completely safe, because there are always highwaymen and everyone now and then has a war, and if one gets mixed up with that one must expect a few bruises. But in these parts men are free, love their independence passionately, appreciate democracy and common-sense; this makes them sociable, however passionately they will defend their rights. And, of course, they are all obedient children of the Pope, that is, as long as he stays away in Rome and is only concerned with their spiritual good. They are also well disposed towards the Emperor, as long as he only comes occasionally and shows off his crown jewels and his menagerie. But none of these gentlemen must interfere with their affairs: if this should happen, they become enemies at once, and all the Lombard cities will league themselves together against the intruder. Nobody minds a little fight occasionally, and anyway anyone can hate to order. That is the state of things north of the Lazio, where in name the Holy Roman Empire begins, but where in fact everyone is his own master.

Here in Lombardy everything is on a smaller scale. There were no leaders of the stature of the Pope or Emperor; the rivalries were local and the alliances confusingly short-lived. But there is an enormous energy in these north Italian towns, which was kept in check by a motive which deserves every respect. It was hardly an expressed ideal; it was more of an unconscious instinct in every one of the people, a sort of feeling for freedom and individuality. This manifested itself in various little ways, small commercial rivalries, or hairsplitting disputations. But its main manifestation was an inflexible resistance to any sort of tyranny, and its greatest triumph was the democratic form of government in so many of the northern cities, which became the inspiration of Italian freedom in this century.

It would have been a much easier task to trace the development of the northern towns, if their ideals had been as clear to their citizens as the popes' or emperors' ideals had been to themselves. As it is, we can only see the general lines in various bombastic speeches, while the really important details become lost in the mass of everyday things. Anyway, their will to independence was so strong that it even excluded any interest in their neighbour's concerns, but was able at most to arouse suspicion. In those uninhibited times it took very little for swords to be drawn and gates to be closed. And there was hardly a year in Lombardy of the *Duecento* when some feud did not occur, some treaty get broken and soon some new treaty made.

The three naval cities of Venice, Genoa and Pisa were frequently at loggerheads, and as frequently allied two against one. Florence's battles were most often with Siena, but differences with Pisa, Pistoia or Arezzo were not unknown. Milan had little love for Cremona, or Bologna for Modena. But the citizens of Modena and Parma 'love one another with a great and ardent love',[2] though this did not prevent one of them sometimes becoming the ally of the enemy of the other. Verona was always in trouble with Padua; and Cremona took the trouble, in order to vex Mantua, to build a dam in the River Po, though the only one to suffer much in consequence was Reggio.[3]

Things began with the ringing of a bell: the storm bell in a sudden danger and the war bell when the city itself was going to start a campaign. In Florence this was the *Martinella*, sometimes called the 'donkey bell'; a month before the campaign it would be put up and then rung day and night, as a warning to the enemy and a reminder to the Florentines to put their affairs in order and see to their armour. Messengers went to recall citizens who were abroad, for every man was bound to serve—in the smaller places often every man from the ages of fourteen to seventy.

There is the *Martinella* again, now joined by all the bells of the city! Here on the steps in the piazza stand the trumpeters, and blow till they are red in the face. When the trumpet sounds this means things are going to begin. Yes, here is the great battle wagon with the bishop and the podestà upon it and all the people packed around it: it is the famous *Carroccio* with the red and white flag, slowly drawn by two oxen all draped in red.[4] It is the most important part of the army; Mass will be said on it before the battle, and fifty of the best warriors keep guard over it. Cremona's wagon, like the Canadian jeeps, has a name: 'Berta'.[5] That of Parma is called 'Blancardo';[6] it is painted white all over, with pictures of the Madonna and the most powerful saints on it.[7] It was a black day, *mala zobia*, evil Thursday, when it fell into the hands of Cremona![8] It was a disaster at Montaperti when Florence, 'the faded flower',[9] lost her grand red wagon to Siena, together with the *Martinella* and everything else; and it was more than disaster at Cortenuova when Milan's *Carroccio* was lost to Frederick. What was left of it he sent to Rome as a trophy, which was exhibited on the Capitol to the everlasting shame of the City of Ambrose.[10]

But there are no gloomy thoughts now. The menfolk are all on the march through the piazza, their freshly polished breastplates shining. A brave sight indeed. Everyone is praying and singing hymns: surely heaven will grant victory. Over there by the city gates the battle candle is alight. Before it burns down the army must march.[11] Everyone goes to war with enthusiasm; the city has been insulted and every war is a holy war— apart from being an exciting adventure, a chance of promotion,

and anyway a change. We must not be misled by the manifestos and solemn speeches, or by the historians who write
about abstract struggles between Pope and Emperor. In the
northern cities men went to war because they liked to: there
was always the hope of having a good time. But if heaven sent
them back shamed and defeated there was plenty of sympathy
when they returned, and maybe they would win next time.

So there they go: the 'Banner of Destruction' is in the lead,[12]
and then the different quarters of the city, marching in the
order chosen by lot, each with their own standard and then the
guilds with their own flags. In Florence the march was joined
by the clowns, the street musicians and even the prostitutes,
each group with its proper flag.[13] The musicians had an
important part: trumpets and drums and cymbals would help
to rout the enemy on the battlefield.[14] After these came the
battle wagon itself, with the principal men at arms. Finally
there marched a corps of women with baskets of provisions
much more varied than the symbol of bread on their banner
suggested. On one occasion the imperial troops recorded the
capture of several wagons loaded with poultry, a novel ambu-
lance wagon full of medical supplies, and even a cart with a
consignment of fans to keep off the flies and the heat.[15]

It was natural that the popes and emperors should sometimes
turn these skirmishes to their own advantage, and then things
became more serious. Usually the Pope profited most by this,
especially when Otto the Guelph, who before the days of
Frederick reigned by favour of the Apostolic See, had won over
nearly half of central Italy to the side of the Pope: Lazio, of
course, and then the Duchy of Spoleto, the whole of Umbria,
the March of Ancona, the Exarchate of Ravenna, and the
greater part of Romagna and Tuscany. Frederick reversed all
this and put in his own governors to ensure the subjection of the
people. But most of the population was really on the Pope's
side: he at least used to leave them in peace, and the worst that
could happen was that he would install a mayor somewhere,
who was obliged, however, to observe the local statutes. Now
things were different, and the cities began to group themselves

into leagues. Even as late as 1286 (36 years after Frederick's death), Perugia and three other Umbrian cities formed a league *ad honorem Matris nostrae almae Urbis*.[16] That sounded well and, after all, committed them to nothing. But only four years previously the Pope had had to forbid Perugia to raze Foligno to the ground. The people of Perugia, who had always been so loyal to the Pope, were so cross about this that they made effigies and burned them publicly: 'There goes Cardinal so-and-so, there goes Cardinal someone else, and here goes His Holiness himself!'[17] In view of such insubordination it sometimes happened that even an anti-imperial city got involved in an interdict, as happened to Florence. It was a curious position when Gregory X was returning from Lyons and being unable to cross the flood-swollen Arno was compelled to go to Florence, which he had hitherto avoided. While he was within the walls of the city he had to revoke the interdict: Masses had to be celebrated and the people flocked to greet their distinguished guest. But as soon as the Pope had gone back came the interdict, so that Gregory X was not a very popular figure in Florence. Things were not much easier for the Emperor, except in the few cities which stuck to him through thick and thin, like Pisa and Cremona. There is a story of a visit of Frederick to Venice not unlike the story of Gregory X in Florence. When Frederick arrived he was received most cordially by the Venetians: the Doge Tiepolo took His Majesty for a state tour of the canals, all the people stood cheering on the quays and there were formal exchanges of presents and relics. But when the Kaiser introduced the subject of his hosts' relations with the anti-German Lombard league and gave voice to some of his authoritarian notions, the attitude of the Venetians changed and the rest of his reception was very cool. The Republic immediately took up the cause of the democratic cities, at least as long as it served their purpose. When later the Kaiser ordered an imperial crown from a Venetian goldsmith the Venetian authorities became very anxious lest such a thing should compromise the Republic.[18]

An emperor who saw himself as a *Sacra Majestas* lording it

over the common crowd of mankind, could conceive no people more unbearable than the Venetians; for they thought themselves as much of a 'Great Mogul' as he did: after all, they laid claim to the whole Levant and had subdued Byzantium itself. Their proud ships were respected even by the Dalmatian pirates; their trade extended over almost the whole of Europe and goods from the world over found their way to their city. In fact, Venice would have had everything her own way if it had not been for her equally ambitious rival on the other side of Italy: Genoa. Every now and then Venice proposed simply to annihilate Genoa, but then Genoa, who at that time gloried in her title of *janua Regni*, 'the gateway to the Empire', had only to call upon the Emperor for help. Thus it was that Genoa never succumbed to Venice. And apart from this, the merchants never really supported these enterprises: such things are not good for trade. Yet if it was a question of keeping the Kaiser away, all the other cities were prepared to join hands with Venice. They were ready to betray him at any opportunity, block his lines of communication with Germany in the area above Trent and confront him with a combined army which was more than he could deal with. How Frederick hated these Lombards, Milan in particular, the home of all heretics and rebels, and all these northern cities which had no respect for his authority.[19] 'Insolent Italians' he called them (perhaps rightly enough),[20] and 'destroyers of the peace of the world', and he felt himself called by God to destroy these centres of unrest and obstinacy.[21] All his life he regretted his failure to do so; he is supposed once to have said: 'If I had one foot in paradise, I should draw it back, if it was a question of vengeance on Viterbo.'[22] German historians even today cannot get over the attitude of those Italian citizens, whom they tend to regard as disloyal and ungrateful.[23]

We must admit that Frederick had more success with them than his grandfather Barbarossa, who never defeated the Lombards, however vigorously his armies tramped through their plain. But the grandson was more of an Italian himself and he knew how to use politics when the force of arms failed.

No city offered him more resistance than Milan, until during the siege he rode up to the walls on his war elephant, at the sight of which the aggressive inhabitants dropped their weapons. They just stared, seeing a *Carroccio* 'high on the back of this astonishing creature', with a flag in the middle and pennants on either side, and Saracens all around it.[24] In 1248, when the animal died, they were all asking whether the *bestia quae vocabatur elephas*[25] really had bones of ivory.[26] Elsewhere Frederick also succeeded psychologically when he put on a fine show for the people and showed himself a real emperor, with a crown on his head and an empress at his side,[27] and maybe he would really have won the whole of Lombardy if he had appealed a little more in this way to their sense of the theatrical. But Frederick had no sense of humour in politics; he got angry too easily and then always lost the game. Sometimes the Lombards won hands down, as in the case of Brescia, where they usually knew their own mind. Their spies had captured a certain Spaniard while their city was being besieged by Frederick. The Spaniard was already a prisoner of Ezzelino, who was sending him to Frederick, but he was intercepted by the Brescians and taken to their city. He turned out to be none other than Calamandrinus, the most famous military engineer of the time. So they gave him the best house in the town and the prettiest girl as a wife. Calamandrinus had had enough of tyrants by now and took up the cause of Brescia. He put their fortifications in order for them and designed new weapons— maybe among them the famous mechanical sling for throwing stones, which the Florentines called *soave*, the 'sweet one'.[28] Anyway, Brescia so soon got the upper hand that Frederick had to withdraw.[29] That was a great day for the northern cities.

But their greatest day came when Frederick was besieging Parma a couple of years before his death. Outside the city he had built a whole temporary town as his headquarters during the siege. Rather prematurely he had called this town Victoria,[30] the church was St Victor's and the coins were called *victorini*. One morning he had gone out for a little hunting in the near-by marshes when suddenly he heard the bell of St

Victor's ringing violently. He galloped back, but it was too late. A handful of men had come out from Parma and taken the confident Victoria by surprise, killed everyone and plundered everything, razing the rest to the ground. They carried their booty in triumph through the streets, including even the imperial crown, which was 'as large as a kitchen cauldron'.[31] But Parma misused their success, as Dante sadly remarks: 'They may have had their victory over Victoria, but they certainly had many pains for their pains afterwards.'[32] It is sad that only too often, for all their passionate love of freedom, the Italian cities through their mutual jealousies opened their gates to the tyrant.

'In those days two horrible women appeared in the skies of Tuscany and covered the land like two hideous clouds entwined with one another in perpetual strife: they were called Guelpha and Ghibellina.' Thus the chronicler Malaspina.[33] These were the Guelph and Ghibelline parties who brought so much ruin to the land. The names of the two parties came originally from Germany, where two factions, the Welfen and the Waiblinger, were struggling for mastery, and it was under the Waiblinger that the Hohenstaufen came to power. When the names came to Italy their real origin was forgotten and a much more romantic story was told by the Tuscan chroniclers. In 1215 there was a young Florentine called Buondelmonte, whose bride to be was from the family of the Amedei. But he abandoned his bride in favour of another beauty. The relatives of the forsaken bride swore vengeance on the faithless youth and killed him one morning as he rode over the bridge across the Arno. This, we are told, is the origin of the feud for which Italians continued to kill one another for a further hundred years, and, of course, it is a much more convincing *casus belli* than hostility between the Welfen, who supported the Pope, and the Waiblinger, who supported the Hohenstaufen. However that may be, the Italian Guelphs became associated with the papal party and the Ghibellines with the imperial, even though the conflict only reached its height after the Hohenstaufen had disappeared.

The struggle involved a large area of Italy and brought much misery. It was, in fact, the sum of many different social, personal and local conflicts. Sometimes it took the form of warfare between the nobles and the people; at other times there were both Guelph and Ghibelline nobles and the people adopted the slogan *Viva che vinze!* ('Long live the winner!'),[34] an undisguised opportunism. It is a mistake to attribute religious motives to it all, even though sometimes the opponents were called heretics, as when Spoleto besieged Foligno, crying: 'Death to the Ghibelline Patarenes!' or when Orvieto issued a statute against 'heretics and Ghibellines'.[35] On the other hand we have already noticed Frederick calling Milan 'the home of heretics and rebels'. In Florence in 1244 when heretics were brought before the inquisition there were both Guelphs and Ghibellines among them.[36] How it was, then, that for instance Spoleto and her allies were all Guelphs and Foligno with hers all Ghibellines? It is impossible to say exactly: it may have been simply what they were used to; or the influence of a particular mayor; or merely the desire to be different from their neighbour in the opposite camp; or even some question of property tied to this or that allegiance. After all, people do need an allegiance, and in those days there was no football to provide harmless but passionate allegiances among the people. So it was that Guelphs and Ghibellines went on hating each other and proclaimed their allegiances in all sorts of ways, their gait, their greetings, their clothes, even their way of cutting bread. And some of these things survived into the seventeenth century, when new allegiances took the place of the old.[37]

The battle went on in both town and country. In the towns, when one party was driven out, their partisans began war on the new régime: arrows and stones rained down from the towers on the barricaded streets. In the countryside adherents of the fallen party were pursued to the countryside where the peasants' farms and hayricks were burnt down. In the towns things were more quickly composed, and anyway law and order could be restored by force of arms, but in the country danger often lingered longer and it was the peasants who suffered.

'At this time there was a bitter war which lasted many years. It was impossible to plough or sow or harvest, impossible to plant vines or gather grapes, or even to live in peace on a farm. Only close to the walls of the city, under military protection, was it possible to cultivate the land. The city guards protected these areas and here agriculture could continue. But elsewhere it was hopeless because of the highwaymen, thieves and robbers, who were attacking every day more openly, taking people prisoner in order to extort ransoms and driving away their cattle to eat them or sell them. And when people did not pay, they would hang them up by the hands or feet, knock their teeth out and put toads in their mouths to make them pay up more quickly. These things were worse than death, and the robbers were worse than demons. Everyone saw the devil everywhere and no one could trust anybody, fearing capture or torture at every turn. And the land was dying, with no one to till it. Wild birds and animals multiplied alarmingly: pheasants, partridges and quails were everywhere, hares, deer and stags, wild oxen, wild boars and terrible wolves. These could no longer find their usual prey of lambs and sheep since the farms were burnt down, so they gathered in hungry packs and howled round the city walls. At night time they would steal into the city itself and fall upon men asleep on their carts in the open halls, and on women and children too . . .'[38] Thus the old chronicler.

It is not surprising that the peasants followed the example of the wolves and sometimes had massed invasions of the towns. In every way they were in a worse position than the townsfolk: they were at the mercy of their masters and of the robbers, and always at the mercy of the weather. One harvest failure, a flood, a plague of caterpillars or a cattle disease could always ruin them, and they had no resources, spiritual or material, to defend themselves or to recover. In this matter the practical Kaiser Frederick was far ahead of his time when he astonished the peasants by ordering an assessment to be made of their land, on the basis of which he would prescribe what should next be sown, corn here, beans there, and so forth.[39] Of course, the

1. This bust of an emperor, damaged but nobly expressive, has been thought to portray Frederick II. The bust, which is life-size, is displayed in the Museo Comunale in Barletta.

2. The main pulpit of the Cathedral of Bitonto has a curious relief which may depict Frederick II and his family. The work, noteworthy for its very ornate ornament, is signed by Master Nicholas, who completed it in 1229.

3. Built by the Emperor Frederick II about 1240 as a residence and hunting lodge, the Castel del Monte dominates the Apulian plain. The severely logical octagonal plan, which is in turn mirrored in the eight corner towers, seems to express the energy and ruthlessness of its imperial patron. The windows and some other details, however, show the penetration of the French Gothic style, then new to Italy.

4. Although the original nucleus of the Castle of Lucera in Capitanata was constructed by Frederick II, the present massive form is due to an architect employed by Charles d'Anjou at the end of the thirteenth century. The vast pentagonal enclosure is reinforced by rectangular and pentagonal towers.

5. This panoramic view of the Adriatic coast of Capitanata as seen from Montegargano shows a key region of Frederick II's south Italian kingdom. The town of Manfredonia, faintly visible in the distance, was founded by Frederick's son Manfred in 1256 to replace the ancient port of Siponto.

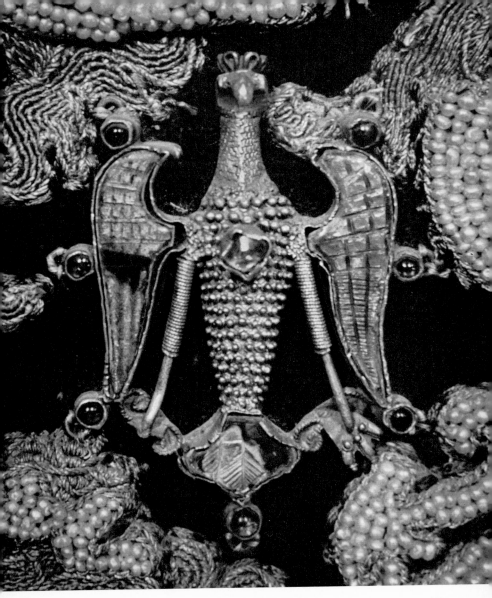

6. The jewelled eagle in the cathedral treasury of Palermo Cathedral is a heraldic emblem of the Hohenstaufen emperors, who were known to contemporaries as the *gens aquila*, the race of the eagle.

7. This miniature of a falconer from a manuscript of Frederick II's treatise on falconry represents the emperor's son Manfred. The manuscript belongs to the Vatican Library (Pal. lat. 1071).

8. The Castle of Termoli in Molise on the Adriatic Coast has a rectangular keep with a curtain wall strengthened by round bastions. This is all that remains of a larger fort built by Frederick II in 1247 to defend the port of Termoli.

9. The pleasure palace of La Zisa in Palermo was constructed by Islamic craftsmen for the Norman King William I in the mid-twelfth century. The stalactite ceiling, mosaic work and rippling fountain represent Moorish work at its best.

10. The five projecting domes of the twelfth-century Church of San Giovanni degli Eremiti in Palermo give an agreeably Near Eastern flavour to this construction of Roger II, King of Sicily (1130–54).

11. Tropical vegetation lends a picturesque charm to the venerable thirteenth-century cloister of San Giovanni degli Eremiti in Palermo.

12. This portrait of Boniface VIII, though it was carved by an anonymous craftsman, brings out the determination and tragic obstinacy of the last great pope of the middle ages. The statue was probably designed to commemorate the pope's authorisation for the beginning of the new Cathedral of Florence; it is now displayed in the Cathedral Museum.

13. With its ancient defensive towers that housed the nobility, the little Tuscan hill town of San Gimignano preserves an important aspect of Italian civic life in the middle ages.

14. The chief monument of secular architecture in medieval Florence, the Palazzo Vecchio, was begun in 1298, apparently after designs of Arnolfo di Cambio. The main body of the building, surmounted by a massive crenellated loggia, is set off by a 300-foot tower.

15. The Palazzo dell'Arengo, or town hall, of Rimini, which was begun in 1204
and rebuilt in modern times, is an imposing block whose broad surfaces are
enlivened by the arcade, shallow loggia and picturesque fishtail crenellations.

16. The pride of Siena, the Palazzo Pubblico, was begun in 1298 and largely completed in the following century. The extremely elegant impression produced by the Palazzo is due to the accent provided by the slender tower and the carefully controlled contrast of glittering white marble and rough-textured brick.

profits of all this went into his own funds and not those of the peasants, because at least in the kingdom of Sicily, but also elsewhere, they were his serfs. But in most parts the peasants, demoralised by hunger and poverty—*colonus ergo fur* was an old law phrase[40]—weary and helpless, fled into the towns. They would be poor here also, but at least they would be secure and free; and the citizens received them gladly, knowing that their flight from the land was weakening the feudal lords.

In this way the balance between agriculture and industry was dangerously upset. The population of many towns increased enormously during the century: the walls of Florence, built in 1160, had within a century to be enlarged to enclose a space ten times larger than before; and in 1220 one bridge over the Arno was adequate, while in 1250 already the fourth one was being built.[41] In 200 years the population had increased from 6,000 to nearly 74,000. Siena and Pisa were both more than half this size; and Venice and Milan in the fourteenth century, including their suburbs, each had nearly 100,000 inhabitants.[42] The devout rhymster Bonvesin da Riva, who belonged to the Order of the Humiliati, and whom we shall meet again,[43] is perhaps exaggerating the figures when he describes his home town of Milan in 1287, but he certainly gives a lively picture of this energetic Lombard city.[44] He tells us that there were no less than 3,000 mills there and 1,000 taverns. The legal affairs of the citizens were in charge of 400 notaries and 200 judges, and there were as many doctors working in 150 hospitals. Eighty teachers and 50 public scribes looked after the more spiritual needs of the citizens, and as for their piety, there were 3,000 altars in 1,345 churches. Two hundred and twenty bells rang in 120 towers, and 10,000 religious prayed day and night for the spiritual needs of the Milanese.

The government of such a community in this individualistic land in this individualistic century would have presented grave problems, had they not been faced here long ago compared with other lands. The ordinary citizens in Italy had formed themselves into a closely knit and self-conscious bourgeoisie at a time when cities elsewhere were still entirely in the hands of the local nobility. For some centuries prosperous citizens had been pursuing their business interests and had organised themselves; their sons were sent to study rhetoric and law, while in other countries students apart from the clergy were almost unknown. The Italian nobility had for a long time had a declining influence; the decline was gradual at first, but became very rapid during the thirteenth century. The people were beginning to make the laws which their lordships had to obey, and the citizens' armies were able to enforce them. No one in 1250 could afford to laugh at the warlike *popolani* in Florence, when they mustered with their shields properly blazoned. They developed, distinct from the nobility, their own fiercely self-conscious way of speaking. One decision of the people of Florence was especially indicative of the new order and was imitated by many other cities: the fortified towers of the noble families were never to be built higher than 50 ells, while many at the time were three times this height.[45] The tower of the Adimari, near the baptistery, which fell down during one skirmish, was 230 feet high.[46] The rivalry of the towers was over for good, when the people at one stroke reduced them to absurdity; and it was not only a matter of the towers.

Since the eleventh century the people had fought for a place in the government of the cities. At first they had their representatives along with the consul from the nobility, but gradually their number and their power increased, and in many places the whole body of citizens would be summoned by a bell and gather to decide the affairs of the city, voting by a show of hands or by acclamation, as is still done today in many Swiss cantons. A church would serve as a parliament house on Sunday afternoons, but it was natural that these crowded 'bell councils' should often become the scenes of noisy lobbyings and gradually only unimportant business was entrusted to them, while the important things were discussed behind closed doors by the mayor and a selected group, most of whom, however, came increasingly from the *popolani*.

The mayor of a medieval town, called the *Podestà*, held a

central, though unenviable, position in the administration.[47]
During his term of office, at first limited to one year, he was
bound by very strict regulations. Once he had taken the official
oath all his business dealings had to cease, and his emoluments
were fixed down to the last penny; the same applied to his
personal expenses. Complete political impartiality was insisted
on—though in the long run in vain. He was always chosen
from the ruling class in another city, and he was forbidden to
visit friends, to go out to meals, or to engage in hunting or
jousting. His household, including his wife, were bound to stay
at home, and there was a censorship of all his letters. Similar
regulations were made by Frederick for his ministers of justice,
and also for the senators of Rome. The man who undertook the
government of a city became the servant of the community,
and like a general on the field of battle he had no more private
life. These 'city generals' were far from being monarchs: the
regulations which bound them were derived from a fear of
tyranny. In matters of finance or war they could do no more
than advise: decisions were not for them. At appointed times
the statutes of the city were read out to them, to be sure they
would not forget or contravene them. During the mayor's
term of office every citizen had the right to bring up any com-
plaint against him, and woe betide the *Podestà* who was found
wanting: it could cost him his position, his salary, his honour,
his freedom and even his life. But for one who discharged his
duties well there were rewards: he was made an honorary
citizen, his portrait was painted in the guildhall and he was
granted the privilege of including the coat of arms of the city
in his own. He would not be re-elected, because this might give
to one man too much influence: at Vercelli any member of the
Council who proposed a prolongation of the office would be
fined a hundred lire; at Vicenza and Novara it was the same;
but at Padua such a proposal would be punished with death.[48]
Yet, in fact, there was a development in this matter, and the
period of office of the *Podestà* was extended by one further
year, then fixed at three and later at five and ten years, finally
becoming an appointment for life and hereditary.

The *Podestà* had with him a whole collegium of officials: envoys, chancellor, notaries, accountants, weights-and-measures officers, treasurers, guards and the secretaries who made records of every meeting of the council. In the south it was the same but they had grander titles and less authority: there they were called grand chancellor, grand constable, grand chamberlain and grand minister of justice, and they were nominated and controlled by the Emperor himself. Among the Lombards the people themselves elected their governing body *per apodixias*,[49] that is, voting papers were solemnly placed in an urn and drawn out by a child. Every man was eligible for these and other offices, provided he were of legitimate birth and married, and —at least at Ivrea—had duly put up his candle at the Lady Altar on the feast of the Assumption.[50] The people's representatives, properly so called, were chosen either in their quarter of the city or in their guilds and they were called the *anziani* or 'elders'. The number of these and their periods of office varied in different cities, but their task was everywhere the same and they possessed considerable power. They genuinely represented the interests of the people and acted as a restraint on the city authorities. The general control of the city was therefore under the mayor, his officials and the representatives.

One of the problems of the sessions of the council was to curb the oratory of the speakers: at Siena, for instance, it was expressly forbidden for anyone to speak unless he had something really new to contribute,[51] while at Bologna another rhetorical danger was envisaged in the statutes of 1267, when it was ruled that any member who flattered the *Podestà* or even attempted to praise him was to be fined twenty florins.[52]

The government of the north Italian towns was not, of course, democratic in the modern sense: it was a middle-class rule from which the poor, that is those who were not owners of property, were always excluded. And perhaps because a middle class was not accustomed to statesmanship its lasting results were limited. The ideal of representation of the people was, in fact, not as effective as it sounds, and the whole system rose and fell with the rise and decline of the guilds, the most powerful forces ultimately being the masters of the various guilds. There is here an interesting parallel with modern times, since the lasting effect of the north Italian systems was the organisation of the people themselves and the influence of these organisations in matters of government.

The guilds were the important thing: a city's prosperity depended on them and even the nobility could not afford to disregard them. In fact, the division between the richer bourgeois and the humbler aristocrats was never very sharp: already in the twelfth century the members of the better guilds intermarried with the aristocracy and they made a common front against the working classes. Thus already as early as this democratic society was already split by clear-cut social divisions. Florence, which is such a typical example and about which we are so fully informed, shows this clearly. Among her seven *arti maggiori* there were indeed different levels of respectability and influence; but they were all far above the fifteen or twenty *arti minori* of the smaller men, the smiths, wine merchants, carpenters and so on. And yet these *arti* seemed a paradise of security to the real proletariat, the servants and labourers, hawkers and peddlers, who were forbidden under pain of heavy punishment to form themselves into any organisations, even religious ones. It is plain that the middle classes went in fear of revolution on the part of the proletariat, and indeed there were occasions of civil unrest when these fears were justified. It was then that the common people grouped themselves together and joined forces with the most left wing of all the guilds, that of the slaughterers, who, accustomed as they were in their trade to sharp knives and bleeding flesh, could become a serious threat to public order.

The common people and the lesser guilds were thought of as the *popolo grasso* as distinct from the *primo popolo* of the seven major guilds. The highest of these included the judges and notaries, who were on friendly terms with the nobility and hated by the proletariat. To the second guild belonged the big-business people of the *Callemala* (the street between the market halls and the Piazza del Duomo), who dealt in home and foreign trade in a very big way and also ran the banks. Lower down the scale were the guilds of the money-changers and the bigger textile businessmen, whose guild was said in the fourteenth century to have had 30,000 members.[53] In the fifth guild were the ordinary merchants. To the sixth guild belonged the retail shopkeepers, as well as the chemists and doctors; while the seventh and last of the major guilds was that of the furriers.

The guilds were in touch with one another, with deputies from each guild, most of whom in the early days were actual workers in their own trades, but who as time went on became professional political representatives in the council of the guilds. Thus gradually the guild council became a rival of the city council and its president came to have a power rivalling that of the *Podestà*: he became the *Potestas Populi* and came to be called the *Capitano del Popolo*. The ascendancy of these men meant the end of democracy. At the beginning, when the guilds served the city under the *Podestà*, they had done great things for the people, but now the *Capitano* so far usurped the power of the *Podestà* that eventually the two offices were combined. Then all the many restraints that had curbed the power of the *Podestà* were thrown off, and it was a turning-point in the story when it was the president of the guilds who received into his hands the banner, the staff and the keys of the city. Sometimes the guild banner became the city banner, as at Verona; but by this time the meaning of the guilds was no longer the same. Everything was in the hands of the *Capitano*, and his son would follow after him. This was the beginning of the *Signoria*.

In the end it was the nobles who had the last word. When a man is *Capitano* of one city, what is to stop him being *Capitano* of ten? Whole areas were swearing fealty to a noble house now: *in dominium et dominos, potestates et rectores in perpetuum*.[54] The bourgeois had got tired of fighting and wanted to do their business and bring up their children in peace. They were convinced that they had conquered the feudal lords; there were no more fortified towers now and now the noble families looked after them and did not rob them any more. But they did not

realise that they were losing their independence and striking
dead their own passion for freedom. Only when the fullness of
the Renaissance had come did they recognise that tyranny had
come, too, and made an end of the Middle Ages with its guilds
and *anziani*. The names of the *Capitani* became the names of
the great city dynasties which we associate with humanist culture and *quattrocento* painting: the d'Este at Ferrara and
Modena; at Verona, after Ezzelino's reign of terror, it was the
Scaligeri; farther north, William of Monferrato and the
notorious Pallavicini; in Milan the Della Torre and later
the Visconti came to power; at Rimini the Malatesta; at Forli
the Montefeltro; and somewhat later the Gonzaga at Mantua
and the Carrara at Padua.

The downfall of the democracies belongs really to the fourteenth century, but perhaps the striving after it in the *Duecento*
stands out more gloriously in contrast. Do democracies always
reach a point of downfall? But history has repeated itself so
often since the days of Hellas that we need not feel discouraged,
for democracy seems to be the phoenix of European politics,
and will always rise again.

4

The People

Then the men of Milan besieged Cremona. They blew upon
their trumpets before the walls, and cried: Come out, you dogs of
Cremona, come out, you rabbits, come and fight. But they of
Cremona durst not.

Annales Parmenses maiores[1]

THERE ARE many small towns on the hilltops which still
enclose a medieval world within their walls: such are Todi and
Orvieto, Spello and Cortona. Rome, Milan or Naples have
changed too much, and Florence is too much a shrine of the
Renaissance. It is in almost any of the hill towns of Umbria that
the Middle Ages are still alive; many things have hardly
changed: the winding road up the hill, the vines, the golden
maize hung up to dry—and the people, a woman still carrying
her pitcher on her head, a boy running past with his goats, a
little girl with a loaf of bread as big as they were ever made, an
old man still speaking the old dialect . . . The walls are still
the same ones, and the city gate, weathered perhaps, but still
bearing an inscription with its date, or a statue or a shield,
still tells its story.

Within the town the steep and narrow streets look now as
they must have looked then—often they still bear their old
names—and a little sanctuary still has its rough medieval
frescoes, which still serve the piety of the people; and the dark
smithy still rings to the same sounds as before. And every now
and then, as the street mounts into the sky, there is a sudden
glimpse of the unchanging hills of Umbria in distant view. At
the summit is the piazza. On one side is the romanesque
cathedral, with its still unfinished façade, its rose window

of delicate stonework, the bronze doors flanked by the stiff figures of the evangelists—and the pigeons strutting about and the swallows flying in and out, as they have always done. Opposite is the massive *municipio*, complete with bell tower and battlements, with its great doorway adorned with the shields of many a *podestà* and guarded by fierce stone lions, and next door is the guildhall equally fortified. In the piazza there will be a fountain, of course, and the inevitable monument to Garibaldi, which is somehow not really out of place here, for it is only one more manifestation of a lively spirit. Then there are the little shops, setting out what a truly Umbrian town has to offer, and townsfolk and countryfolk mixing there as they come to bargain and to buy. The magnificent women with fair hair, such as one sees in the pictures of Lippi and Botticelli, are now rarely seen in modern Florence, while in the hills all the girls seem to have the almond-shaped eyes of Perugino's madonnas. Like the local wine with its single and most appropriate name, *Sole*, the old ideas remain. You would not be surprised to hear: 'that lot of Guelphs. Here you are among decent Ghibellines.' Things have not changed much since the days when the citizens in their free time brought stone and sand to build this cathedral,[2] with a song on their lips that was more patriotic than pious. The painter of the unimportant madonna in the church, or of the almost unknown patron saint above an altar, may have gone, but his madonna and his saint remain. The bell founder may be long dead, but his bell still rings. . . .

It is otherwise in the northern towns: the pursuit of success along the trade routes brought many changes which never touched the secure and remote hilltops. The Middle Ages were swept away from Vicenza and Padua along the road to the Brenner, just as they were carried away from Pavia, Piacenza and Ferrara by the River Po. As for the ports, they could hardly resist the new influences: they gradually got wide new streets with trams, enormous piazzas with baroque churches and factories, and the few really old *palazzi* are huddled away in back streets. Sometimes on the edge of the town there remains an old quarter, now in reduced circumstances, which can show us something of what the old town must have been like before the days of progress, before there was a Piazza Garibaldi or a Via Cavour, or a Jesuit church with altar pieces by Guido Reni.

It is often difficult for us to realise how unhygienic things must have been by modern standards, with the wooden houses crowded together, under the constant threat of the twin horrors of fire and plague. Anything could start an epidemic: a returning crusader or a wandering beggar could bring the disease, and the rats, dunghills and drains, or absence of them, would help to spread it. Nobody bothered about hygiene: on the contrary, it was suspect, and one of the most unchristian habits of the Emperor Frederick was considered to be his addiction to a daily bath, even on Sundays, 'from which it is evident that he had no regard either for the commandments of God or for the feasts and sacraments of the Church', concluded the chronicler.[3] Such care of the body may have been considered the devil's business, but the people's contempt for material things took them more quickly into the hereafter than they liked. Two or three cases of fever or plague would start an epidemic, and within a week all the resources of the doctors and nursing brothers were exhausted. Processions and blest candles were of no avail now, and the dead were too numerous for the bells to be tolled for them. Within a month whole quarters or even whole towns would be wiped out. The other horror was fire. At any time whole streets would be reduced to ashes; in 1232 the principal quarter of Florence, near the cathedral, went up in flames, and within two years the whole section of the Oltr' Arno from the Ponte Vecchio to the south gate was destroyed by fire, started by the torch of a passer-by on Christmas night; and this is far from being a full account of the damage by fire in ten years of the city's life.

The ordinary people cared little about their private dwellings: they were usually of a temporary nature, since people had always spent most of the day out of doors. Churches and public buildings were constructed with care, mostly of stone. With increasing prosperity, a craze for building began, and the chroniclers fill their records with accounts of new constructions: a new bell tower, perhaps, or a fountain, or a statue. The *Podestà* of Florence carried on his own august shoulders the first bucket of lime for the new Ponte alle Grazie, whose graceful single span bridged the Arno until 1944.[4] At the end of the century they made a pleasure garden where the Cascine are today; there was even a fishpond there but no trees so as not to spoil the view of the other people there.[5] About the same time people began to spend more on their own houses, especially outside the immediate centre of the town, and large houses became the fashion, with a loggia, reception rooms, bedrooms, kitchen, stables, cellar and bakehouse.[6] Outside the city walls were the hospitals and poor-houses, managed by nursing brothers, and farthest out of all was the leper-house, which never had any fear of being raided, since both soldiers and robbers were terrified of going near.

By evening the environs of the city became completely deserted; at the Angelus bell the gates were closed,[7] and before long all would be quiet in the city as well. When darkness came there was another bell, the *campana bibitorum* or 'topers' bell', which was the signal for the taverns to close and for the drinkers to go home. A little later there was a third signal, the *coprifuoco* or curfew bell, which told the citizens to put out their lights and to cover their fires. Anyone who was seen outside after this was liable to severe punishment, for the darkness often provided cover for robbery or insurrection, whatever party, Guelph or Ghibelline, was in power. Once a man came out of his house at night, shouting and screaming, and was at once arrested and had his hands cut off, since he was accused of shouting: 'To arms! To arms!'[8] There were very few people officially allowed in the streets at night, carrying a lamp: priests and notaries, doctors and midwives, and of course the night watchmen. All had to be silent until the religious houses rang their bell for matins; then the slaughterers went to their work, and gradually other people, until the seven strokes in the morning, when the city gates were opened again.

The whole life of the community was regulated by bells: they rang before the morning Masses, before the offices in the monastic churches and for all kinds of daily tasks in the town, as well as for special occasions. The city bells were usually the most tuneful and also the loudest and there were special bell-ringers for each. Hence, of course, the importance of those tall towers on the municipal buildings of Florence, Siena and other cities.

Whenever a war was declared or a peace was achieved, whenever a king or an emperor or a prince of the Church was coming, the bells rang. They summoned the town council, they summoned the guards and resolutions taken *sine campana* were reckoned invalid.[9] The favourite story book of the century, the *Novellino*, still speaks of the 'plaintiff's bell'. This goes back to the time of Charlemagne, when it was said that anyone who had suffered an injustice had the right to ring that bell, and then the authorities would examine his case.[10]

Great store was set by the bells and much care was taken about their fullness and beauty of tone; they were the pride of any city throughout Europe.[11] To capture a city bell in war was the greatest triumph; and many stories were told of miscast bells—in other cities, of course, of bells which were cast without a headstock so that they could never be hung, of the monster bell which the boastful Manfred had cast and which was so big and heavy that no one could ever ring it.[12] There was the famous bell at Parma that was so badly made by a scoundrel from Pisa that it literally rang itself to pieces and crashed down from its wooden frame, but even then it managed to serve justice, because it shattered the foot of a youth who had been kicking his old father.[13] Still, it was a sad day for that city when they had to find a hundred pounds for a new bell.

Among the sounds of the city, after the bells came the city trumpeters.[14] Every town had at least one and he had a busy time. Whenever the battle wagon was brought out or a proclamation made, or when the magistrates came to wreak vengeance on the house of their victim, the *tubatores* were always there, blowing their trumpets. Envoys were always received and sent off with trumpet blasts from the shining silver instruments, bound with silken cords.

Meanwhile the citizens were busy folk, members of the guilds had to work hard at their trades to qualify for membership; people were always at work, the weaver with his shuttle, the blacksmith with his hammer, the baker at his oven and the dyer over his tubs. Membership brought many benefits: in sickness one went to the guild's own hospital, in death one was buried in the special graveyard, one's widow would be cared for and one's daughters would receive a dowry. This meant not only hard work, but also strict surveillance; weights and measures were regularly checked and any infringement was taken as an offence both against society and against God. A just price is as important in morality as it is in business and an honourable firm understands this . . . Perhaps nowhere in the world was the law of supply and demand considered so carefully as the will of God as in the energetic guild city of Florence at the time when Dante was young. Men were convinced that a state of spiritual bankruptcy at death was as bad as a financial failure, and worse. The guilds therefore adopted measures which had been carefully thought out, guild patrons were honoured, guild churches built and the most proper behaviour was insisted on within the premises of the guild; there was to be no betting, in their inns no women of easy virtue or waitresses of that type were admitted. Meals were usually only served to travellers, because a proper guild member was expected to have his meals at home.[15] The council in Florence also took into account another human weakness when it issued its first law against blasphemy: there was a scale of penalties according to the standing of the offender: 20 lire for a nobleman who spoke ill of God or the Virgin Mary, but only 10 lire for a commoner.[16] It was not like Rome, where the guilds were a mere appendage of society, a little circle of businessmen who had their shops down there in the *Via delle Botteghe oscure*, 'the Street of the Dark Shops', under the Circo Massimo! No, this is Florence, 'the great city, spreading her wings over the sea and the earth'.[17] Here in Florence the learned Giovanni Villani was writing the history of his own city, full of his impressions of Rome which he had recently visited, noticing how 'as Rome sank, Florence rose'.[18] For him, which was the most important year of the century— the year when Francis founded his order, or when Aquinas published his writings? The year when the Emperor Frederick died, or when Charles of Anjou defeated Manfred? No, for Giovanni Villani it was the year 1252, when the first gold florin was minted, the real, genuine, world-famous florin.[19] With this first-fruit Florence came to the forefront of the commercial world and henceforth a network of trade spread from the Mercato Nuovo and the Callemala into the whole of Italy and the world abroad. For more than a century Florence had devised tariffs and customs from which only pilgrims and travellers who came *pro civitate videnda* were exempt.[20] And these regulations not only protected the home products, as they do today, but they also controlled the whole system of weights and measures and coinage, which differed from city to city according to its prosperity. Thus the bushel of Parma was reckoned as six *sextarii*, while that of Ferrara counted as twenty, because more corn was grown there.[21] The Florentine bankers in their imposing stone *palazzi* had lists of every currency there was: from the humble penny, the *denarius* of the market place, to the *imperiale, augustale* and *bisanti* of the kingdom of Sicily. The merchants thought of nothing but rates of exchange and they were mocked by Jacopone, the Franciscan poet who loved poverty:

> You can treasure your fiorini,
> your ducati, carolini,
> smeraldini, genovini:
> just a lot of junk to me![22]

The names of many of the coins of the time bespeak their origins in different Italian towns: nevertheless, even today the lire and florins of Florence, the ducats of Venice, the carlini of Naples and the pistols of Pistoia are reminders of the importance of Italian monetary operations for Europe. Nor is it surprising that the oldest commercial law and the oldest system of book-keeping both come from Italy. But at the same time the worst

usurers were found there: everyone knew the danger of falling
into the hands of the moneylenders of Asti, who would ruin a
small man by demanding $43\frac{1}{2}$ per cent interest. They were
scoundrels, until it was time to die, when they were converted
and founded a hospital or church with their blood money.[23]

This spirit of enterprise made things lively in those north
Italian towns. Their trade representatives covered half the
world, from Provence to the Levant, doing business in the wool
markets of England or at the trade fairs of Venice and Genoa.
There was a regular textile industry at Milan, and Lucca had a
special line in cloths and brocades—together, of course, with
their *Volto Santo*, the crowned crucifix of the weavers' guild,
which brought people from all over Europe. Nor was Sicily
outside their orbit: it remained the granary of Italy and the
source of oil supply. More recently the silk industry grew up
there, which the Emperor had given to the Jews as their
monopoly. Trade was not so easy in the Empire under the
Hohenstaufen, because there was government control of salt,
iron and steel, while the banks, public baths and abattoirs were
mostly Government enterprises and foreign merchants were
obliged to live in special quarters in the ports. Naturally the
Government purse did well by these arrangements and the sale
of Sicilian corn brought in one and a half millions during the
Tunisian famine; Frederick may not have been a very devout
man but he knew his Bible well enough to follow the example
of Joseph.

All this travelling made the Italians into cosmopolitans and
foreigners in the small towns aroused less curiosity than they do
now, 700 years later, when the patterns of travel have altered.
Travellers' hospices were to be found everywhere and many
bridges had been constructed, some built upon piles in the
rivers, while others were laid upon pontoons. There was also a
considerable traffic on the rivers themselves, and this is the
setting for the story of the famous tame raven of Cardinal
Gregory of Montelongo at Ferrara: unfamiliar guests at the
hospice would be woken up at night by the bird's imitation of
the boatman's cry, 'Anyone for Bologna? Anyone for Doiolo?

Anyone for Peola? Hurry along, please, and get aboard with your luggage: we are sailing now!' The unfortunate travellers would hasten downstairs only to spend the rest of the night on the quay below. The story is told by Fra Salimbene of Parma in his chronicle,[24] and gives evidence of regular passenger sailings on the Po at this time.

Then there is the question of slavery; all important people had slaves, and one could always have a pagan slave, even though serfdom for Christians had long been abolished. There were quite busy markets in Rome, Florence and Venice, and then there were the 'little souls' one could buy at the ports and feel quite a philanthropist in consequence, for these were Christian children from the Levant whose own parents had sold them, and who were entitled to their freedom after a fixed number of years' service.[25] Incidentally, the lot of serfs was generally not too hard. Their masters were too practical to make it so.

Then there was the question of the Jews. Outside the ghetto in some places they were distinguished by wearing the star of David, in other places they wore a blue tunic, but the bearded figures mixed freely with the people in the piazza and their position seems to have been more favourable in Italy than elsewhere. The Emperor Frederick had a particular interest in the Jews and their faith and he gave them special protection. He did not approve of their conversion to Christianity any more than that of the Saracens, since this would have robbed him of the special taxes he levied on them and their special distinguishing marks. At the same time he took the trouble to investigate the usual medieval stories of Jewish ritual murders of children, showed them to be false and officially forbade their circulation.[26] The Pope also was concerned with the protection of the Jews, and at the beginning of each new pontificate the Rabbi of Rome laid before the new Pope the scroll of the Law, and heard from the lips of each new Pope his approval of the Law and his repudiation of the faith of the blind Jewish people who failed to recognise the Messiah who had come so long ago.[27] But this ceremony guaranteed for the Jewish community the right of asylum during the current

pontificate, and if they also paid their tribute of one pound of
pepper and two of cinnamon they were left in peace in their
quarter by the Tiber. They had their own trades and their own
businesses. There was never any persecution in Rome, unless
we except the ruling that the penalty for murdering a Jew or a
Saracen was only half that for murdering a Christian,[28] though
the penalty was anyway much more than the one hundred lire
which the two working lads had to pay for murdering a nobleman in Florence in 1280, when the Government was hardly
aristocratic. In anticlerical Padua the penalty for killing a cleric
was for a long time only thirty-two dinars, and so many people
availed themselves of this cheapness that the penalty had to be
increased.[29] One gets the impression that these penalties, apart
from being punishments, became a kind of source of revenue,
for as the prosperity of a town increased the penalties became
less. Indeed the fiscal arrangements of a medieval town often
show great ingenuity and people had to pay heavy prices for
their security. Every trade was taxed, including usurers, professional receivers of stolen goods, prostitutes and their em-
ployers.[30] There were taxes on slaves, paid servants, oxen, and
even so much per wheel of one's vehicles, taxes on every fire-
place in one's house, purchase taxes on foodstuffs and especially
on salt—the notorious *gabella*. Sometimes the tribute took the
form of compulsory labour; not only were servants bound to
serve their masters but all citizens were bound to work for the
community. In general people saw to it that their money was
not squandered; in good times they would get something for it
and on the whole prices were just. In fruitful years things were
cheap and could be bought sometimes at a fifth of the price in
other years or in other places.[31] In hard times distribution was
careful and stern measures were taken against smuggling and
black market.[32] The city council itself organised supplies and it
was remarkable that in this way during the first holy year,
1300, in Rome no less than 200,000 visitors a day were catered
for with cheap foodstuffs available on the markets for both man
and beast.[33] Frequently retail prices were controlled, as in the
case of the fishmongers of Reggio during Lent 1285, who put

up their prices and were forbidden to sell their fish, and the
butchers who were threatened with a similar boycott if they
did not improve after Easter.[34] Unfortunately the chronicler
does not tell us what was the reaction of the people; it must
have been a struggle between the desire for righteousness and
the desire for good food.

The ordinary medieval street scene was a man's affair, the
few women one would see about were mostly from the lower
classes, for the ladies of good family seldom went out, and then
not on foot; for one thing the clothes they wore, with their long
trains, made it impossible. 'The train of my dress is worth more
than all the rest put together,' said a young lady to Fra
Salimbene, who was much interested in such matters.[35] And
there was an outcry from the ladies when a certain cardinal
ordered under pain of excommunication that their dresses were
to be shortened 'to reach to the ground and then only one-and-
a-half handbreadth longer, whereas before they used be one-
and-a-half armslength longer', and moreover they were to
cover their heads with veils. This was a blow to the fashion
designers and hairdressers, until they found a way out by
designing veils with silk and gold decorations which made the
ladies 'ten times more attractive', as Salimbene observes.[36]
Apart from this enslavement to fashion there is not much more
evidence about the ladies' behaviour in the *Duecento*, for their
lives were spent indoors, with occasional concerns about
charitable works, which indeed caused several of them to be
included among the saints. In the whole of Hell, apart from a
few biblical or mythological characters, Dante only meets a
single woman. This was Francesca da Rimini, whom he
addresses with special tenderness as she expiates in the Second
Circle the one sin which it was possible for a woman to commit.
All the other sinners in Dante's Hell, gluttons, misers or
traitors, were men.

About life indoors there is only scanty information, though
certain rules of deportment and table manners have been preserved, such as those given in rhyme by the good Brother
Bonvesin of the Humiliati in 1270. He explains that nowadays

it is impolite to drain one's glass at one draught or to attempt to speak with one's mouth full, to put one's elbows on the table or to drink too much even if the wine is very good. 'My friend,' he continues, 'hold your glass in both hands, taking care not to spill it. Always turn aside if you have a fit of choking, and never utter an oath if the soup is disappointing. Do not take the whole loaf if your neighbour is expecting to share it. If you find a fly or some other creature in your food, say nothing about it. Do not poke your ears or scratch your head; do not stroke the dog if you still have to use your fingers for eating; never lick your fingers or pick your teeth with them . . .'[37] It was usual for two neighbours at table to eat from one plate and it is perhaps not surprising that quarrels sometimes had their beginning in some disagreement at this point: it has even been suggested that the troubles between Guelphs and Ghibellines began at a feast given by a young Florentine on the occasion of his knighthood.[38] Two worthies were quarrelling over the best portion on their plate and before long their neighbours took sides. A large meat platter was thrown by Oddo Arrighi at the head of the young Buondelmonte. Oddo attempted to atone for this by offering him his niece, but when the young man rejected the offer he was murdered on the bridge over the Arno.[39]

This young man was not the only one who met his death on a public thoroughfare, nor would the incident have caused much surprise. In fact, it was more surprising when a nobleman died a natural death; such an event would receive special mention in the chronicles. To be murdered was an ordinary risk for any nobleman and for the ordinary citizens all the ensuing duels, funerals and lawsuits were part of the theatre of life which was theirs by right, rather as Western films are today.

Italian law in the later Middle Ages was a mixture of Roman, Lombard, ecclesiastical and local law and differed in each north Italian city. In the larger cities there were at least seven different law courts for different kinds of offences, but the ordinary people preferred to go to the local courts of arbitration, where arguments of piety or sentiment carried more weight than before the professional lawyers.[40] Legal processes were in part extremely primitive and in part fully realistic. For centuries there had been protests against invoking divine judgement, yet animals were often brought to court, given counsels for their defence, cross examined (usually in their absence) and condemned to mutilation, exile or death. There were still traces of this extraordinary system in Italy in the eighteenth century.[41] Imprisonment and torture were principal elements in the administration of the law in the *Duecento*. One only has to read the verses of the half-starved Jacopone da Todi, produced in the years of his imprisonment, to feel almost physically the miseries of the chains, the stench, the cold and dampness, and the unnerving silence of those prisons.[42] At least the Florentines left their victims to spend their last hours in the open air, if a dried-up well can be so considered.[43] At this stage the worst was over: the tortures of the 'iron bit', 'the Spanish boot' and the 'neckband' were past, the dripping water that turned one crazy, the branding, the foot-roasting and the boiling fat.[44] Of course, the judge would only have recourse to torture in extreme cases, he was personally responsible for seeing that the torturer did not go too far, and a doctor's statement was required to show that the candidate was physically fit enough to undergo torture, which in any case was not to exceed one hour per day. Man's inhumanity to man remains a very strange thing. The death sentence was also carried out in ways more gruesome than the mere scaffold, gallows or wheel: victims were left to sink in a bog; were poisoned, impaled, boiled or roasted; were deprived of sleep till they died; were walled-up or buried alive, each sentence being proper to a particular crime.[45] The Emperor Frederick ordered rebels to be thrown from a cliff into the sea, but first of all they were to be sewn into a sack together with a dog, a monkey and a viper, 'so that as they drowned they would be devoured by the terrified animals'.[46] When he describes the torments of Hell, Dante was, in fact, drawing upon everyday experience of his time.

Dante also reminds us of a punishment that was little less

than death, when 'midway on the path of life' he was banished
from Florence and was henceforth a homeless exile. What this
meant to a man can only be realised when we understand the
bond between the citizen and his city, and the terrible implica-
tions of the sentence: 'Your wife we declare a widow, orphans
your children. Your goods become common property. Your life
and limb we commit to the beasts of the field, the birds of the
heavens, the fish of the sea. We give you the four winds as your
only shelter, no rest and no home shall be yours. Every man's
right to peace and protection is hereby denied to you.'[47] The
exile carried these words with him and even if he fled to
another city he remained without a home and with no civil
rights. Only the mighty spirit of one exile enabled him to see
his journey through the hell of exile as a 'divine comedy' that
led him to the light. . . .

Life was hard even because of the land itself; hardly a year
went by without some natural disaster. At Christmas-time in
1223 Verona and Brescia were wrecked by earthquakes[48] and in
the same way in 1231 the Colosseum in Rome began to fall
down, and at San Germano the wells fell in and became
poisoned.[49] Every summer the rivers dried up and every winter
they overflowed and broke the bridges. In severe winters the Po
froze over and the knights of Reggio held tournaments on the
ice while the women danced.[50]

A good quarter of the year was occupied with festivals and
all restraint was abandoned at carnival time. Then even the
impoverished peasants placed torches above their cottages,[51] so
that the landscape was a carpet of lights; wars would be forgotten for the moment, the rich people of the city would
provide food and games and the *Podestà* would have a dance
floor laid down in the piazza.[52] Another festive occasion would
follow the death of the bishop: after a tearful funeral his successor would be gaily welcomed, the clergy would be there in
full dress, the army and the guilds with trumpeters, fiddlers
and bells. Or it might be the state visit of a neighbouring lord,
when boys in white would go to meet him waving palms[53] and
the women would dance him a welcome at the city gate, while

all kinds of treasures in the form of carpets, rugs and silken hangings would be spread out from every window along the route of the procession.[54] A more homely reception was that given to the Count and Countess of Namen by Florence in 1270: first of all they spent their money on cloth and sweetmeats in the market, where they were thoroughly cheated, and then joined eagerly in games of chance, which old and young together played near the river.[55] The people in their curiosity reckoned them among the city's attractions, together with the clowns and a group of Saracens, who were busy telling fortunes and challenging people to games of chess.[56] The local sanctuaries outside the walls would be another occasion for merry-making, and the whole town, led by the *Podestà*, would go out in procession with banners and music, and if times were good everyone would be provided with new clothes.[57] At the turn of the century the festivals begin to have a Renaissance character, and the first *maggio musicale* was held in Florence during one period of peace. During two months there would be a series of festivals of costume, singing competitions and banquets. There was even a kind of club in the Oltr' Arno district, whose members wore white and went dancing and singing through the streets. Minstrels and clowns came from far and wide and went away well supplied with clothes, money and drink.[58]

In Padua a festival of flowers was organised when the prettiest girls went under a bejewelled silken canopy and the young men covered them with flowers and fruit.[59] This was in the springtime and the rich merchants appeared on the sports field with the latest novelties they had brought from abroad:

Ambianti palafren, destrier di Spagna,
e gente costumata alla francesca,
cantar, danzare a la provenzalesca,
con istromenti novi de la Magna.[60]

Ambling palfreys, steeds from Spain,
People in costumes made in France,
To sing and go dancing à la Provence,
New instruments from Allemayn.

All very lovely . . . but it would not be long before the bitter feud between Padua and Venice would be resumed; it was much more fun really to challenge your neighbour and defeat him and then put up a monument about it. 'I, Florence, came here' was engraved on a stone by the sea at Pisa, after the victory of 1222.[61] Fifty years later the city paid no less than 4,000 florins to the Prince of Anjou for the pleasure of laying waste the hateful town of Poggibonsi, so that not a wall, not a church, not a well remained.[62]

These were the things the menfolk talked about in the evenings; most of them had been on one of these military expeditions, some had been abroad on business, someone had been on a crusade and all of them could tell a yarn. There were also the professional travelling story-tellers. History and fable became indistinguishable; King Arthur and the Round Table, Charlemagne and the diabolical Emperor Frederick and the fabulous treasures of the King of Bohemia all became mixed together.[63] Stories grew up about strange animals from the unicorn of the East to the hairy monster with teeth, paws and a tail which a fisherman took out of the sea the other day at Ostia,[64] and the dragon which the bold mountaineer Peter of Aragon saw with his own eyes fly out of a mountain lake.[65] Crusaders had their stories of crocodiles, which they took for snakes, and of tigers, which they thought were a kind of lion.[66] One wiseacre, respected as a biologist, maintained that salamanders were the creatures of the Devil, full of noxious humours, which poisoned apples and pears.[67] The best stories naturally were heard in the ports, where the world of the thousand-and-one nights was at hand. Yet the stories from the Levant were believed by everyone; these were no fables, they were histories of adventures. Many a Genoese and Venetian travelled on business as far as the Persian Gulf and described to his family the Indian merchants with their white turbans, offering for sale at Hormuz their loads of 'plants and spices, jewels and pearls, silks embroidered with gold, elephant tusks and suchlike',[68] brought there either by ship or by overland caravan. Amid all this description of the wonders of Asia sometimes there inevitably came the mention of the name that struck terror in every heart: Ala-ad-Din, the old man of the hills. Everyone knew of his magic castle at Alamut in the mountains by the Caspian Sea. Here he trained his men, giving them a magic drink called Hashish, whence they were called *Hashishin*, and they had killed so many people that the word 'assassin' remained in the languages of the West. At Alamut, it was said, there was a garden of paradise, with all the trees and flowers of the world, with fountains flowing with wine and honey, with tame animals everywhere and dazzling marble temples where the most beautiful maidens danced to fiddles and lutes. 'All this,' Ala-ad-Din would say to his men, 'I will give you, if falling down you will adore me. Heaven awaits you if you fall in my service.' The good citizens at home listened to all this and drank it all in. This Oriental picture of the Garden of Eden was attractive; such people must be dangerous and doubtless the crusaders would come across them; in fact, it was said that Conrad of Monferrato, King of Jerusalem, had been killed by these very fanatics.[69]

Everyone knew that beyond the Turks were the Tartars, and beyond them the Chinese, and central Europe had already had Tartar invasions. But in Italy the chief authority was that of the Franciscan from near Perugia, whom the Pope had sent to their King, Khan Kuyuk, in his tent dwelling at Karakorum. In all the countries which the Franciscan had visited on his way back there were copies of his diaries, and everyone knew all about the Tartars, how many wives they had, how they got drunk on horse's milk, how they lived and dressed and buried their dead. But better still were the stories of the men who had their hair in pigtails and wore garments of silk; a Venetian called Marco Polo had visited them and had quite recently written his memoirs while he was a prisoner of the Genoese. He had so many stories about the Chinese Emperor's millions that he got the nickname *il millione*, but there must be some truth in his yarns, though everyone knows the Venetians are great liars.[70] The good people were puzzled to think how big the world is and were full of admiration for the courageous men who went so far without getting lost. There was even a story current about a magic needle which always pointed north, but, of course, it was understandable that the sailors were unwilling to speak of it, for who would care to admit that he navigated by means of magic?[71]

And so in the evenings the stories went on . . .

5

The Saints

Faciamo laude a tutti sancti
colla vergene maggiure
de buon core cum dolçe canti
per amor del cre a to re.

To all the saints we give our praise,
And to the Virgin greater,
And songs with all our heart we raise
For love of our Creator.

Hymn from Cortona[1]

HOWEVER WE approach Assisi we are immediately seized
by its character. From Spello it seems to cling to its hillside
with the castle above and the great basilica below; from the
plain it rises like a fortress out of the ground; from Perugia it is
merged into the distant hills, but is instantly recognisable; and
when we look up at Assisi as we mount the road from the plain
we have the view that the dying Francis had, half-blind though
he was, when he turned and blessed the city he loved so well.

The character of Assisi is the character of Francis. At one time it must have been very much like many another hill town of Umbria, proud, self-conscious and quarrelsome. The castle and the chronicles bear witness to this. But since Francis lived there it has been different: the little town is less compact and built up within its walls than are Orvieto or Todi, even though the old crafts still produce the finest glazes and the best embroidery of Italy, and even though trade still flourishes—though much of the trade lives on the holiness of the place. And why not? For its holiness is part of its character. Assisi speaks to us more of Francis than Siena does of Catherine, or Padua of Anthony, or, for that matter, Rome of its martyrs. It stands aside from the world's traffic as a shrine of St Francis and his friend St Clare.

In Italian history interest is focused upon different areas for different reasons and in different times. Thus in the *Duecento* for the history of the Emperor the focal point is obviously Sicily and Naples, while for the papacy it is Rome and for the democratic trading cities it is the north. As we set out to study the spiritual life of the *Duecento* the focus is upon Umbria.

Umbria is itself a symbol; as the *Duecento* forms a passage between two cultures, so Umbria lies between the ancient Latium and the humanistic Toscana, for better or for worse between the Middle Ages and the Renaissance. There is a freedom about its great plain which has something of the Campagna about it, and round it are the hills which share certain qualities with the valley of the Arno. Here the people do not live under the curse of an Empire that has passed away and the sun is milder. The little towns are more like hill fortresses, enclosing churches and palaces alike. Here the schools of Foligno and Spoleto were painting their pale frescoes and their pictures of Christ in torment on the Cross. Jacopone da Todi was typical of Umbria, and perhaps also that John the Baptist of the West, Raniero Fasani, leading the ranks of his Flagellants at Perugia; but before either of these, St Francis had preached up and down Umbria and from here his spirit had spread through the length and breadth of Europe.

The preaching of St Francis and the legends that grew up around him have a peculiar quality of possessing an increasing appeal as they spread farther both in time and place from their first utterance. The way he spoke to the wolf and to the birds, his miracles, his stigmata, the whole world of the Portiuncola, all belong to Umbria, but God alone knows how many people in distant places and centuries later have drawn consolation from them. Umbria is the source of a devotion that is both merry and stern: Francis's Song to Sister Death and Jacopone's dark pictures of skeletons and worms are separated by no more than forty years and forty miles—only Perugia of the Flagellants lies between them, but they all belong to Umbria. To the north the learning of Bologna was laying the foundations of the *Divina Commedia*, while the last medieval genius of the south was building his *Summa theologica*, more upon the scholasticism of Paris than upon the native piety of his homeland. It is perhaps significant that at the beginning of the century Pope Innocent III came to die at Perugia, and that at its end, when all was ready for the move to Avignon, the Tuscan Giotto was busy painting at Assisi, and in Florence the young Dante was beginning to turn from the sorrows of this world to his heavenly Beatrice. The point of cultural focus was slowly moving northwards.

The saints of Italy often reflect very clearly the countryside from which they came. Thus Francis and Clare could hardly come from anywhere but Umbria, and they represent so perfectly the *devotio* of their century. At the end of the previous century, much farther south and in quite different countryside, there lived a powerful contemplative spirit who came to have an important influence on the piety of Umbria in the *Duecento*.

This was Abbot Joachim of Flora, the prophet who died in Calabria about the year 1200 and reflected the strong and silent character of his own land, with its wild hills and rough vegetation, trackless as the Sila which was his hiding place. The dark and mysterious speculations of the Greek and Levantine thinkers found a home in his brain, just as the Byzantine hermits did in the caves of his native land. The countryside of southern Italy is more like Spain or Palestine than the pleasant landscapes north of Latium. It is only in the springtime when the merciless sun has not yet dried everything up that we can realise that Magna Graecia is indeed part of the same land. In a sense it was like this with Joachim, for only in his early years could we guess that he was a compatriot of Francis. His sudden conversion at the sight of Byzantium stricken by the plague reminds us of Francis's experience when he embraced the leper; and Francis's vigorous action, when he threw down at his father's feet his money and clothes and stood there naked before the horrified judges, is not unlike that of Joachim, who stripped off the silken clothes he had worn as a Norman lord's page boy and cut off his curly blond hair, which had been so much admired, as a sign of renunciation of all his past. It is the same with some other details of his life. When he was on the road in the Lord's service he would have a donkey with him which carried a portable altar and the necessities for Mass, so that as soon as dawn came he could celebrate amid the silence of the dew-laden morning.[2] One day the weather was dull as he was preaching in the church, when suddenly the sun came out; he stopped his sermon and invited the people to come outside with him and greet the sun as he intoned the *Veni Creator Spiritus*.[3]

But we must not take the parallel too far; this is a far cry from the spirit of the *Fioretti*. When Joachim went out to greet the sun it was with no poetic ecstasy as with Francis's canticle; for Joachim the sun was no more than an important symbol which required explanation. Francis loved all created things, Joachim asked questions about them and sought their significance, their prophetic meaning. His approach was entirely intellectual, not poetic, his prophetic warnings are not in the style of the Old Testament. His attitude was more like the Spaniard Ignatius and the Fathers of the Desert than like Francis: indeed, during the first years of his conversion he visited the holy places in the Syrian desert, sometimes leaving the reformed Cistercian abbey he founded in the mountains of Flora and going to preach his grim threats of damnation to frightened popes and cardinals. At Palermo he addressed the Kings of Sicily, France and England in terms of Jonah's message to sinful Niniveh. He is more like the stiff Eastern mosaics of Monreale than like the gentle frescoes of Giotto. Unlike Francis, he does not see Christ either in Bethlehem or Geth-semane. He cannot wait for Christ to set aside his humanity: he sees him on Mount Taber; more often on Patmos, uttering his terrible warnings. 'Mine to declare the war: yours to take up arms! Mine to mount the hill and watch for the approaching foe: yours, when I give the sign, to take prudent flight!'[4]

The battle was at hand; none of Abbot Joachim's hearers had any doubt about that and the calamities would be worse than any before. Sin in the world had opened his eyes to the meaning of scripture and now he must announce the end. From the Bible he had learnt the meaning of history, he had seen its great pattern. Thus he proved himself an expert in scripture, but not in the wider field of theology. An angel had promised him insight into scripture, but no further gifts. In consequence he worked at his profound but peculiar and subjective commentaries, which in spite of his orthodox intentions came into conflict with the teaching of the Church. Basing himself upon various correspondences between the Old and New Testaments and the evidence of many obscure passages from the Pentateuch to the Apocalypse, he maintained that both before and after the Incarnation the seven seals must needs be opened and the seven ages must come and go. There was but a short time now and the seventh age of the world would be finished. Then, after the Old Testament King-dom of God the Father, and the New Testament Kingdom of God the Son, there was to dawn the Kingdom of the Holy Ghost.

In his *Liber Concordantiae* Joachim shows how clearly the Book of Esther foretells what will happen: 'Now on the seventh day, when the king was merry, and after very much drinking was well warmed with wine, he commanded [them] to bring in Queen Vashti before the king, with the crown set upon her head: to show her beauty to all the people.' 'Could not even a

Jew see the meaning of all this? The first six days of the feast signify three years, the time of Christ's teaching upon earth. The seventh day will be the moment when the faithful will become drunk through the outpouring of the Holy Spirit.'[5] Even plainer is the story of Judith in scripture: 'And Judith was a widow now three years and six months.' This is the same as 1,260 days, so that Judith is the Church, who outlives Christ her spouse not 1,260 days but as many years.[6] The year 1260 would therefore be the great turning-point, but Joachim himself did not yet take all that precisely in a literal sense. It seemed certain to him that the Judgement was at hand. In every rumour he heard already the footsteps of Antichrist; and night after night he awaited the Coming of the Lord. But his main theme was the need for penance. He was a prophet whose forebodings had a great influence on his time, his was a hand raised in warning, a trumpet that did not cease to sound. Men must be prepared, but it was useless to count the days: for although he knew in principle when the Kingdom of the Spirit was to come, the coming itself was more important for him than the time. *Temerarium est finem mundi quarere*,[7] he said, but this advice too often went unheeded.

The saints of Italy indeed reflect their own countryside and when their teaching is uprooted and planted elsewhere it sometimes changes its character considerably. Thus the younger generation of Joachim's followers in the north, with their militant creed but no desire for speculation, took his general warnings and turned them into positive programmes. Joachim's dark broodings in the Calabrian hills were transformed into plain vision in the busy northern towns; the end of the world was at hand, the Antichrist was plainly Count So-and-so, as the Angel of the Apocalypse was unquestionably the local saint, and Rome was Babylon without a doubt. At first sight it would seem that the development in the north of Joachim's ideas represents an important trend in the *Duecento* from the south to the north, if it were not equally probable that these same ideas would have come to the fore, whether there had been a Joachim or not. If there had not been a prophet, they would have invented one, for the general tension which characterised life in the middle of the century was ready to turn the gentlest legend into a fearful revelation, and it would be a serious mistake to consider the tender mysticism of the time without the background of the genuine belief in the end of the world, especially as the fateful year 1260 drew closer.

Let us go back, however, to St Francis, who lived at the beginning of century (from 1182 to 1226) and was as far removed from those dark forebodings as the Song of Songs is from the Apocalypse. Above all it is the warmth of his lovable personality that comes through the great mass of historical evidence about him.

At first Francis wanted to be a knight and a troubadour. So he took part in a battle with Perugia in one of the many local wars, after which he proposed to go south and earn his knighthood fighting against Frederick. But for a year he was kept as a prisoner of war at Perugia, after which his great journey to the south never got beyond Spoleto, where he was held up by illness. There were too many knights in Italy now anyway, but too few beggars who begged for the love of God. Thus he came back to Assisi. Somehow his father's prosperous cloth business seemed too small for him now, and all the merry parties meant nothing to him any more. Not that there was anything wrong in the noisy *bonhomie* of the young people. But in the long run there is nothing more unpleasant than the tradesman who wants to be a nobleman, the bourgeois who wants to be an artist. A person who has no vocation to be either a tradesman or a bourgeois suddenly feels nauseated by it all. Tomorrow all this pretence will be over and they will take a wife or a bread-earner and will themselves become the worthies they had previously despised—just so do they now scoff at him as he flees from the little town: as artist or pilgrim, whatever God wills. So—or even worse—it was for the young Francesco di Pietro Bernadone, who did not know what he wanted, or what was wanted of him, until the Crucifix of San Damiano spoke to him.

17. The massive and self-contained Town Hall of Pistoia in Tuscany (1294–1385) has a fine ground floor portico of broad, pointed arches. The three storeys of windows exhibit undulating Gothic profiles.

18. The cathedral with its three Gothic portals and three rose windows occupies one side of the main square of the central-Italian hill town of Todi. On the near right is the rugged face of the town hall.

19. Perugia's famous thirteenth-century fountain, the Fontana Maggiore, shows the concern of the authorities in this as in many other Italian cities to combine improvement with beautification. The fountain displays an extensive series of figures and reliefs by Nicola and Giovanni Pissano and Arnolfo di Cambio.

20. The abbey of San Giovanni in Fiore, picturesquely situated at the lower edge of a south Italian town, was founded in 1189 by the revolutionary prophet and mystic Joachim of Fiore.

21. Looking from the Rocca Minore, or small fortress, this view of Assisi highlights the Cathedral of San Rufino with its fine tower (left) and the Rocca Maggiore, or large fortress (top right).

22. The town of Cortona is located on the slope of the Valdichiana spur of the Apennine Mountains. Crowning the hill is the sixteenth-century Medici fortress.

23. The town of Assisi, which retains many characteristically medieval houses, perches precipitously above St Peter's Gate. The gate is surmounted by a defensive crenellation or battlement.

24. The cobblestone paving, unplastered walls and tile roofs of this street in Anagni, near Rome, give a vivid impression of the popular quarters of Italian cities in the middle ages.

25. The elegant church of San Lorenzo in Verona (begun about 1110) has a narrow two-storeyed nave covered by a pitched wooden roof. The architect has used the contrast of banded and plain surfaces to emphasise the function of the load-bearing piers and arches.

26. The Castle of Monteriggione, which is mentioned by Dante in his *Inferno*, was built by the Sienese in the thirteenth century to guard the frontier with Florence. The great perimeter wall is buttressed by fourteen square towers.

27. In Verona the tower of the ancient abbey (left) and an isolated campanile (right) frame a masterpiece of Italian romanesque architecture, the Church of San Zeno. In a pattern formed by the measured accents of the strip buttresses on the façade stands the Lombard porch with its bronze doors and flanking sculptural decoration. (See plate 39)

28. The façade of the Church of San Pietro, which stands just outside Spoleto, is noteworthy for the inset sculptural panels showing figural scenes and animals. (See plate 29)

29. This scene of a peasant ploughing affords a glimpse of medieval agriculture, the way of life of the overwhelming majority of people. The panel is part of the façade of the Church of San Pietro, near Spoleto. (See plate 28)

30. The clarity and precision of the arcades of the cloister of Sant'Agostino in San Gimignano represent the essential spirit of Tuscan architecture.

31. Rising in the centre of Bitonto in Apulia this late twelfth-century cathedral forms an imposing mass of dark stone. The narrow centre field of the façade is surmounted by a rose window.

32. This fresco scene in the Upper Church of San Francesco in Assisi represents
the Dream of Innocent III. Having declined to authorise the Rule of St Francis's
new order, the pope had a dream in which he saw Francis supporting the Lateran
Basilica which threatened to fall. Innocent then speedily granted the friar's

God recognises in each of his children an attribute of his own and has a special word for each one of them. To Joachim he spoke in symbols, but to the darling of Assisi in that early springtime of 1206 he said something quite plain and simple: 'Go and rebuild my house.' The young man looked up and suddenly noticed that there was indeed a large hole in the masonry. He could even see the vine tendrils that belonged outside and the sky beyond, and as he looked he saw the swallows flying in and out through the hole. There was sense in the Lord's command and he immediately got up and began to look for stones to repair the poor little chapel.

Many other people would not have understood the command and would have thought it must be a symbol of reforming the Church or the clergy, and would have set out to do so as Arnold of Brescia or Peter Valdes had done and like them become merely pseudo-reformers. But Francis took the words literally and in so doing he began their symbolic fulfilment: by literally carrying those stones to the chapel, he was beginning the great work that would indeed repair many ruins throughout Europe.

Francis founded an order, in fact he founded three orders, the friars, the nuns and the Third Order for layfolk. The story is well known to history and in every century the Friars Minor have been the tireless infantry of the Church. But it is not the founder who gives such a special charm to the century and draws people from every century back to him: it is Francis of Umbria, the troubadour. It is the young man who went through the woods singing, with no other possession than the old tunic given him by the bishop's servant. When he met the three surly robbers he announced himself as 'a herald of the Great King', but they only threw him into a snow-filled ditch. It is the beggar, singing in the streets which had known him as a smart young man, singing as he begged for building stones. When the people laughed at him he soon laughed with them, and they stopped laughing when one of them distributed his possessions among them and went with Francis, and another gave away half his money and others came running to join him. Fifteen years later there were five thousand and by the end of the century thirty-five thousand of them.[8]

It is Francis of Umbria himself who is the centre of attraction, Francis the minstrel who began the love song to Lady Poverty, who was obeyed by the animals, who wept because 'Love was loved no more'. He held festival with all creation in his *Cantico del Sole*, he heard the song of the angels, he was seen raised from the ground on the hilltops and he went to the rocky fastness of La Verna to receive the seraphic wounds of Christ. This is the Francis of the *Fioretti*, and it is as useless to discuss their historical accuracy as it is to discuss the realism of Giotto's frescoes. These things are his own people's offerings to their own saint and even if certain adornments may be unauthentic, they present a living picture of the man. They include all the poetic spirit of that restless century and though the background of the scene may, like a medieval painting, have no accurate perspective, it is authentic Umbrian landscape all the same.[9] Lake Trasimene is still there, framed in its blue hills; and the old legend of the battle between Rome and Carthage has been overlaid with the forty days of Francis fasting there in his hut of branches and leaves, a legend not of blood but of blossom. The little island is still there, looking like a small green leaf floating on the surface of the lake. Here he built his hut and prayed alone for forty days; he took half a loaf with him, out of humility, it was said, so as not to resemble Christ, who took nothing.[10]

The spring of water is still there in the Appenines where Francis sat down one day after begging his bread. The handsome Fra Masseo had done well on his quest, and he remarked that Francis with his unprepossessing appearance had brought less. Francis found this most amusing and, placing the bit of bread that he had received upon a graceful smooth flat stone, he began to sing the praises of Lady Poverty, the good bread, the lovely stone and the bubbling water. Masseo, who was still inexperienced in the ways of the new Jerusalem in Umbria, could not understand his joy over a picnic without a plate, a knife and a tablecloth.[11]

Another time Francis was trudging barefoot through a

snowstorm from Perugia to Assisi and was trying to explain to his shivering friend where perfect joy was to be found. He told him to imagine that they came to a hostel and were refused, beaten and sent back into the snow for the rest of the night. 'Then,' he said, 'if we take it patiently and merrily, thinking of our Lord's pains and that we can suffer these things for love of him, then, my friend, you can really say this is perfect joy.'[12] Anyone who visits this vale of Spoleto and does not feel this perfect joy has made the journey in vain—even if it is Goethe looking for the temple of Minerva.[13]

Then there was the famous night when St Clare came from San Damiano to have supper with St Francis. Years before she had fled from her noble family and been dedicated to God by Francis at Santa Maria degli Angeli and had become the mother of all Poor Clares. During the years she had remained with her nuns, shut up at San Damiano and living a life of prayer and penance. Francis thought it would do her good to come out and visit Santa Maria degli Angeli again. So she came with one of her nuns and they began a frugal meal under the trees. Francis was speaking of the love of God so wonderfully that they all became rapt in ecstasy and a supernatural light began to glow round them and all the forest became bright. The local people, seeing the light, came hastening to the place with all their fire-fighting equipment. When they arrived they found the company round the humble table rapt in contemplation. 'Then they understood that the fire was divine and not material fire, and that God was in this way making plain by a miracle the fire of the love of God which burned in the souls of those holy friars and nuns, and they went home greatly consoled and edified.'[14]

Yet in the *Fioretti*, for all the happiness about 'perfect joy', there is a note of sadness. It is like the sadness of autumn, when one knows that the summer is past. It was in the nature of things that the Umbrian idyll could not last for ever. The order was growing up and some organisation became necessary: 30,000 troubadours, each going their own way, would soon produce disaster. They had to have a rule and then a system of provinces and ministers and guardians. Huts were almost bound to give way to stone-built friaries and amid all sorts of privileges the service of Lady Poverty became less strict. This could not be prevented and realists cannot complain, but it may be regretted and none did so more than Francis himself. But he was no organiser and somehow the order had grown out of his control. He handed over the reins of government and that decided the whole fate of the order. Among the brethren there rose up a body of spiritual administrators who guarded him like some relic, received his words with veneration and then went their own way. He retired to his Sinai at Fontecolombo above Rieti, and wrote his rule, but then Brother Elias, the General, intentionally or not, managed to lose what he had written. Francis knew that a rule which gets interpreted out of recognition or which loses all its force through wholesale dispensation is all but useless. As a last attempt to keep his sons on the road of total surrender, which he saw as the only way, he wrote his Testament. It is written in quite unadorned Latin, not philosophy or literature, but a human document of a simple soul who had won the battle for heaven, but had lost the battle on earth.

In this wise the Lord brought me, Brother Francis, to penance. When I was still living in my sins, the sight of lepers was distasteful to me. Therefore the Lord himself guided me to them, and I showed them mercy. And when I departed from them, it seemed as if what had been distasteful to me was now turned to sweetness both for my spirit and my flesh. Thus I lived for a time, until I turned from the world altogether. And the Lord gave me so great faith in his Church that I had but one prayer: Lord Jesus Christ, we adore thee, here and in all the churches of the world, and we praise thee, because by thy holy Cross thou hast redeemed the world. . . . Later, when the Lord had given me brethren, no man shewed me what I should do; the Almighty alone revealed to me that I must live by the rule of the gospel. This I wrote out in a few words, and my lord the Pope approved it for me. And those who came to lead this life gave all their possessions to the poor and were content with a worn tunic, a cord, and breeches underneath. They did not wish to possess more.

The clerics amongst us recited the Divine Office as did the rest of the clergy, and the lay brethren said their beads; gladly we visited churches to pray there. We were unlearned and considered ourselves inferior to all. I have worked with my hands, and desire to continue to do so; and I earnestly charge all the brethren to practise an honest trade. Those who know none should learn one, not for the sake of gain, nor to earn money, but for the sake of good example and to dispel idleness. If for our labour we receive no reward, we should make the Lord's table our refuge and beg alms from door to door.

The Lord revealed to me the greeting we should use: The Lord give you peace. The brethren should be on their guard against accepting churches or friaries or any such that men might wish to build for them, unless such buildings be in accord with holy poverty, to which we are vowed in the rule, and which will have us live ever as strangers and pilgrims.

Most strictly also I charge the brethren, that none should ever make bold to seek privileges from the Holy See, either personally or through another, neither for a church nor for a friary, nor should they seek any special patronage or formal authority to preach. And above all, should they be unwelcome in one place, let them flee to another, there to do penance with God's blessing . . .

Let none of the brethren say: Here is a new Rule. For this is but a reminder, an admonishment, an encouragement; it is the testament which I, Brother Francis and least of all, leave to my blessed ones, my brethren, that we may lead our Catholic lives according to the rule, to which under God we are vowed. And the Minister General and all other Ministers and Guardians are bound under obedience not to add anything to these words, and not to remove anything from them. And they should keep this document always by them, together with the Rule. And I strictly charge all my brethren, both clerics and lay, not to set up interpretations of the Rule or of these words, as if to say: This, or that, is to be understood in this, or that way. The Lord gave it to me to write the Rule and these words simply and plainly: simply and plainly therefore you should understand them, and keep them with a holy perseverance to the end . . .[15]

But within five years of the death of Francis the papal bull
Quo elongasti declared his Testament to have no binding force,
interpolations were made in his rules, and the order received
one privilege after another. Prosperity had come to the order,
and the Church was playing safe. But there was much heart-
rending among the few who remained in the little cells and
the caves of Umbria, protesting their fidelity in 'The Legend of
the Three Friends', the Mirror of Perfection' and the 'Little
Flowers of St Francis'.

The *Poverello* of Umbria is probably the most characteristic
saint of the Italian *Duecento*, but he was not the only person
renowned for miracles and holiness in that restless age. There
were many others within his own order and elsewhere, among
the Dominicans, the Servites and the Humiliati; and indeed
this troubled century was a time of remarkable growth of
sanctity.

In Portugal in 1220 a certain Ferdinand, an Augustinian,
exchanged his habit for the rough tunic of the Franciscans.
Why he then changed his name to Antony we do not know;
the use of a 'religious name' was still at the time unknown
among the Friars Minor, but his early biographers tell us that
he was called 'Antonius' because of the strong tone of his
voice, *alte tonans*.[16] However that may be, he has become
known to history not as Ferdinand of Coimbra but as Antony
of Padua. There is a certain international quality about Antony
that stands in immediate contrast to the essentially local
atmosphere of Francis, and it was only by a sort of chance that
he came to Italy. Moreover, he had not joined the Franciscans
for the love of poverty or humility; he joined them because
he wanted to share the martyrdom among the Moors which five
Franciscans had suffered in Morocco in 1220. But the Lord had
other plans and he ended up in a shipwreck on the coast of
Sicily, it is said not far from Taormina. He was typical of the
international spirit of the time and just as his connexion with
Italy and indeed with the Franciscans was almost a matter of
chance, so also was his connexion with Padua, where he only

came to live shortly before his death in 1231. But the fame especially of his miracles had preceded him and the people at once claimed him as their own, not the least vehemently perhaps when it was a question of his shrine and his canonisation.

When we look at the character of Antony, especially once we have eliminated the sentimental view of him which has so long prevailed, we find a person in almost every way different from Francis. He was not a typical Franciscan: he had none of Francis's charm and typically Italian poetical attitude to life, none of Francis's vigour and carefree joyfulness: he was a Portuguese, corpulent, sickly, diffident. Francis was by nature a lover, Antony was an apologist, preaching to people to serve God, while Francis was imploring them to love him. The same contrast appears even when the legends about the two men are similar. Francis talked to the birds simply because he loved all creatures, while Antony addressed the fishes to confound the people of Rimini who had refused to listen to him. Francis tamed the fierce wolf of Gubbio, which crouched down before him in an attitude of penance, while Antony used the donkey as a piece of apologetic, when he made it kneel down before the Blessed Sacrament to convince unbelievers.

But when this quiet, learned friar mounted the pulpit he became transformed and his words became a sword of fire. What was the power of Antony's preaching, the magic of his words? We shall never know. Yet we know that thousands came to hear him and that the largest churches were always packed to the doors. Shopkeepers shut up their shops, farmers forgot their harvests, housewives left their children untended, people threw up everything to come and hear him with never a fear, for the holy man would help in any trouble. Hardened heretics came as a joke, thieves came to ply their trade among the audience, but before the end they would be sobbing aloud and proclaiming their change of heart. There are some preachers whose sermons we can read and feel the power of their oratory: Berthold of Regensburg or Bernardino of Siena for instance, with their vivid and acute language and imagery, possessed by the spirit which uttered through them. None of this is evident with Antony: his sermons as we have them are mere chains of quotations and similes, rather in the style of the Fathers, but with none of their clarity. Presumably the true preacher can rarely be confined to a book, his gift is something that belongs to the moment and vanishes, like the gift of the singer or the actor, unless perhaps his actual words are taken down at the time, as were those of Augustine. Antony had no such person—or at least only one, who was a poor amanuensis—so that at best all we have seem no more than compilations of ideas and the whole secret of his power eludes us. Yet after his death this man became known as the greatest wonder-worker of Christendom. It is not surprising that the memory of Antony remained most vivid in the northern town of Padua, rather than in the Franciscan midlands, for northern Italy was the scene of the more erudite and doctrinal preaching which we associate with the work of the Dominicans.

So we come from Francis's land of 'perfect joy' through Antony to the centre of learning at Bologna, which was the headquarters of St Dominic. If the power of Antony's preaching eludes us, the actual quality of Dominic's words eludes us too, for we have no actual reports of his sermons at all, though we know well enough how enormously attractive his preaching was.

Dominic's was a very different character from that of Francis, although legend tells us that the two men became friends. This is indeed likely, since in so many ways they are complementary: Francis was a poet who spoke to the common people, while Dominic was first of all a teacher who addressed himself to the university world. Francis's message was uttered with a carefree spirit which failed when it came to planning an order in this world, while Dominic's brilliant legislative mind not only conceived but effectively produced a worldwide order with the most perfect organisation. The figure of Francis soon became surrounded by legend—and this was typical enough of the man—while the history of Dominic is so precise that often we can follow him almost from day to day. Again, unlike

Francis, Dominic's life is intimately bound up with the establishment of his order and the formation of his followers, and such was the precision of his formation that they at once began to continue their master's work in precisely the same way as he had started. The approach, again unlike that of Francis, is primarily one of conviction; people need instruction first and it was natural that this approach should attract men already endowed with an intellectual formation, so that Dominic's first recruits came mostly from the universities. But with all his intellectualism Dominic had an intensely attractive personality and was a born leader; there is an astonishing wealth of evidence of the devotion he inspired, of the warmth of his friendship and of his unfailing kindness to all. Indeed, the secret of his character seems to lie in the combination of the qualities of leader and friend, and the secret of his sanctity in the combination of his leadership in the battle to spread the love of God and his friendship to fulfil in his own person the love of one's neighbour.

It is often said that Dominic cared little for Lady Poverty, but nothing could, in fact, be wider of the mark. Franciscan legend has it that he learned of the virtues of poverty from Francis and this may well be so, but the fact is that he was insistent to the point of severity on the observance of poverty by his friars. For the Dominican, poverty is not an end in itself, it is rather a means in the struggle for truth against the Albigensian rigorists on the one hand and the easy-going clergy on the other. It was Thomas Aquinas, the Dominican, who later wrote: 'Spiritual perfection does not consist essentially in poverty . . . which is rather an instrument of training towards perfection.'[17]

Dominic de Guzman was born in 1170, or more probably in 1172, in Castile. The earlier part of his life was spent in Provence, preaching to the Albigensian heretics there, and his first visit to Italy was in 1215. During the remaining six years of his life he spent much of his time there, mainly in Rome and at Bologna where he died in 1221. St Dominic became a saint of Italy as it were by adoption, for although he had started the work of his order at Toulouse, its great development spread especially from Bologna among the northern cities of Italy. His work in papal Rome and in the centre of learning at Bologna had a profound effect upon the thought of Italy at the time, though in popular appeal and local legend he naturally never rivalled the attraction of his friend St Francis. Crowds of pilgrims never came to his tomb in the way they did to that of Francis, and his canonisation thirteen years after his death was not so rapid as the two years that followed the death of St Francis. For the people of Umbria the '*santissimo Francesco*' was their own saint, not to be compared even to the '*santo Domenico*' when the meeting of the two is mentioned in the *Fioretti*.[18]

Here, then, are three great saints of the Italian *Duecento*, with their shrines at Assisi, Padua and Bologna: three saints who now belong to Italy, where their bones lie. But two of them came from abroad; it was only Francis who was born upon Italian soil, which also became his grave.

6

The Faithful

O vita penosa,   Life is a labour,
continua battaglia,   Unending the strife,
con quanta travaglia   O what a battle
la vita è menata . . .   To struggle through life.

                    Jacopone da Todi[1]

IT IS difficult for us today to picture to ourselves the character
of the ordinary people of medieval Italy. We are well enough
informed about the leading personalities, the rulers, the
writers, the civic officials—and the saints. But surely these are
the exceptions; their deeds have been recorded in history
because they were exceptional people. We are well informed
even about their piety, or lack of it. But what of the piety of
the ordinary, uninstructed people? The old beliefs, centuries
old perhaps, belonging to a remote past before ever Christianity was preached, often live on in the backgrounds of
people's minds in the form of superstitions. Here and there in
thirteenth-century Italy there are hints of ancient superstitions
surviving among the people, while the theologians were
developing their theology.

Europe had indeed become Christian, but the process of
ousting the old beliefs was inevitably slow, even when it was
a process of transforming them. As the abbeys began to
multiply they became strongholds of faith and holiness and
the local gentry perhaps could through their education, so often
drawn from the abbeys, share something of their understanding. But what of the unlettered peasants in the fields? In the
cities it was better; there were the cathedral schools, the

occasional sermons. But it remains a fact that saints are few enough, other than priests or religious, between the martyrs of the Early Church and the time of St Francis. Small wonder, then, that the people took to their hearts the new preachers of the *Duecento*, the Franciscans and the Dominicans, for they were a new generation of apostles.

Everyone knows the story of the dream of Pope Innocent III, how he saw the Lateran Basilica, the mother church of Christendom, about to fall down. Huge cracks appeared in the walls and the whole building seemed in danger, but the piazza was deserted and nobody cared, until a little man in a shabby tunic came along and with his own little shoulders propped up the cathedral until it stood again fair and square upon its foundations. The Pope awoke. He had seen the little man before. Was he not the penitent from Umbria who had already been to see him about a rule for himself and his friends and was coming again tomorrow with the recommendation of his bishop?

So the story goes that Innocent did that day what he previously had no intention of doing: he let the little man have his way. Thus in 1209 the Friars Minor were founded and once more the conversion of Italy had begun again.

The parallel between the dream of Innocent and the divine command to Francis to repair the church of San Damiano is obvious enough. But it is not so easy to see exactly where St Francis set to work to repair the building that was the Church itself. It was not a matter of theology, and anyway that was not his *métier*. The reform of the clergy? In this too he did not succeed, though his example will have had some effect. But he and his friends came to do what the clergy were too often not doing: talking to the people. It is after all the ordinary faithful who are the solid stones out of which the Church is built. In all the confusion of the thirteenth century it was these solid stones that were falling apart, so that the building seemed in danger of falling down. So the Lord sent his stonemasons to 'repair the church', as he said to Francis. The Franciscans and Dominicans set to work to repair the wreckage of Italian Christendom. There are those who see the troubles of the thirteenth century as the seed-bed of the Renaissance: be that as it may, the work of the mendicant orders belongs properly to the Middle Ages. Each of them had their own weapons, but they had a common enemy, the monster of ignorance among the people, and this they hunted down with their preaching and even where necessary by means of the Inquisition.

Dominic's penetrating mind saw the task clearly enough and his whole order was designed to deal with it; but Francis was much less certain of his programme; his first concern was the spiritual danger which threatened both himself and his brethren. Francis was like someone trying to fish something out of a pond and finding to his surprise that he was pulling out the whole contents of the pond. His own personal life of penance began to be shared not only by his few companions but by hundreds and thousands, and from being a personal affair of his spiritual life became a world-wide apostolate. This is probably why his vocation was not to direct the machinery of an organisation offering spiritual direction to the world, but rather to give the inspiration that enabled such an organisation to start. The ecstasy of the beginnings was to pass away—as an ecstasy in this life always does—and give way to a calm understanding of the needs of mankind, which was more likely to endure. In the order of the Friars Minor this practical common sense, which struck coins out of the gold of grace, received a name and shape: that of Brother Elias.

Brother Elias is the most controversial figure in Franciscan history: so much has been written about him, beginning with contemporary or near-contemporary sources, mostly with the heaviest prejudices for, or more frequently against, him, that it is difficult to estimate his true character.[2] Even his parentage is uncertain: according to some he had been a mattress maker and part-time schoolmaster at Assisi, according to others a notary at Bologna. His name has been given as Elias Bombarrone and it is likely that he came from Umbria and certainly was a person of education and great natural accomplishment. It would seem that he joined Francis with a genuine desire for the Franciscan way of life and a real devotion to the saint, and that the two men became close friends. This seems evident from the first edition of Thomas of Celano's life, before it was altered in the light of subsequent events. Thus it was that in 1221, when St Francis decided to hand over the reins of government, he appointed Elias as Minister General of the Order. After all, Francis knew that he was no organiser and Elias seemed to have the necessary qualities.

Elias was still General at the time of St Francis's death in 1226, and as such he informed the order of the event. He was a personal friend of Cardinal Hugolino, a great admirer and friend of St Francis, who became Pope as Gregory IX early in 1227. The Pope was eager for the proper veneration of St Francis, and as well as canonising him in 1228 he desired that a fitting monument to him should be erected at Assisi. This task he formally entrusted to Elias, and the building of the great basilica began at once under Elias's personal direction. Money was collected and the work went on at unheard-of speed, so that the lower basilica was ready to receive the saint's body as early as 1230.

Meanwhile the general chapter, summoned by Elias, had taken place at Whitsun 1227 and another friar, John Parenti, had been elected Minister General, though Elias in virtue of his personal commission remained in charge of the building. The idea of this magnificent church, although ordered by the Pope, seemed to many of the brethren to be in serious contradiction to the spirit of St Francis, and there were many who opposed it. Yet at the chapter of 1232 Elias was once more elected General.

Although Elias signed his work in the basilica as *Frater Elias peccator*, a change seemed to be coming over his character. A sort of *folie de grandeur* caused him on pretexts partly of health, no doubt justified, and partly of the importance of his business, to abandon poverty and simplicity in his way of life and to turn to a mode of living little short of luxury. During his second generalate (1232–9) he received heavy criticism within the order on other scores beyond the matter of the basilica and his mode of life. His highly organised government was accused of being autocratic and even cruel and his personal representatives or 'visitators' in the provinces assumed dictatorial powers in his name. He favoured the equality of the laybrothers—a matter hardly alien to the ideas of St Francis—but thereby angered the more educated priests among the brethren, who had through their superior education arrived at many positions of government in the order, and were now being overridden by the authoritarian demands of the General. In fact, it was suggested that his re-election in 1232 was brought about by the block votes of the laybrothers; and it was certainly the efforts of the Ministers Provincial, most of whom were priests, which brought about his deposition in 1239. Not the least of his troubles was that he undoubtedly saw himself in the role of peacemaker between the papacy and Frederick. In this he was supported by Gregory IX himself and he had already become a personal friend of the Emperor. This alone was a danger to him, and the Franciscans in Italy, who were solidly Guelph, naturally suspected their General of being all but a Ghibelline.[3]

Thus a strong feeling grew up in the order and in 1239 the Pope was asked to depose him. At first the Pope was unwilling and Elias's personal influence nearly won the day, but eventually the Pope agreed to the request, and while speaking of Elias as St Francis's friend and expressing his own personal esteem for him, he formally deposed him. It must be admitted that Elias took it badly; he refused to obey the next General and was excommunicated, only to be absolved on his deathbed in 1253.

Many of those who wrote after his disgrace in 1239 spared no pains in underlining his weaknesses, such as Salimbene, who was among his loudest critics, asserting that he had spent the order's money on his own luxury, that he kept his own cook and servants, and used a horse even for the shortest distances.[4] After 1239 Elias became entirely separated from the order and threw in his lot with Frederick, which did not improve his reputation among the brethren, so that gradually he came to be regarded as the originator of all the subsequent dissensions, the source of relaxation, a Judas to St Francis and the author of every departure from the founder's rule; a sinister figure and the evil genius of the saint.

At the same time the transition that occurred after the time of St Francis was inevitable. Certain privileges were bound to come when the brethren were preaching in the churches instead of the open countryside, when they became university lecturers as well as simple penitents. Many were the discussions about the rule: the professors began to dispute about the 'spirit of poverty' and the '*usus pauper*', and whether it was not more in accordance with this to have a thick habit of good material rather than a cheap one, for the good habit would not only last longer but would increase devotion in a chilly choir.[5] While the zealots were disapproving of these innovations, the moderate party were progressing: more sinners, they claimed, were converted by theology than by mere piety, and therefore study was necessary and libraries and properly built friaries to house them.

Times were changing and it was useless to resent these things. It was useless to compare the holy folly of Francis with the growing needs and weep over every new or neater habit, every expensive manuscript or every dispensation from the rigours of the early days. One day some of the modern young men in the order were showing old Brother Giles one of their new and up-to-date friaries with the greatest pride. 'All that's missing is the women,' said the old man.[6] But he was one of the old school and lived in a hermitage and still begged his bread even when invited to dine with a fastidious bishop. What of the famous Brother Juniper, whom an important delegation came to visit and found him playing with some children in the street? And Brother Leo, 'Brother Lamb-of-God', who was so troubled about these things that he fled to the fastness of Greccio and wrote the *Legend of the Three Friends* together with Angelo, the converted knight, and Ruffino, the stern ecstatic? And Brother John, who lived at the top of La Verna and so loved God that his burning heart could find no rest, and 'as if drunk with the Spirit, would leap through the kitchen garden into the woods or run to the church, driven by the fire and strength of the Spirit'?[7] What had these men to do with universities or ecclesiastical privileges? They were the forerunners of the party later labelled 'spiritual', who were extremists and enthusiasts, withdrawing themselves from the rest of the brethren and writing their manifestoes (such as Angelo Clareno's *Chronicle of the Seven Persecutions*). Many of their accusations may be unfounded, but there is something in the ring of them at the end of the thirteenth century that reminds us of the terrible warnings of Joachim at the end of the twelfth. These fiery sons of the gentle Francis were the real heirs of Joachim: Jacopo dalla Massa, Pietro da Macerata, Ubertino da Casale, Corrado da Offida and Pier Olivi, that clever man from Provence. They cried down condemnation on the order that was no longer the Order of St Francis, they attacked their superiors and even the Pope, whom they called Belial upon earth. Of course, they were repressed, persecuted, excommunicated, and in the fourteenth century even burnt as heretics. Perhaps they really were heretics, for that is the tragedy of the 'spiritual' party, that after all their zeal and struggle they came to possess less of the heritage of Francis than their moderate opponents, his joy, his humility and above all his charity. It was not with their help that St Francis would 'repair the church', for his true helpers were the practical and moderate men of the later age. By the time that the order was exerting its greatest influence on the ordinary people, its spirituality had lost its 'extraordinary' and ecstatic qualities, and was composed largely of the rather dull and ordinary Fathers whom we meet in the pages of Salimbene of Parma. This was perhaps as it should be, because the ordinary people probably needed Christianity presented to them in an ordinary way. It was a lewd and lascivious world they were talking to and these good friars, whose poverty and obedience—and even sometimes their chastity—were hardly on a heroic scale, were performing a gigantic task; they were breaking down the age-old barriers between priests and people, they were preaching virtue and administering the sacraments and they were zealous about their work.

The development of the Order of Preachers was a much more peaceful story. St Dominic, the founder, had a very clear idea from the start of what he wanted it to be; there might be differences of opinion about details, but never about the main ideal of the order. Most of his recruits came from the intelligentsia and frequently from academic careers, and the mode of life he demanded of them did not differ so violently from the life they led before as did the mode of life of the early Franciscans. They were trained to be preachers: 'study is the bending of the bow: the arrow flies in preaching'—a remark of a medieval French Dominican which sums up the idea.[8] They specialised in preaching; when there was to be a sermon by John of Salerno, or Peter of Verona, or the beloved Master General Jordan of Saxony, or Jordan of Pisa of almost legendary eloquence, no church or piazza was large enough for the crowds who came to hear them and sometimes people would come the night before to secure a place. It was their preaching that established the popularity of their order, for there was a fact about the Dominicans which made them unpopular in certain quarters, the fact that early in their history the management of the Inquisition was placed in their hands. Of course, there was rivalry between them and their Franciscan brothers, but what the Franciscans achieved through their simple friendliness the Dominicans achieved through their eloquence. Thus both orders contributed equally to the great rebuilding of faith during the *Duecento*, and it is perhaps significant that there is a Dominican version of the legend of Pope Innocent's dream where it is Dominic who saves the Lateran basilica from falling down.

Gradually, however, the differences between the two orders grew less, chiefly through the adjustment among the Franciscans of their attitude to studies. As soon as the objections of the 'spiritual' party in Umbria had been reduced to silence, the Friars Minor began to write and teach, hoping soon to get as many students and professors as the Friars Preachers; but

it took them a long time to catch up. Salimbene tells of an
occasion when a learned Dominican was staying with the
Franciscans and hardly expected them to know anything about
the bible. But when a mere Franciscan was able to argue with
the master point by point the community became wild with
delight.[9] This very enthusiasm showed their eagerness to be
able to compete. The learned Bonaventure was a great asset
to the Franciscans, and though on various points he disagreed
with the Dominican Thomas d'Aquino, the two men were the
best of friends and they stood shoulder to shoulder in resisting,
and overcoming, the bitter attacks made in Paris in 1255 on
the mendicants by William of Saint-Amour on behalf of the
secular clergy. This occurrence perhaps more than anything
brought the two orders together.

The jealousy of the diocesan clergy towards the new orders
was a serious thing at that time. With the old monastic orders
there had never been any difficulties: they lived in their
abbeys, remote from the ordinary people. But these new
mendicant orders were settling in the towns, threatening the
authority of the parish clergy, drawing the people away from
the parish churches, and, it had to be admitted, depriving the
diocesan clergy of certain sources of revenue which from time
immemorial had been theirs. Generally the popes supported
the mendicants, but Salimbene merrily tells a grim story of
how Pope Innocent IV, incited by the seculars, had deprived
the Franciscans of certain of their privileges, when suddenly
he became ill and a fortnight later died; whereupon his
successor, fearing a similar fate, immediately revoked the
impious decree.[10] The conflict between the secular clergy and
the mendicants broke out again at intervals, as at the synod
which had set out to deal with a genuinely urgent matter
regarding the threat of a Tartar invasion, instead of which the
whole time was taken up with wrangling about certain rights
contested by the Friars Minor and the diocesan clergy.[11]

Among the many other religious orders which came into
being in Italy in the thirteenth century the most important
were the Servites and the Humiliati. In the year 1233—a year

we shall notice again in a sacred context—it happened that
seven young Florentines in one night dreamed the same dream:
it was the night of the Assumption and each of them saw our
Lady in such dazzling glory that from that moment the glitter
of this world lost all its attraction. The seven of them together
at once took a small house near the city gates, to the great
displeasure of the seven noble families who had no time for
devotio without *decorum*. But the young men's *devotio* was so
solid and so good that after a few years the *decorum* came of
itself, and where the humble house had stood by the gate there
now stands the magnificent church of the Santissima Annun-
ziata. Seven years after their sevenfold dream, the young men
founded the Order of Servites, the 'Servants of Mary', which
had a rapid growth. Their great saint was Philip Benizi, whom
they left to look after the cows until they discovered that he
had been at the Sorbonne. He then became superior and
finally General of the Order, achieving a remarkable fame as a
preacher and wonder-worker, so that at the death of Pope
Clement IV he was elected Pope, but managed to decline the
honour. With all his graceful aristocratic charm he is a typical
Florentine saint. It was under his influence that the equally
aristocratic Juliana de Falconieri founded her Order of Mantel-
late, but her story would take us into the next century.

At the beginning of the *Duecento* the Order of the Humiliati played an important part in the confused society of the time.
Its members combined a secular occupation with their religious
life; in Lombardy in particular they were weavers and formed
an important link between the guilds and the monasteries. As
well as their second and third orders who continued to ply their
trades, there grew up a first order of clerics, drawn mainly
from the working classes and in consequence having an influence comparable to that of the Dominicans and Franciscans.

Every kind of religious habit was to be seen on the roads of
Italy, and at first the people eyed them with caution. There
was no doubt about their hostility to the first Franciscans, who
had thrown up their possessions and begged from others: there
had been all too many thieves and parasites who had claimed to

be saints. When they came for the first time to a town as often
as not the people greeted them with catcalls and mud slinging
and it was only gradually that they won respect. 'I would not
belong to them, even if it got me straight to heaven!' cried one
smart young man to Brother Giles as he trudged along in his
shabby tunic.[12] The majority regarded the Apostles of poverty
simply as hypocrites, but gradually they came round, for whatever their ignorance and superstition may have been, there was
a kind of basic faith in those people. A childish faith perhaps,
but a desperate faith amid war and oppression and mistrust and
fear—and a terrible dearth of selfless priests to guide them.
This is why they clung to what religion they had. If a famous
preacher came they would flock to hear him. If there was a
rumour of a miracle whole towns would go wild with excite-
ment, everyone would come out with their crosses and banners
and would weep and sing and promise anything to God or to
His saints. It was the century of the eucharistic miracle of
Bolsena, which directly influenced the institution of the feast of
Corpus Christi (1263), and in this century our Lady's house at
Nazareth flew of itself to Loreto (1295). But many of the
miracles, alas, were only tricks, as in the famous case at
Cremona. A humble barrel maker named Albert had recently
died there. At once one miracle after another took place at his
grave and no sooner was his picture hung up at St Peter's
church at Parma than miracles began to occur there too. No one
had noticed this humble workman before and suddenly he had
posthumously become a wonder-worker. Shelters were built for
the sick all round the church, Masses were celebrated in the
piazza, pious confraternities were founded in his honour, and
meanwhile the barrelmakers were reaping a good profit; then
the toes of the saint, which had been taken by Parma as relics,
turned out to be cloves of garlic. After this the miracles ceased as
suddenly as they had begun. Similar things occurred in many
other cities.[13] Such things, however, were no more than a kind
of religious parallel to the sensationalism which the people
found in the turmoils of civic life and strife. Thus the main
feature of the social life of the *Duecento*—organisation—is so

extraordinarily characteristic also of its religious life in the multitude of confraternities and what are now called 'secular institutes' in the religious sphere. It is open to discussion whether this organisation in medieval Italy sprang from an awareness of unity among the people or, as is more probable, from the extreme individualism and mistrust of each group, which caused them to organise themselves in self defence. However that may be, the hundreds of associations on the basis of trade, locality, piety or amusement formed the cells out of which the small guild systems of the towns developed.

Among the most important organisations were the military orders, with the spiritual ideal of chivalry at the time of the crusades. God's warriors, clothed like St Michael with the armour of light, bound themselves to serve Christendom in obedience and chastity according to the needs of the Church. The idea was of French or Spanish origin rather than Italian, and the Knights Templar and the Knights of St John who guarded the holy places, together with the Mercedarians who were dedicated to the redemption of captives in Mohammedan hands, are hardly our concern here. But in the thirteenth century similar military orders were brought into being in Italy and many towns had their *militia* of Christ or of our Lady. The best known was the *Ordo Militiae beatae Mariae*, founded in 1233 by the Dominican Gerard of Parma. Its members retained their own possessions and were far from poor, so that they soon received the nickname of the *frati gaudenti* or 'jovial friars'. Many of them attained high office, where, however, they pursued their jovialities so that Dante met some of them in Hell,[14] and before long Our Lady's militia was wisely demobilised.

The confraternities were usually based upon the parish church. Some were associations for the performance of charitable works, while others existed for purposes of devotion. And there were the Third Orders, or associations of people living in the world, but under the jurisdiction of a religious order. The most important of these was the Third Order to which St Francis gave a rule in 1221. The action of St Francis was not as novel as is sometimes supposed, for even apart from the weavers of the Third Order of the Humiliati there were other similar examples previously.[15] But the Franciscan 'Third Order of Penance' had a special importance through its connexion with the powerful First Order, and as long as its members practised the strict rule of the seraphic founder they remained a powerful influence in civic life. They were Christians who took their faith seriously, and though they wore secular clothes they refused to carry arms, to take oaths, or to indulge in doubtful amusements. They can never have been very numerous, but their influence was out of proportion to their number, and everywhere they ran hospitals, leper colonies and hostels for pilgrims. Their womenfolk sewed and cooked for the poor and organised rescue work for the poor and provided poor girls with a dowry. Travellers and pilgrims could get a free bath at their hostels; unwanted babies were placed in the stone cradle that stood at the door of their orphanages and were taken in; the sick, the prisoners and the possessed were all cared for. All these good works began with small local groups, among whom the Franciscan 'Tertiaries' had a leading place. Later, when on the one hand some of the zeal of the Third Order had declined, and on the other hand an uneducated and fanatical element had brought the ideal into disrepute, the Franciscan Fathers were less ready to support the movement, as a writer from the circle of St Bonaventure explained in his treatise 'Why the Brethren do not support the Order of Penance'.[16] The Franciscan Fathers found themselves held responsible for all the faults of their tertiaries, for their quarrels and even their illegitimate children and for all their decline in fervour. It was a wise move when in 1289 the whole Third Order was reorganised and given an entirely new rule, which more or less remains its rule today. The Dominican Third Order had grown up about the same time, but its chief period of influence was after the thirteenth century.

These Third Orders, composed as they were of married layfolk pursuing their ordinary business yet living by the sacraments and Chrstian ideals, had a profound effect upon medieval

Italian piety outside the cloister. Many outstandingly holy men and women drew their inspiration from them.

There was the Tuscan moneylender Luchesio, who was wholeheartedly engaged in climbing the social ladder by means of his money,[17] when he met St Francis, who pointed out to him that this was not the only object of human striving. The moneylender never forgot that beggar; he sold all he had for the benefit of widows, and orphans and pilgrims, and set out for the plague-stricken marshlands with a donkey loaded with medical supplies. At first his wife laughed at him, until she also came to understand and became his devoted assistant, earning her honourable title of *Buona Donna*.

Then there was Novellone, the cobbler of Faenza, who went eleven times, barefoot, on pilgrimage to Santiago de Compostela, praying as he walked; a true son of Francis.[18] And what of the pious and learned Guido, the glory of the tertiaries of Cortona?[19] And Peter, the devout comb maker of Siena? And Bartolo the leper of San Gimignano, who bore his terrible fate with such joyful resignation that he was called 'the Job of Tuscany'?

There were holy women, too, among the tertiaries. In Viterbo there was the little girl, St Rose, who did not cease to proclaim her allegiance to the Pope and upbraided the people for submitting to the Emperor, confirming her message with miracles, until she was forced to leave the city.[20] At Foligno wonderful visions were granted to the widow, Angela; while Margaret of Cortona was doing penance for her early life as a courtesan, living in her small cottage by the piazza.[21] Both these saints heard the voice of the Holy Spirit, each of them in turn being assured that she was the most loved of all women.[22] The conduct of Margaret in some respects strikes us nowadays as completely hysterical; by the way of penance she devoted herself day and night to the sick and poor, but neglected her own little son so that he threatened to throw himself down a well,[23] though later he was sent away to school and eventually became a Franciscan. Sometimes she would wake up the whole town at night with the loudness of her penitential wailing: 'Wake up,' she would shout, 'wake up, people of Cortona, and drive this sinner from your midst with stones!' Another time she interrupted a sermon with the cry of Mary Magdalene her patron: 'Have you seen my Lord? Know you where they have laid him?'[24] But it is in her many conversations with our Lord in ecstasy that her importance as a saint and mystic appears, and many miracles occurred after her death.

Then there are the hidden saints: Zita of Lucca, who went to heaven by her life as a humble maidservant; [25] and Fina of San Gimignano, who (like Lydwina of Schiedam in Holland) had a whole lifetime of pain.[26] Finally, back in Florence, in a bare room within one of the rich banking houses, there was the young widow Umiliana de' Cerchi, leading a hidden life of penance, fasting and weeping to atone for the dishonest dealings of her rich brothers next door.[27]

Perhaps this Florentine woman is a symbol of all the hidden goodness that made up for the all too open evil of the time. There must have been many such, in fact: who now remembers the nobleman of Pisa, whom Dante calls 'The good Marzucco',[28] who had the cowardly murderer of his son in his power and yet forgave him, becoming a Friar Minor at Santa Croce? It was typical of the age to regard it as a dishonour to renounce bloody feuds, while recognising as saints Francis whose poverty contrasted with its greed, Marzucco whose forgiveness contrasted with its hatred and desire for revenge. In the most widely read story book of the time there is a little story which is as it were symbolic of the counterpart of goodness to so much rivalry and violence in that age.[29] 'How a banker did a great almsdeed for the love of God. Peter the banker was a rich man, but he became so kind that for the love of God he began to give away all his possessions to the poor. And when he had given everything away, he went and sold himself and gave the whole price to the poor.'

7

The Sinners

Ahi, serva Italia, di dolor ostello,
  nave senza nocchiere in gran tempesta,
  non donna di provincia, ma bordello!

O Italy, poor slave at sorrow's door,
  a ship without a steersman in the storm,
  no gentle lady thou, but merest whore.

Dante, Purgatorio[1]

GOD HAS always given his people of Italy many saints to assist them; this is how he spoke to his faithful Margaret of Cortona:

> Who are those who betray me as Judas did? They are indeed those who talk, laugh, eat and drink, and sleep with their fellow-men, and then murder them for the sake of money.
>
> Who are those who bring me before Pilate to accuse me? The judges who with false evidence and lying speeches condemn men to death.
>
> Who are those who pull out my hair? The goldsmiths, merchants and artisans, who think only of their greed for money.
>
> Who are those who scourge me at the pillar? They are those who go about the countryside attacking men and tying them up, in order to extort a greater ransom than they can pay.
>
> Who are those who slap me in the face and strike me without ceasing? They are those who do violence to priests and religious; and he who seeks their life, even should they deserve it, is as one who plucks out my eye.
>
> Who are those who dare to ill-use my cheeks and my beard? The unhappy usurers who rob themselves of all hope of salvation.

Who are those who prepare a cross for me so narrow and small that I have nowhere to lay my head? Those who unjustly claim land for themselves and drive people out of their homes, compelling them to become beggars, robbers and thieves, and to lead a life of shame.

Who are those who blindfold me like a criminal? The adulterers.

Who are those who dare to spit in my face? Those who blaspheme my holy name and those who paint their faces.

Who are those who nail me to the cross? Those who produce false coins.

Who are those who divide my soul from my body with gall, myrrh and vinegar? Those who commit the unnameable sin against nature.

Who are those who mock me on the cross? Those who look upon my holy body on the altar, and deny their faith in me.

Who persecutes me as Herod did? Every bad priest. And now know this: as much as my mercy is shown to them now, so much shall my justice overtake them, when the time comes for the punishment of their crime.

And know this too, my daughter, that among Christians today there are more Jews against me, than ever came running before Pilate at the time of my Passion. [2]

If no one had told us of Luchesio, the kindly moneylender, of Marzucco who forgave the murderer, of Margaret, the converted sinner, and of Umiliana, who renounced the banker's riches, we might have thought that usury, murder, sins of the flesh and ill-gotten gains were the usual thing in everyday life at the time; and they were evident enough. But there they are, these holy people upholding Christian living in a society whose everyday life often seems frighteningly remote from such an ideal.

Yet there is a difference between the medieval sinner and his modern counterpart. Today there are many psychological theories to explain, and perhaps sometimes to explain away, the phenomenon of sin. In the Middle Ages it was simpler: the sinner knew that he was a sinner: he admitted that he had sold his soul to the devil. Conflicts in souls and in society thus became

more tense, but the moral aspect of the whole epoch became
more simple: almost always good and evil were judged by the
same standards. Therefore the burden of sorrow was greater
for those who had to look on helplessly while evil overpowered
the children of God: 'All the virtues proclaimed by Jesus are
being rejected; the poor, the peaceful and the simple are no
longer the chosen ones of his Church; all that Jesus proscribed
and condemned, avarice, oppression, material gain, possessions,
power—all this stands in the place of the beatitudes and the
love of our neighbour, renouncing all that the early Christians
stood for.'[3]

The popes of Rome in the *Duecento* we have seen to be a
series of men, some strong, some weak, while some were
geniuses and others were limited, and some again were born
diplomats, while others were too innocent; but few of them
were saints, though none of them were rogues. Yet a glance before
and beyond our century shows us that within the *Duecento* the
Church was not as unfortunate in her pastors as at certain other
times. Of course, there was nepotism, which thrives on any
kind of corruption, and there were cardinals who were hardly
more than courtiers eager for worldly gain: *cardinales carpinales*
as the Latin joke had it.[4] The devout and sober Bishop Jacques
of Vitry could not disguise his disappointment after a visit to the
papal court: 'I found that many things at the curia were
entirely opposed to my ideas: everyone there is so busy with
earthly and transitory affairs, with the business of kings and of
kingdoms, with lawsuits and cases, that there is no time or
opportunity to speak of spiritual things.'[5] His Franciscan compatriot Hugh of Montpellier does not mince his words when he
addresses the cardinals, and his confrère Salimbene has eagerly
put it all down:

> As soon as the papal consistory is over you hasten to the dining
> room and eat and drink magnificently; then off to bed for a
> thoroughly good siesta. For the rest of the day you loaf about your
> apartments, simply exhausted with idleness, or else you amuse
> yourselves with your pet dogs or your jewellery or your
> nephews or your horses, and see to it that you have plenty of

servants, well turned out, an elegant house, and of course evidence of distinguished parentage. That is all your daily task. You don't care what pilgrims there may be lying exhausted in a village outside the city, or who needs food or clothing or just a visit, or who ought to be ransomed or even buried. You could surely convert the whole world if you did what the Wise Man says in Proverbs: 'Run about, make haste, raise up thy friend', or again, 'Deliver them that are led to death, and those that are drawn to death forbear not to deliver.' People will believe you rather than other priests. . . . Why don't you do it?[6]

Perhaps the common people did not have such a close view of the lives of their prelates, but they had certainly long ago lost confidence in them. Therefore they hailed as a saint the Franciscan who had just refused a bishopric when they saw him begging through the streets of Perugia.[7] And as in France, the people were talking about a terrible letter, recently un- earthed, written in blood from the bottom of Hell by none less than Lucifer himself, in which he addresses in affectionate terms his dear friends, the prelates of the Church.[8] It was also observed that *Praelatus* and *Pilatus* were not dissimilar words.[9]

Both history and literature provide evidence about the depravity of certain prelates. In a time when the moral stan- dards of the Middle Ages had not yet been forgotten the gifts and moral standards of a man of the Renaissance stand out sharply in the person of the young Florentine cardinal, Otta- viano degli Ubaldini. He wrote poems which show genuine talent, and he chose his furniture and vessels for the table with the most perfect taste. But the writing of love sonnets does suggest a lover, and the buying of *objets d'art* does suggest money, so that the young cardinal soon had a reputation of being an unscrupulous intriguer and money maker as well as a tireless woman hunter. He thanked his chamberlain for his devoted service by making him Archbishop of Milan. This man, Otto Visconti, was a member of a heretical sect, but a fact of this kind was no worry to his patron. When Otto died the cardinal had him buried in a tomb of red marble, but it was said that the man was such a heretic that the marble twice turned itself black.[10] Dante coupled the names of Ottaviano and 'the Second Frederick' among the heretics in Hell.[11] But while the emperor's Averroism did apparently form a basis to his philosophy of life, it would seem that the cardinal's heresy was chiefly the pursuit of frivolous pleasure and the utter neglect of spiritual things.

Otto Visconti was not the only heretic to occupy a Catholic see. There was, for instance, the Bishop of Parma, the scene of whose deathbed is described by Salimbene in the most matter-of-fact tones: 'He lived a short time and died at Mantua, a heretic and accursed. When during his last illness they brought him the body of the Lord, he refused to receive it saying that he did not believe any of that. When they asked him why he had accepted the bishopric, he said it was for the sake of the money and the honour; and so he died without the sacraments.'[12] There were many bishops who opposed the Pope in their politics and even mocked at his sacred office. On one occasion we read of the people rising against such a pastor and making a tumult before his palace, so that the bishop fled by a back door.[13] But for the most part they contented themselves with pointed stories, like that of the red marble tomb of Visconti, or that of the dog which lifted its leg before the tomb of the Bishop of Reggio.[14]

In these circumstances it is not surprising that the life of the diocesan clergy was not always edifying, and that sometimes their main interest was in money and material gain, business deals in relics and indulgences and the squandering of tithes on their concubines. 'Lazarus the begger lies at the gate and Christ himself is weeping outside the door. And within? The houses of the clergy are more like comedy or farce within: among the dogs and birds there are the fools and jesters, the singing girls and the ugly voice of flattery. In all that noisy company, amid the drums and cymbals, the flutes and organ, how can the fear of God find a place?'[15] It was not suprising that none less than Pope Innocent III (or another under his name) wrote the famous work 'Of the contempt of this world'[16] and gave utterance to what was in the minds of many when he wrote: *Qui nocte Venerem amplexantur, mane vero Virginem venerantur.*

Many of the clergy could not write and could hardly read. Some of these, whom the Florentine wits called *clerici fittizi*, had only been ordained to escape the courts of justice; they thus lived merrily abroad by trade and adventure, but as clergy refused to pay their debts. Quite often parish priests ran public-houses in order to provide for wife and children. There is a story of a Franciscan who went to a village church to say Mass and found everything dirty and unkempt and the altarbreads fly-blown, and no girdle among the vestments, so that he had to borrow the housekeeper's belt, and every time he turned to say *Dominus vobiscum* the bunch of keys on it rattled.[18] Another story of Salimbene's, perhaps equally exaggerated, but perhaps equally with an element of truth, is that of the woman who came to confession to a Franciscan father with a knife in her hand. She had been raped by a tramp and three priests to whom she had gone to confession, one after another, followed the tramp's example. After the Father had given her absolution, he asked her, 'And what is that knife for? What are you going to do with it?' She said, 'Truly, Father, I would have killed myself with it if you had behaved like the others.'[19] Are these perhaps slanders against the secular clergy? Maybe. But there is too much evidence for us to deny their general slackness; and one chronicler, for instance, tells in the most everyday terms how in his own home town a priest was boiled to death as a punishment for murder.[20]

But let us not delay any more over the sins of those whose vocation it was to do good in the world. *Chè voler cio udir è bassa voglia*: 'To want to hear such things is base desire', says Virgil to Dante.[21] One thing is certain: although Christ promised that 'the gates of hell shall not prevail', those gates sometimes came very near doing so during the late Middle Ages. Dante's objectivity in the *Inferno*, peopled by so many of the *Duecento*, is indeed the dark counterpart to Francis's golden age, but it would be unjust to condemn the Church of Rome for the evil state of the world at the time, for though she had a part in it, it was not of her making. It was a time of crisis, the end of an age, and at such times decay is in the air like poisonous fog and no one can protect himself against it. It is not right but people in distress are seldom right. Even the unspeakable Ezzelino addressed thus a captive legate:

> How is it possible that our holy mother the Church can still survive, when under her wings one Christian can be unjust to another, and her own servants can condone robbery and oppression? You are surely aware that those who came to Padua with you, calling themselves Christians and warriors of St Peter, robbed and murdered other Christians, extorted tribute from them, and reduced many to the state of widows, orphans and beggars. And then they make the strange claim that they were acting in the name of the Church, which had given them a free hand and never mentioned restitution of their ill-gotten gains.[22]

It is easy to point a finger of scorn at Ezzelino, of all people, for preaching, when we know that his own cruelty yielded nothing to that of the papal forces at the siege of Padua; but that does not make the accusation less true, or remove the bitterness of those thousands who went to seek their salvation elsewhere.

In the Middle Ages if men turned to seek their salvation outside the Church it was not in enlightened scepticism, as it would be today. Throughout the centuries there have been wild olives growing out of the root of Rome, when the ancient tree seemed to wither. These wild branches have usually grown when an atmosphere of decay seemed to smother the life of the tree; but of the wild olives that grew in the *Duecento* no trace remains today.

It is significant that the two great heresies of the late Middle Ages came from France. It is said that the Gallican spirit has always been ready to be independent of Rome; but it is otherwise in Italy, where Catholicism is a national heritage and so bound up with the people that no local heresy has ever survived for long. No lasting enmity with the Church has been native to Italy. Even Italian communists today will not hesitate to take off their hats as they pass a shrine of the Madonna in the street, and this is the weakness of Italian communism, however strenuously the official Marxist propaganda may deny it. But communism has shown up the weaknesses of native Italian anti-clericalism, which cannot measure up to the imported doctrines from Russia. In the same way any local heresy in the medieval Italian towns could not measure up to the French Waldensians and Catharists.

The Waldensians were convinced Christians. The severity of their life was a protest against the luxury of Rome, an accusation against the Church which struck home. Under the name of 'the Poor Men of Lombardy' they were found principally in the north, where, in fact, they were more effectively countered by the exemplary life of the Humiliati than by the denunciations of the Inquisition. It was understandable that some people attributed Waldensian sympathies to Francis also at the beginning and regarded this as one of his merits.

Much more dangerous than the followers of Peter Valdes were the Catharists, who under the name of Albigensians had flourished in Provence. Their dualism was hardly Christian any more, and it is difficult to see wherein lay the attraction for simple folk of this grim Manichaean doctrine. At least the Italian people were not likely to accept the idea that Christ was neither God nor man, but an angel who only appeared to suffer on the cross: this was therefore nothing but a hideous instrument of torture which ought to be destroyed wherever it appeared. Nor were they likely to find consolation in the theory that man was created by the devil, who kept him captive in a sorry series of reincarnations. The *consolamentum* of the Catharists was not likely to win them over from the Catholic sacraments, and the suicide ideal of the *endura* could hardly have held much appeal for hard-headed, common-sense people like the north Italians.

But it is doubtful whether a large number of people has ever left the Church on theological grounds. Simple people never understand these things, but they did go to catharist sermons; how were they to distinguish the ascetical heretic from the begging friars or austere hermits they already knew? Were they not all good men, practising what they preach? These men were preaching virtuous living and crying down the abuses everyone knew about, and often going in danger of their lives because of it. Who was to know the difference?

It is interesting that the Italian heretics, Waldensian and Catharists alike—the two groups were tending to fuse into one another anyway—preferred to be called 'Patarenes'. The name comes from the *pataria*, the second-hand or old-clothes market at Milan, and therefore has a flavour of the ragged proletariat about it. Moreover, about 1060 there was a riot of the people of the *pataria* against the rich married priests of the time in Lombardy. The name thus carried an overtone: it was a revolt of the proletariat linking hands with the new heresy: a social as much as a theological revolution. How much doctrine came into it, it is difficult to say, but it was in the main an emotional reaction, and an accusation by the common people of the Church, which, it must be admitted, had in such large measure abandoned them.

The preachers, and especially all those who held official positions among the Patarenes, belonged to the circle of the 'Perfect': they lived the lives of saints, rather like the saints of the Stoa or of Buddhism. They were never known to lie, they refused to take oaths, they renounced many foods, they never touched a woman and they sought death as the only ultimate prevention of sin. The example of the 'Perfect' was not obligatory on the ordinary people, but the people were influenced by it in so far as they admired it. This influence was disastrous, because the hatred of life—for the true disciple, life was the work of the Devil—made the Catharists into complete nihilists, and their belief in dreary reincarnations undermined the family and the whole accepted order of Christian society. Thus the Catharists are as it were the first wave of anarchy to attack Western Christendom. Christian society was sometimes overthrown throughout a whole province; the Church then lost all control and Catharist bishops set up their sees and ruled as they pleased. Small wonder that the agnostic politician Frederick II, tolerant as he was of Jews and Saracens, turned against the heretics and persecuted them with fire and sword. The Italian Patarenes, although numerous, remained a minority; hence they were able to carry on their activity only in secret; it is only through the trials of the *perfecti*, who did not lie and had no fear of the death-sentence, that we can learn something of their mode of life. In the north there was no city without its Catharist centre; Florence, through her lively trade with the south of France, counted hundreds of heretics, in Poggibonsi we find a proper Catharist school, and Viterbo and Treviso seem to have had a kind of Catharist pope. But the centre of the whole movement remained Milan: *omnium haereticorum, Patarinorum, Luciferanorum, Publicanorum, Albigensium, usurariorum refugium et receptaculum*,[23] in Frederick's comprehensive phrase.

We know how the heresy was finally brought to an end. After a fairly long period during which both Church and State attempted to restore the balance by means of preaching and persuasion, final recourse was had to extreme means of saving European society: the Albigensians were annihilated by the hundreds; the State took the lead, first the King of Aragon, then France—Innocent III reluctantly agreeing—and finally Italy. It was 1224 when the Emperor Frederick issued the first edict against the heretics in Lombardy.

The progress of the trials of the heretics was very varied: in some places they jostled the victims along to the stake with great applause, while elsewhere they hunted the inquisitors out of the town. The first inquisitors were mostly Dominicans, some of them being convert Patarenes. The most important of these was Peter of Verona. As a student at Bologna he had heard St Dominic preaching there in 1221 and from that moment he had vowed himself to the defence of the Catholic faith. Gregory IX appointed him inquisitor for Lombardy, where for twenty years he fought the Patarenes, until on Maundy Thursday 1252 he was murdered by them on the road from Milan to Como. His position as leader of the Inquisition brought him a rapid canonisation, though subsequent devotion to him varied from veneration to execration: as late as 1299 a blacksmith of Bologna was brought to trial for having spoken disrespectfully of the holy martyr.[24] When today we look at his serene portrait at San Marco we cannot help wondering how much is his character and how much is the art of Fra Angelico.

But there is no doubt about Peter the Martyr's eloquence. The Florentines would pack the Piazza Santa Maria Novella to listen to him spellbound; new orders and confraternities sprang up under his direction, and he became the centre of popular devotion in the city. But when, relying on his immense popularity, he attempted an indictment of the heretics, a riot broke out and he was compelled to leave Tuscany.

Among those accused of heresy there were a number of prominent people, doctors, bankers, professors, merchants and monks, who had been ordained as 'perfect' by the imposition of hands. In the trials of 1244 there were members of both the Guelph and Ghibelline nobility, the Neri and the Pulci, who at some time had harboured an heretical bishop. Those who renounced their heresy were obliged to wear a yellow cross on their breast and shoulder, and to stand at the church doors on Sundays as public penitents, as a warning to both Christians and Patarenes. Such conversions were rare, however, and in fact the obstinacy of the heretics was more profitable to the State and to the judges than their penitence, since all the heretics' possessions came into their hands. Sometimes even the dead were condemned as heretics, especially if there was a profitable confiscation in view.

After these grim and fanatical Catharists the purely Italian heresy presents a very different picture. Here we are best informed about a sect who called themselves the 'Apostles', founded by a frustrated Franciscan of Parma. This was Gerardino Segarelli, of whom the Franciscan Salimbene, also of Parma, has nothing good to say,[25] although his invectives do not enlighten us as to how far Gerardino's views coincide with those of the Patarenes. At any rate his movement found supporters among the poorer people. One of the stories told about him by Salimbene was that he stood by a vineyard and called out to passers-by, 'Go ye also into my vineyard', to the ultimate detriment of the owner's harvest. He held frenzied meetings when the whole assembly would at intervals shout *'pater, pater, pater'* and nothing more. At other meetings the 'apostles' would 'strip themselves of all things' and stand naked in a circle round the heap of their discarded clothes. At one time it is said he had 4,000 followers, whose spiritual care he gave to a certain Fra Dolcino and to his 'spiritual sister' Margherita. Gradually the spiritual element disappeared and it became a rebellion of the *pauperi* against the wealthy. How much relation with the Patarenes the 'apostles' had cannot be established, but the whole thing eventually came to an end when the last of the movement were attacked by the plutocrats, who had been upset by their 'communism', on a hill near Vercelli in 1307 and killed.

There remains one strange area among these human aberrations that needs to be examined, and that is the world of magic. It is not generally realised how large a part magic played in everyday life in the Middle Ages. It had its influence both among the uninstructed and among the learned, and numbered among its adherents on the one hand simple superstitious folk and on the other hand the professional court magicians, who were consulted on affairs of state and were expected to prophesy the outcome of a given political undertaking. The common people, of course, relied on their old traditions and intuitions, but the educated people turned principally to astrology, which, it must be emphasised, was not considered a pagan thing, nor, at any rate at first, as something occult. The Emperor Frederick's learned astrologer, Michael Scotus, lived long in the memory of Italy as a mighty magician. He was called a 'second Apollo', and he always went about wearing a steel helmet, because of his foreknowledge that he would meet his death through a falling stone—which did, in fact, happen, in spite of the helmet. This Scotsman, trained in

Spain, combined an immense erudition with the sharpest wit.
Frederick, who had become suspicious of everyone, was always
pressing him for evidence and proof of everything, and it was
said that the astrologer always had the right answer. He had
several arrows to his bow: he was expert not only in astrology,
but also in mathematics and philosophy; he translated several
treatises of Aristotle, and his *Physionomia* was one of the most
widely read books of the *Duecento*.[26] Under him was a regular
college of augurs, ready to advise the Kaiser about everything,
even down to the best time to approach his wife in order to
beget a son.[27] Astrologers and magicians from all the known
world were sure of a welcome at the Hohenstaufen court, and
there are many contemporary anecdotes about the Emperor's
clever questions and the astonishing answers he received.

Several cities had their own oracles. At Modena there was an
astrologer who had only one eye and had come from Brescia. He
made quite a good living at his trade, until one day they asked
his advice about a suitable day for starting a campaign, adding,
'And if we don't get the victory you promise, we'll come back
and poke out your remaining eye.' The night before the
appointed day, however, the magician, 'fearing it might not
come true, took up all his earnings, and disappeared without
saying good-bye to anyone'.[28] Parma also had her prophet, the
cobbler called '*Asdenti*' or the 'toothless' *per contrarium*,
'because he had such huge and irregular teeth that he could
not speak clearly', about whom Salimbene also tells us that he
was 'pure, simple, God-fearing and courtly (*curialis*), that is,
having great urbanity, but illiterate, though he had such an
enlightened mind that he understood the works of those who
foretold the future, namely, Abbot Joachim, Merlin, Methodius
and Sybilla, Isaiah, Jeremiah, Hosea, Daniel and the Apocalypse, as well as Michael Scotus'. People came to him from
everywhere, learned and unlearned alike. But fifty years later
Dante put him with his head turned backwards in Hell, in the
company of Michael Scotus and Guido Bonatti, the court
astrologer of Montefeltro.[29]

The cradle of the black arts was known to be half-Moorish

Spain. All the necromancers and nigromancers of repute, who had mastered the craft of magic and were able to conjure up the dead with the greatest of ease, studied in Toledo, just as the theologians went to Paris and the law students came to Bologna. Sometimes there were Italian students at Toledo, like Philip, later Archbishop of Ravenna, who had gone there to study magic, but was told by his master: 'You Lombards are no good at this; you had better leave this to us Spaniards, and you go to Paris and read theology', which the future archbishop promptly did.[30]

But even if the Italians could not compete with the Spaniards, they certainly made their experiments at home: Siena was the Toledo of Tuscany: nowhere did they know as much about magic formulas and magic plants.[31] During their campaigns with Florence magic played an important part. Although the Sienese proclaimed the Virgin Mary as the real victor at Montaperti in 1260, and all the pictures of the time showed her as such,[32] there were those who wondered whether she could have done it without the help of magic. For already they had the 'secret weapon' of the old 'Greek fire', which worked on the enemy at any rate like magic. In all Italy only Siena had the formula and production was in the hands of a doctor, Simon, and an apothecary, Bartolo. The chief ingredient was petroleum and the army that possessed this weapon had the advantage from the start over an enemy who only had old-fashioned bows and slings. Siena in any case had a reputation for magic and one had to admit that the city was impregnable. If their spies could enter the enemy camp, they were less interested in capturing war documents than in acquiring portraits of the enemy leaders; once they had these, they could be worked upon with magic formulas, and the enemy was in their hands, but only if they remembered to bring a young girl to take part in the magic. Still more effective, however, was the preparation of their magic powder; then the women, who could easily have access to the enemy's camp, would strew the stuff among the tents and along the paths. Was the magic powder some poison that affected the horses and mules? We shall never know; but what is much more interesting is the people's belief in its magic powers.

It is a curious thing that these eminently reasonable people from the north of Italy were so fascinated by these occult forces. Probably it was but a part of the universal fear that dominated the land in the middle of the century, a phenomenon that we shall discuss in the next chapter.

8

The Penitents

Torniamo a penetenza
che el tempo è 'mcomenzato
con degiunio e astinenza
e guardiamce dal peccato,
chome fe' Christo nel diserto:

chi'l farà n'averà merto.

Now let us turn to penitence:
  The time is coming in
For fasting and for abstinence
  To keep us free from sin;
With Christ come to the
    wilderness
  His own good prize to win.

A hymn of the penitents of Gubbio[1]

AFTER MANY hours' travelling through the night, how
welcome the daylight is once more. Dante felt this as he came
out from his long journey through the darkness of Hell, and
set out through the dawn towards the mountain of purgatory:

> Per correr migliori acque alza le vele
> omai la navicella del mio ingegno,
> che lascia dietro a sè mar sì crudele.[2]

> And now the little ship of my own mind
> to run in better waters hoists the sail,
> and leaves that cruel ocean far behind.

The *Duecento* was a time when a whole people was emerging
from darkness into light, with much of the darkness of a
violent and superstitious world remaining, but also much
light of a new age and a new kind of holiness. It was a period
of chiaroscuro, of intense contrasts of light and shade. It was
like Holy Week in the liturgy, when after the bleakness of

Lent we suddenly come upon Palm Sunday with the cry *Hosanna* from the people, only to be followed by the cry *Crucifigatur* and all the darkness of the Passion, in turn to be transformed by the festival of light at Easter and the repeated *Alleluia*.

Soon after the death of Francis, there seemed to be a fulfilment of promise through all the length of Italy, and somehow people found themselves suddenly, and rather to their own surprise, at peace. Only at Messina did the sounds of war continue, for Frederick had little time for peace. But in the north there came into being a whole popular movement towards peace, with an eager desire to make an end of warring. The beginning of the movement can be ascribed to the year 1233, which came to be called the 'Alleluia year'. It was a remarkable year in which the cause of St Dominic's canonisation was opened, our Lady appeared to the seven holy founders of the Servites and the novel order of the *Frati Gaudenti* was begun. But still more interesting was the appearance in the cities of Tuscany of an extraordinary man, whose signature, as it were, was the threefold cry of joy *Alleluia, alleluia, alleluia,* and who gathered the people with the blast of a small trumpet, 'which sometimes filled us with terror and sometimes filled us with sweetness',[3] and who was therefore nicknamed 'Benedictus de Cornetta'. He was a friend of the Franciscans, and perhaps his little trumpet put him in mind of the ivory horn which the Sultan of Acre gave to the *poverello* and with which he also was said sometimes to have summoned his hearers.[4] But Benedict was much more of a showman: with his black beard and rough black tunic with a huge red cross all down the back, his preaching made a great impression. He interjected invocations which the people recited after him, or he got little boys to sing them, and then he would play on the trumpet again and so resume his sermon. The people were delighted: they would give up their feuds and restore stolen goods, and they held burning candles and green branches in their hands as they listened to him with tears of penance running down their cheeks, and then once again they would sing with him his chant of *Alleluia* and other acclama-

tions, of which we find one still a hundred years later in a
Florentine song book:

Alleluia, alleluia
From the height the King of kings
Down to man his friendship brings![5]

Everywhere Benedict de Cornetta found enthusiastic supporters
among the young men who helped to draw people into his
following by their eloquence, but sometimes also by their
charlatanism.[6] The chroniclers tell us of 'Alleluia preachers' at
Cassino,[7] Modena, Reggio, Milan and throughout the Po valley.
It seems that they adopted a special style of their own and as
late as 1285 Salimbene tells of a man who could imitate the
style of the preachers and wonder-workers of 1233.[8] And, of
course, the Italian people enjoyed it all, as they always do
enjoy anything theatrical. But at the same time the 'Alleluia
preachers' did genuine good work: enemies were reconciled,
exiles were recalled and whole cities sometimes came under
their spell. One of the most important of these enthusiastic
preachers was the famous John of Vicenza, the Dominican who

worked in Ezzelino's area round Treviso. His was a short
enough career, but it was packed with excitement.[9] He had a
triumphal progress through Padua, Treviso itself, Brescia,
Mantua and Vicenza. Everywhere there were miraculous cures,
and it was said that he raised ten people from the dead and
that when he preached no sinner could resist him. Even the
unspeakable Ezzelino himself, who saw the power of his cruel
government threatened by this preacher, wept hot tears when
Fra Giovanni appealed to his conscience.[10] All over Lombardy
the peace campaign was bearing fruit. Verona even went so
far as to invite him to become the governor of their city, but
Florence on the contrary would have nothing to do with him;
they refused his offer of mediation in their continuous war
with Siena and forbade him to enter the city: 'He'll only want
to bring some more dead to life, and we have got enough people
here already,' they said.[11] But Verona was a special case;
they had suffered so much at the hands of Ezzelino and had
had so much trouble with the Patarenes that they hardly
knew where to turn; so they made the holy man their dictator
and before long his home town of Vicenza did likewise. He
organised a vast festival of peace near Verona and hundreds of
thousands came from all over Lombardy and listened to a
self-conscious sermon of Friar John on the text 'My peace
I give unto you'.[12] As *podestà* of Verona he acted quickly and
it is said that in three days he had sixty leading heretics sent
to the stake. But all this power went to his head and it became
evident that he had no real aptitude for government. The
great alliance of the northern cities which he had hoped to
achieve suddenly became no more than an alliance to bring
about his downfall: he was thrown into prison and disappears
from the scene. Within two months the people were as
divided as they had ever been and the peace campaign was
ended.

Man has always been ready to interpret events in terms of the
will of God, or of the gods, and to see them sometimes as trials,
sometimes as proof of divine favour.

Thus it was that towards the close of the Middle Ages natural calamities came to be regarded not only as direct visitations from on high but as divine warnings about the future. Men's terror was less concerned with the present punishment than with what it presaged. In the mid-*Duecento* the first reaction to an earthquake, flood or eclipse was not so much to save what could be saved from the disaster (however ready the wealthy merchants were to do this, too), but rather to prepare to save one's soul against the impending judgement; people hastened to confess their sins, to be reconciled to one another, to make restitution and quickly to take up good works. Who was to say that this time it was not the beginning of the end? The rich gave away their goods, the mayors assembled their people in the piazza and preached terrible addresses to them, moving them to tears. Frightened women rushed through the streets with screaming children in their arms, the theatres were empty, the churches were full. These natural disasters did not happen just by chance—even if it afterwards turned out to be no more than a passing storm. After all, there was the earthquake at Rieti which occurred while a stern pope was reading to the people the gospel of the first Sunday of Advent about the 'signs in the sun and in the moon and in the stars, and upon earth distress of nations'.[13] When the people were in that mood any thunderclap sounded like 'the last trump'. The prophecies about 1260 as the great year of distress had struck deep into the consciousness of the people.

> *Cum fuerint anni completi mille ducenti*
> *et seni decies post partum Virginis almae,*
> *tunc Antichristus nascetur daemone plenus.*[14]

When the whole sum of years, thousand two hundred and sixty,
Shall be filled from the year when the sweet Virgin gave birth,
Then of demoniac spirit great Antichrist shall be born.

No one knows now who wrote those lines which everyone was repeating to himself as the fateful year drew on. His identity is lost, as is that of Merlin and the Sybils, of the author of the commentaries on Jeremiah and the Apocalypse, or the explanation of the prophets discovered by a Jew under a rock near Toledo,[15] which sounded like the visions of Abbot Joachim of Calabria speaking once more of the terrible year 1260. Now was the time to return to Abbot Joachim: the old covenant was with God the Father, the new covenant was with God the Son; and then would dawn the age of the Holy Ghost, a thousand years of heavenly love, when flesh and blood would count no more. The new age would begin about 1260, as was plain from both the Old and the New Testaments. This was the teaching of Abbot Joachim, but it is by no means certain how far he saw himself as precisely foretelling the future, or realised the effect his prophecies would have, or how exactly many people thought they were being fulfilled, for he himself wrote: 'He who reads what I have written without a super-natural insight, will certainly be led by evil minds into a false interpretation.'[16] If prophets have ever doubted their own 'supernatural insight', then certainly not the prophets of the *Duecento* who were called the 'Joachites'; perhaps it was just this assurance which led people to regard them as false prophets. Yet they stirred up a whole nation to a state of frenzied excite-ment, which can hardly be considered as anything but 'a false interpretation' of the abbot's words.

The reign of the Holy Spirit would come, but first would come his herald, the Angel of Destruction: Antichrist would rage through the world, tearing up and taking with him every evil weed, to give place for the good corn of the Spirit to grow, for only the clean of heart shall be citizens of the new kingdom. All the rest, the wicked and the impure, the faint-hearted and the lukewarm (whom Christ shall vomit out of his mouth), all those who have forgotten his Passion and mocked at his mercy, shall be destroyed. Who was to know whether he was perhaps among the number of the damned? Jacopone cried out his warning to the world:

Or se parrà chi averà fidanza!

Now those that have been
faithful shall appear!

La tribulanza ch'è profetizata

The turbulence and trial that
men foretold,

da onne lato veggio tonare.

I see is thundering on every
side.

La luna è scura, el sole
ottenebrato,
le stelle del ciel veggio
cadere;
l'antiquo serpente pare
scapolato,
tutto lo mondo veggio lui
seguire;
l'acque s'ha bevuto da onne
lato,
fiume Giordan se spera
d'enghiuttire,
lo popolo de Cristo devorare.

Dark is the moon and
shadowed is the sun,
I see the high stars falling
from the sky;
Now the old snake is loosed
upon the world,
And every man I see goes
after him;
On every side the water he
has drained,
The Jordan he would swallow
if he could,
And Christ's own people now
he would devour.

Lo sole è Cristo che non fa
mo segna
per fortificare li soi servente;

miracoli non vedemo che
sostegna
la fedelitate nella gente;

question ne fa gente malegna,

obproprio ne dicon
malamente,
rendendo lor ragion nogl
potem trare.

The sun is Christ, who gives
no more a sign,
Whose servants thus he
fortifies no more;
No miracles are seen that
might sustain
The sadly stumbling faith of
common folk;
Now evil-minded men begin
to doubt,
While blasphemies are
uttered without shame,
And answer there is none
that we can give.

La luna si è la ecclesia
scurata,
la qual la notte al mondo
relucía,

The moon enshrouded is the
shadowed Church,
Born to shine in the dark
night of the world

papa e cardinal con lor
  guidata;
la luce è tornata en
  tenebría;
la universitate clericata

è encorsata e pres' ha mala
  via.
O sire Dio, chi porrà
  scampare?

Le stelle che del cielo son
  cadute
la universitate reliosa;

molte de la via si son partute,

entrate per la via pericolosa;

l'acque del diluvio son salute,

coperti i monti, sommerso
  onne cosa.
Aiuta, Dio, aiuta lo notare!

Tutto el mondo veggio
  conquassato,
e precipitando va in ruina,

come l'omo che è enfrenecato,

al qual non può om dar
  medicina;
li medici si l'hanno desperato,

ché non glie giova encanto
  nè dottrina:
vedemolo en extremo
  lavorare.

And kept on course by
  cardinals and pope;
But now is all her brightness
  become dim,
When every rank of all her
  holy priests
In headlong haste has gone
  the evil way.
Lord God, is still a remnant
  to be found?

The high stars that have
  fallen from the sky
Are all the cloistered people
  of the world:
How many from the path
  now fall away
And enter on the dangerous
  high road!
Still rising are the waters of
  the flood,
And sinking are the hills, the
  valleys drowned.
O help us, God, to swim
  against the tide!

I see the whole world shaken
  as with pain,
Tumbling, splintering, down
  to the abyss,
Like a man frenzied, mad
  beyond repair,
For whom remains no
  human remedy:
Physicians have abandoned all
  their hope,
No science and no magic can
  avail:
We can but stare and watch
  the agony.

Armate, omo, chè se passa l'ora	Up now to arms, o man, the hour is come,
che possi campare di questa morte,	The last chance of escaping from this death;
chè nulla ne fo ancora si dura,	Never a death so hard has ever been,
nè altra ne sarà giamai si forte;	Never a death so strong shall be again;
gli santi n'aver molto gran paura	A mighty terror grips the very saints,
de venir a prender queste scorte;	When they behold the fate that lies before;
d'esser securo stolto me pare.	Only a fool would feel no need to fear.
Or se parrà chi averà fidanza!	Now those that have been faithful shall appear!
La tribulanza ch'è profetizata	The turbulence and trial that men foretold,
da onne lato veggio tonare.[17]	I see is thundering on every side.

At every street corner there were the wandering preachers and hermits, the half-crazed Joachites and the feverish 'spirituals', all shouting about the Last Things, but also all ready to decamp in a hurry should there be any trouble with the authorities, who had little understanding for their message. But the people crowded round them, or hung out of their windows, or climbed up on to anything to get a better view. They listened in sinister and unwonted silence, with all the sins of their lifetimes staring them in the face. They looked at one another in terror. Has Antichrist already been born? Is he perhaps here in our midst? The preachers were not agreed about his identity: some said it was Frederick, who cannot be dead, because as everyone knows he cannot die; others said it was Ezzelino, or the Minister-General Elias, or the King of Spain. At another street corner there would be a Ghibelline who was saying that without question the Pope was the Antichrist. But whoever it was, one of these days he would show himself as the herald of the End, and woe to those whom he took away as his slaves.

People beat their breasts, went to confession and did penance. Salimbene tells us that the priests were so busy with confessions that they had no time to eat.[18] All sorts of prophecies, riddles and rhymes were circulating; there were even stories of babies in arms who suddenly spoke and uttered warnings.[19]

> Now once there was a Roman
> Hit a Roman on the head,
> And the Roman by a Roman
> Was offered Rome instead;
> So the lion climbed the mountain
> And became the fox's friend,
> But when he put on leopard-skins,
> He met a sudden end.

That sort of thing. Who was the lion? The last Hohenstaufen, Conradin? Or someone else? And who was the fox? Everyone made the prophecies fit their own ideas—as people have done since Delphi. People were quite accustomed to apocalyptic symbols: Pope Gregory IX had spoken of Frederick as 'the beast with the claws of a bear and the jaws of a lion', and Cardinal Raynerius of Viterbo (Abbot Joachim's own pupil) had likened the Emperor to both Lucifer and Antichrist.[20] The Joachites so often used such symbols, that they became quite commonplace, so that it was perfectly natural that Dante should later introduce the three symbolic animals at the beginning of the *Inferno*.[21] Moreover, strange animals were familiar to all who knew of Frederick's menagerie.

Thus the phantoms of the uneducated people hung like an evil dream over Italy in 1260. Only a handful of sceptics from the more educated classes remained untouched by it all. There is a story of twelve young knights of Siena who had listened to one of these penitential sermons and had not been impressed: they had won the battle of Montaperti, they were well off and wanted to enjoy themselves, so instead of starting a confraternity of penance, they started a *brigata spendereccia* or 'spendthrift brigade' and had a good time.[22] But what was this compared to the thousands in desperation? The masses could not be turned back now, coming as they did to the fateful year through a series of calamities, failures of harvest, famine, atrocities and a plague so severe they gave up tolling the bell for burials.[23] Then the year arrived and penance spread like an epidemic, with the hills of Umbria as its centre where no one ever knew the happy mean between rapture and despair. It was in the piazza at Perugia that Raniero Fasani first appeared, a dishevelled and emaciated hermit scarcely twenty years old. This was a change from the gaiety of Francis and of Benedict with his trumpet. It was said that Raniero belonged to the 'spiritual' party of the Franciscans. Now he had found a letter which had been written in heaven,[24] and which no one could decipher until the bishop laid it on the altar during High Mass, after which its message became clear: Do penance, do penance and scourge yourselves!

And so they did. There was Raniero, clothed in nothing but a sack, with a scourge or 'discipline' in his hand. The people made their disciplines from string and improved them with thorns and bits of wire. Raniero took the procession through Perugia: he went ahead, shouting and scourging himself as he went, and all the crowd who followed him did likewise. He led them out into the country, going wherever the spirit moved him. Southwards they went, roaring through the Campagna to Rome; then north again through town after town towards France. Everywhere people laid aside their work and joined the *disciplinati*: the farms were deserted, the markets were still. For a whole year, throughout one winter and one summer, Italy chastised herself.

Such was the fear of the Lord that came over the land, that rich men and poor alike, old and young—including some boys down to the age of five years—went two by two as in a procession through the towns, all naked except for what modesty required; each one had a discipline in his hand, and sighing and weeping scourged himself upon the shoulders until

the blood flowed. They went as if they had our Saviour's
Passion in reality before their eyes, and they sang penitential
songs begging God's mercy and imploring Our Lady's help, that
he should be appeased through the countless penitents who
were bewailing their sins. Not only by day but also by night,
hundreds, nay thousands and tens of thousands of them
marched through the towns in bitter winter weather with
candles in their hands, going from church to church led by
priests with crosses and banners, to prostrate themselves before
the altars. The same happened in country villages and hamlets,
so that the fields and hills echoed to the cries of those who
called upon the Lord.

During this time all music and secular songs ceased. Only
the grim chanting of the penitents was to be heard. . . . And
not only men's hearts, but the very stones were moved, and the
most obdurate could not restrain their tears. Even the women
took part in their own way in these pious exercises, for they had
similar devotions indoors, and not only ordinary women of the
people, but also some distinguished ladies and their daughters.
Also during this time almost everyone who had a quarrel made
peace with his neighbour; thieves and robbers gave back their
stolen goods, and other criminals proclaimed their sorrow for
their sins and mended their ways; prisons were opened and the
captives released and exiles were permitted to go home.[25]

This was the account of a monk of Padua, and the same things
could be seen in almost any town of Tuscany or Lombardy:
countless chroniclers recorded the same, though sometimes
with less eloquence. More than 20,000 men went from
Bologna to Modena,[26] where the whole city joined them. From
there they passed on Monday of All Saints to Reggio, where
all the authorities, led by the *Podestà* and the bishop, went
scourging themselves through the streets.[27] On Tuesday of
All Souls the whole crowd went on to Parma, whence, together with the Parmigiani, they went to Piacenza, and thence,
with the addition of the Piacentini, to Pavia.[28] For three
whole days they disciplined themselves in Genoa, going from
church to church both in the centre of the city and in the

suburbs.[29] There was an icy wind blowing in the streets, but
no one caught a chill, so James of Voragine tells us, because the
fire of love kept them all warm. Some of the most enthusiastic
disciplinati had begun with the loudest scorn,[30] and blessed
were the scorners who were converted and became flagellants,
though Salimbene knew some who remained obdurate in
their impenitence; but apart from being despised by the
others, 'some misfortune quickly overtook them and they
either died or became gravely ill'.[31] But a worse fate doubtless
awaited those impious rulers who dared to forbid the penitential exercises: Obizzo d'Este who issued an edict against the
flagellants, Manfred of Sicily who treated them as heretics, and
Pallavicini of Cremona who put up a gallows for any of his
subjects who joined them.[32]

Nevertheless the terrible year 1260 came to an end; the
world was still there, Antichrist was not unmasked, the Holy
Spirit had not taken possession of any throne on earth. The
disciplinati went home, the Joachites disappeared and everyone
breathed again.

The storm had passed; perhaps the crisis had increased
devotion in northern Italy and had brought men closer together, but there was certainly one great treasure that it left
behind: a song. The folk-song of the *disciplinati*, which all the
chroniclers noted as an indispensable accompaniment to this
scourging; this folk-song outlasted them. The impressions
of the chroniclers are various: the monk of Padua speaks of a
'*cantio lugubris*', while James of Voragine tells of the '*cantiones
angelicas et caelestes*'. But the song which Bartolomeo Scriba of
Genoa has preserved for us as the most popular song among the
flagellants,[34] and which has found a place in countless manuscript municipal song books, sounds to our ears neither particularly lugubrious nor celestial. The most primitive text belongs
to a Phrygian marching tune, so serious and noble in its
melodic line that already here we see that genius for a tune
which is so typical of the Italians and is exemplified in this
earliest document of their tradition:

Madonna Sancta Maria—

mercè de noi peccatori——

faite prego al dolçe Christo

Ke ne degia perdonare——

Holy Mary, Lady mine,
Sinner though I be,
Pray that that sweet Son of thine
Mercy show to me!

This was not the only song the penitents sang; it seems as if during that anxious year they made the discovery that the greatest pains can be relieved by a song, and thus it happened that all those pains of the *disciplinati* gave birth to a great national heritage of popular song. When the great procession was disbanded, people grouped themselves into small confraternities of penance and continued to discipline themselves; but they also continued to sing, and before long they forgot the scourges but remembered the songs. Wherever one went up and down the countryside people were singing. This indeed is Italy. From all the fears and psychoses, all the prophecies of doom and wildly distorted penitential practices, at the end melodies are born. Perhaps this was Abbot Joachim's era of the Holy Ghost after all, with the new and eighth gift of the Holy Ghost, which surely is music.

The *Compagnia dei Laudesi* is a phenomenon which has no parallel in western Europe. This is understandable enough, since no people has such natural gifts both for organisation and for music as the Italians. There were indeed local and trade associations already in the tenth century, such as that of the fishermen at Ravenna and the 'Confraternity of the people of Santa Maria in Gradi', founded in a parish at Arezzo in 1070, and the line continues unbroken to the guilds and the Third Orders of the Humiliati and the Franciscans and Dominicans in the *Duecento*.[35] The year of the flagellants, 1260, enriched social life with a new kind of association: that of the *disciplinati*. Out of this emerged later the *laudesi*: associations of those who felt that penitential exercises were necessary to their spiritual welfare and who looked back at the processions of the *disciplinati* as a health-giving experience. At their meetings they scourged themselves and performed various penances; they were known by various names: *disciplinati*, *battuti*, *scopatori*. Often their members belonged to one parish, sometimes they were all men of the same trade, but songs were always an essential part of the idea.[36] The rules of the confraternity were no less strict than those of the early Franciscan tertiaries: they were bound to attend their meetings regularly, avoid rowdy gatherings and dances, hear Mass daily, go to confession weekly and not to carry arms. They had their own chaplains and often ran a hospital for the sick or aged. In the privacy of their meetings they scourged themselves and wore a kind of long habit which left their backs uncovered, which can still sometimes be seen on the figure of a pious founder on an altar piece as late as the fifteenth century. 'Then one of the brethren shall rise and stand before the crucifix and devoutly sing a *laude*; he shall then kneel down and all shall discipline themselves in silence for the space of an Our Father and a Hail Mary.' Thus the regulations at Siena. At Assisi the *laude* was to accompany the scourging 'in order to move the hearts of the brethren to penance and tears, wherefore they should pay more attention to the meaning of the words than to the voice of the singer'.[37]

It soon became a mark of quality to belong to a confraternity, and in Florence alone at the end of the century there were sixteen such confraternities, which increased in the next century to twenty-four; in central Italy there were about seventy in all and in the north more than forty.[38] All ranks and conditions of men had their own confraternities, and, as in the days of the flagellants, membership gave a certain standing: at Parma, for instance, anybody insulting a member of the 'Brethren of the Cross' ran the instant risk of having his house pulled down. If someone wanted to enjoy some esteem in the town, it was prudent to join the confraternity or at least to support it.[39] A far cry indeed from the anxious days of 1260.

The singing flagellants came to have a regular place in the civic life of the late *Duecento*. Led by their chaplain and their *capitano*, usually a prominent layman, they held their processions.[40] The brethren of Assisi went down the valley to the Portiuncola, singing the 'Lament of Our Lady'.[41] The brethren of Gubbio, walking behind the banner of the confraternity and carrying lighted candles in their hands, visited the churches and sang songs to Our Lady.[42] Several confraternities in Florence soon gave up the scourging, and did much of their singing out of doors, but they were forbidden to sing anywhere near a convent of nuns, for at that time, we must remember, a lament was not so far removed from a serenade.[43] The brethren of Bologna were more strict and conservative, and singing was only permitted together with the scourging and indoors.[44] But such restrictions were becoming rarer, and by the turn of the century the song had almost entirely ousted the scourge. Before long the meetings turned into public concerts and the important place was now not that of the chaplain but that of the copyist, whose task it was to copy out the words and music on vellum that was placed on the music stands. Some groups began to consider whether they could afford a regular music master; the rich parish of Or San Michele in Florence opened a regular school, where songs were learnt on Sundays.[45] In other places they hired professional singers, who for a few pence and a jar of wine would be prepared to sing at their processions and funerals.[46] By this time the songs had already lost their simple, firm and friendly character; they had

become virtuoso pieces of coloratura, their melodic line had
become languishing and catchy. The strict flagellant assemblies were blown up like a massive medieval stronghold by the
Renaissance—explosive if pleasant, sweet-sounding concerts.
They sang 'before the picture of Our Lady of the pillar, under
the loggia',[47] the miraculous picture of Or San Michele with
its wonderful colouring, or before the tender, dreaming
'Rucellai Madonna' of Duccio di Buoninsegna, which was
specially venerated by the *laudesi* of Santa Maria Novella. It
was still the same veneration as was practised by the *disciplinati*
of fifty years before with their song '*Madonna sancta Maria*',
but now there was a new elegance about it.

Florence was a city that belonged to the whole world, but in
the remoter parts of Umbria and Tuscany the old devotions
continued for centuries. In Holy Week the penitential
brethren were on the road day and night; whole cities were
turned into a Way of the Cross and everyone wound their way
through the little streets with songs and with scourges. A huge
cross was carried in front of the procession and other men bore
the other symbols of the Passion: the veil of Veronica, Peter's
cock, the pillar of the scourging and the scourge.

Timorosa pietança
la corona fie a vedere,
la croce, i chiovi et la lancia

co'i patì gran martire,
l'aceto e'l fele k'ebbe a bere
che i fo dato colla spongia,
quando in croce fece pugna
per noi misericordioso.[48]

O, fearful reverence,
To see the crown of thorn,
The cross, the nails, the spear—
 the pain
By the great martyr borne;
The vinegar and gall to drink
That on a sponge they gave,
When on the cross he fought for us
And loved, that he might save.

In one place on the procession they would halt and perform
the Washing of the Feet, in another the Kiss of Judas, in yet
others the Scourging and the Lament of Mary. Towards the
end of the nineteenth century in some villages on Good
Friday they still blew on cow-horns, so that the mournful
notes should bring to mind the sorrows of our Lady.[49]

In the streets small Calvaries were put up and adorned with spring flowers,[50] and some craft-guilds kept watch, faithful to the practice of the *Duecento*, in the churches during prayer and hymns, until the bells of Easter rang.[51]

What can we understand today of this chiaroscuro of Italy's *Duecento*? Can we still share the merriness of the Alleluia folk and still beat our breasts with the flagellants? Many today are more inclined to dismiss these things as hysterical phenomena; they find no place for the idea of penance and often reduce sin to a psychological twist of character. In that case the message of St Francis becomes reduced to mere sentiment, if not to folly.

It is too easy to dismiss as hopelessly primitive the devotions which live on today among the simple people in the Appenines, who hold to the traditions which were as real to their forefathers as they are to them. Seven hundred years is a long time, and humanity has learnt many things, but if we take the trouble to look back down the centuries we find that the human spirit has not changed, and that the joys and struggles of mankind so long ago are not, after all, so far removed from his joys and struggles of today.

9

The Scholars

Chi se speja in la doctrina
scrita de li gram doctor,

e no menda so error
degno è de disciplina.

He who studies every letter
Written down by learned
men,
If he's not becoming better,
Ought to go to school again.

Genoese jingle[1]

AT THE beginning of human history, we are told, man disobeyed God and in consequence a veil was cast over his intelligence, so that he no longer enjoyed the faultless clarity of understanding, with which, together with the angels, he had been endowed at his creation. From that moment began man's struggle to understand the meaning of things, and his restless search for knowledge, which sometimes as we look back seems painfully slow, but at other times seems to penetrate the mystery with the most astonishing rapidity.

Probably in every age men have thought that there never had been such progress in human knowledge and achievement as in their own, and that never before had any generation so far outstripped its forebears as their own had done. Yet, in fact, the knowledge of every age builds upon the achievements of the past, and every age makes its contribution to the continuous development of human thought and discovery. The thirteenth century made its contribution as did every other age, and it may be said that even if its contribution to the actual store of human knowledge was small, its most outstanding contribution was to effect an ordering, an organisation, a sorting out and an assessment of the contents of that store.

There have been various periods in the history of human thought when progress as it were calls a halt and pauses to put in order the accumulation up to date, to recapitulate and to think over the ancient problems in new terms. It is the glory of the thirteenth century that it was such a period, and probably never before had there been so intense a rethinking, a criticism of previous thought, a reassessment of the ancient heritage. There was a new passion for reducing things to a system: '*la passion de l'ordre*', Emile Mâle calls it.[2] Doubtless he is thinking of France, yet two of the greatest thinkers who reassessed the achievements of the human spirit at this time were Italians: Dante and Thomas Aquinas.

Criticism and order: these seem to be the two main characteristics of the learning of the *Duecento*. It would be a facile observation to show that on the one hand the lack of logic together with a blind acceptance of authority was always thwarting criticism, and on the other hand that the lesser devotees of order were only too often reducing their very systems to absurdity. Moreover, we all know that a passion for order sometimes pressed things into the strangest preconceived patterns and invested facts with the most arbitrary meanings. The significance of numbers, for instance, often took the place of serious observation, and facts were reduced preferably to a pattern of three (in honour of the Trinity), or else seven or twelve. Thus it is nothing strange that a chronicler, observing ten factors in the downfall of the Emperor Frederick, should hasten to find two more 'in order to complete the dozen'.[3] In so doing he was but following the fashion of his time, which no longer seems strange when we see it applied to abstract argument and symbolism, as in the balanced layout of the *Summa* when it achieves a systematic and all-embracing clarity, or in the mystical treatises of Bonaventure where the very strictness of the pattern produces a poetic rhythm of genuine beauty.* Much more important was the attitude of reason, the spirit of criticism and logic, to the

* A plan of Bonaventure's *Triplex Via* is given towards the end of this chapter.

traditions and legends of the time. Here also St Thomas provided the solution by marking off clearly the frontiers of the natural and the supernatural, reason and revelation. Yet the time was hardly ripe for the majority of writers fully to grasp the significance of these distinctions; men had for too long rested on their creed instead of applying their reason; the authority of the ancient writers was unquestioned and the favourite method for several centuries—and the safest, too— had been to write in the form of commentaries upon the standard works.

But in the *Duecento* things were changing, there were enlightened spirits who were beginning to realise that things were not untouchable simply because they were ancient, and it was possible to observe afresh and to call things in question without being impious.

When at the end of the century the Genoese James of Voragine was writing the lives of the saints in his famous *Legenda Aurea*, he certainly tells some remarkable stories without the slightest embarrassment; after all, we know that God does work miracles, so why should anybody question them? But when his authorities come down to historical details, he does not hesitate to pursue the matter. There is a delightful passage, which is absolutely typical of the spirit of the time, at the end of Legend 101: he has just told the story of the seven young men who fell asleep during the reign of Decius and woke up some centuries later, and then he adds that 'it is open to question whether they really slept for three hundred and seventy-two years, as is usually stated; for they woke up in the year of the Lord 448, while Decius reigned only for one year and three months and that was in the year of the Lord 252; from which we must conclude that they slept only for a hundred and ninety-six years'.[4]

There is a constant interplay of common sense and nonsense, of rational observation and complete fable in those servants of the learned world, the chroniclers. The good Salimbene is always formulating laws of nature, which he has deduced from his observations, as when he says: 'It is a general rule that a plague among cattle is followed the next year by a plague among men.'[5] In another passage he recounts the discovery in 1283 of the relics of St Mary Magdalene at Saint-Maximin in Provence, although both Sinigaglia and Vézelay already laid claim to their possession. The chronicler then suddenly makes the acute observation that 'it is plain that the body of a single woman cannot be in three places at once'.[6] In an earlier age this would have presented no difficulty, for the bodies of the saints were credited with unusual powers; while in a later age the authenticity of all three would probably be denied.

The finest fruits of thirteenth-century learning, and those which have had the most effect upon subsequent ages, are undoubtedly in the field of theology. This field had been well worked over during the preceding centuries, and the best minds were applied to the task. Yet in the learned world of the Italian *Duecento* secular studies had pride of place, and the great majority of the *studiosi* were laymen.

There was a certain tradition about this in Italy, for south of the Alps there had never been the same ascendancy of the clergy in studies as there had been in other lands. Already in the ninth century the cities had their schools of rhetoric, where laymen were taught by laymen, and whose standards were a match for those of the cathedral schools of the clergy. As soon as the Lombard cities became aware of their importance, the sons of well-to-do citizens began to pursue further education, quite apart from any ecclesiastical association, and this continued when the city schools became universities. In most cases they received what we should call a general education and became notaries, lawyers and doctors, but not theologians, for faculties of theology were seldom to be found in the Italian universities. Clerics who wished to study theology usually went to Paris. Italy's oldest university, the medical school at Salerno on the gulf of Naples, had only this one faculty; and its mentality was materialistic and semi-Arabic. As far as we know, it was founded in the eleventh century and its importance was chiefly local; after a hundred years it was overshadowed by the young university at Bologna and disappears from the scene, especially later when the medical faculty at Montpellier had become the centre of medical studies in Europe.

The tendency at Bologna was also towards materialism, as indeed it was in all the other universities which came into being during the thirteenth century. There were at least nine, but once we understand how vague the distinction was between a grammar school, a city school for higher studies and the private instruction of a single teacher, we are no longer surprised to find some sort of academic institution in almost every town. They were springing up everywhere, sometimes with a charter of either the Pope or the Emperor, but sometimes simply with the reputation of a particular professor who drew students from all over Italy.[7] The cities themselves were eager to start academies and took a great interest in their progress: Bologna was glad to be able to have upon her coins the proud words 'Bononia docet'. They were an alert people who then began to take possession of learning; the students however brought not only life but money to the town, and for this reason the city authorities were usually prepared to make a modest outlay towards the expenses of running their academy. When the students knew there was public money involved they sometimes took undue advantage of it and troubles with the city authorities ensued. The next step was for a group of students and their professors to decamp and start again in some more hospitable place. This was the way that the universities of Vicenza, Arezzo and Padua began and indirectly also those of Vercelli and Siena. The new towns felt honoured and did all they could to welcome the students. Vercelli earmarked five hundred of the best lodgings in the town for the students coming from Padua: only the houses round the market place were exempted from the scheme.[8] The lodgings were made cheap: nineteen lire was the highest figure. The students (the lads were called *domini*) got their provisions at cost price and the town undertook the upkeep of fourteen professors. Siena also took a lot of trouble over its university: in 1246 the city council voted fifty stivers to be paid to a herald, who was to 'go through the towns and villages of Tuscany and invite students to come next year to Siena to study law under Dominus Pepo'.[9] This was a most successful device, and a little later Perugia did the same in Umbria.[10] The kingdom of Sicily had its own university at Naples, founded in 1224 by Frederick. He brought many famous and learned men to Naples, having added a special incitement about its 'salubrious situation',[11] and moreover he made the choice of Naples obligatory on any of his subjects in search of higher studies. Nevertheless, the attraction of Bologna was growing, even though Frederick with his usual energy simply declared that university to be closed—a gesture which continued to amuse Bologna long after the university of Naples had come to an end.

Eager youths would come from near and far to attend these schools, which were called *studia*, and it was they themselves who formed the *universitas*, although this term gradually came to be applied to the whole body of men, including the professors. The student corporations governed the whole academic world: their leaders were able to hold their own against the city authorities, and relations with the teaching staff were often tense. At first the corporations had the status of simple guilds, whose function was to protect the interests of students far from their home towns, so that at Bologna, for instance, students who came from the city itself, the *scholares cives*, did not belong to the guilds. Originally therefore the *rectores scholarium* were representatives of the student body and were usually students who were priests, because if a layman were leader he would have no authority over any of his fellow students who were members of the clergy. It was strange enough that the two faculties of law and medicine were crowded with priests and clerics, but in 1219 these two faculties were permanently closed to all the clergy by Honorius III on the grounds that they encouraged worldly ambition.

Before the various corporations settled themselves into the two large groups of the *citramontani* and *ultramontani*, each country had its own guild. The Tuscans and the Lombards had organised themselves, as had also the French, who included in their number the English and the Normans, and the Provençals, who included the Spaniards and Catalans.

The citizens had sorry tales about the behaviour of the young seekers after learning: fights, murder, robbery, theft and other scandals were the order of the day. In the accounts of the German group broken windows form a regular feature: *item pro vitris fractis* . . .[12] The various nations do not show up much better than in Paris, where Jacques of Vitry tells us that 'the English are drunkards, the French proud and effeminate, the Germans hot-tempered and lascivious, the Lombards avaricious and cowardly, the Romans deceitful and quarrelsome, the Sicilians tyrannical and cruel . . . and as for the men from Brabant, they are bloodthirsty incendiaries and robbers'[13]—but we may hope that there were not many of these in Italy! It is not surprising that the patience of the city authorities was sometimes sorely tried, and that the city, forgetting their pride and their original welcome, occasionally drove their guests, together with their *rectores*, out of the gates. But what of the professors? At first they attacked the students' corporations with the very learning which the students had come to seek: they explained that the corporations, in fact, did not exist, since according to Roman law there could be no such guilds except on a basis of a trade.[14] But the students did not trouble much about their juridical existence: the guilds were there anyway. Moreover, the professors were powerless, since they depended entirely upon these wretched guilds, being appointed by them and paid by them, and now the students were claiming that they ought to administer the oath to the professors, give them permission to leave the city, punish them if they came late to the lecture room or finished early, or if they made a mistake or avoided a difficulty.[15] If a professor wished to marry he only got one day off, and there was little he could do for his wife, because the fees the students paid were miserable: 'they want to learn, but they don't want to pay,' lamented the learned Odofred.[16] Poor teachers were always looking out for a job in another city where they could earn a little more; so that finally the city authorities of Bologna were compelled to pay a reasonable salary to the professors. Now the academics could breathe more freely, and soon they began to organise themselves, too: parallel to the *rector scholarium* appeared their own *rector scholarum*, with gradually increasing power. (How much that one letter 'i' meant!) The *rector scholarum* was the one who conducted the examinations and conferred the degrees, and in this quarter at least the students could not interfere.

Every programme of study obviously had to begin with the seven *artes liberales*. This was basic study in every city or monastic school, and at the universities was by far the most frequented faculty, though it was the least esteemed. Everyone still learned his grammar from the *Ars Donati*, which had been written about a thousand years before. Modern teachers would not be able to sleep if they had not a new edition of the textbook; but the old method produced more profound and better Latinists than the elaborate systems of the present time. The oddest Latin of the simplest chronicler still far surpasses the Latin essays of our grammar school students. There was little concern with philology in the *Duecento*: the new French and Italian dialects were useful for peasants and artisans, but of little interest to scholars. Few knew Greek, Hebrew or Arabic. Latin was the thing, and they taught and wrote in Latin. The time was not ready for etymology either: if an explanation of a word was given, it had more to do with edification than with linguistics. Thus James of Voragine explains in his Golden Legend 141: 'Mauritius comes from *mare*, the sea; and *cis* which means "to vomit" or else "firm"; and *us* which means "the counsellor" or "the hastener". Or else it comes from *mauron* which Isidore says is Greek and means "black". For Maurice had in himself the sadness of the sea, because he lived far from his home; and he vomited, because he cast away all excesses; and he was firm in his martyrdom, and black through contempt of self.'

The most outstanding grammarian of the century was Boncompagno da Siena, who regarded Cicero as his precursor and laid down the law in all fields of learning. He is said even to have designed wings with which to fly in the air.[17] Less eccentric were his colleagues Guido Faba, and Bene of Florence, who wrote the *Candelabrum dictaminis*.

The *Duecento* produced more in the field of mathematics than of grammar. Leonard of Pisa, who played Voltaire to the Emperor Frederick's Sans Souci, was the man who introduced Arabic numbers to the west, and in his *Abacus* published one of the most interesting mathematical treatises of the Middle Ages. The exact sciences were held in great esteem at the Hohenstaufen court, for the Emperor had a passionate interest in all that concerned the earth and the cosmos. The problems of those days were more eagerly discussed in his circle of lively minds than in the somewhat unenterprising schools of rhetoric of the time. Is the shape of the earth flat, or round, as Aristotle thought? Why does fire come out of volcanos? What about the water on the earth? Everyone knows that it all comes from the springs of the sea and that it is all connected either above or under the ground; but then why is some of it sweet and some salt? Dante was perplexed by the same problem[18] and was no more satisfied than Frederick with the explanation that salt water is older. Frederick used to put all kinds of questions to the savants whom his friend Al-Kamil sent to him: such as, Why do things half submerged in water look as if they were bent? What is the explanation of the specks one sometimes sees in one's field of vision?[19]

These conversations at the imperial court, keenly continued later by his son Manfred, put us in mind of the symposiums of the Florentine Renaissance. It was a remarkable company: Michael Scotus, the Levantine occultist Master Theodore, the silent John of Palermo, the talkative Pier della Vigna, and all the clever Sicilian courtiers together with learned Arabs and Jews. The Kaiser was for instance discussing a text of Maimonides, where it is explained that at ritual purifications the Jews use the ashes of a red cow; now he, Frederick, had recently read

that the Indians use the ashes of a red lion for the same purpose:
is there any connexion between the two? And why in both cases
should the creature be red?[20] Here Frederick was close to
historical sociology. How interested he would have been in
the journals of Brother John of Plano Carpini near Perugia,
who in the middle of the century went on behalf of the Pope
to the Tartars as far as their headquarters at Karakorum.

In a certain sense the science of geography was a discovery
of the thirteenth century; never before had there been so much
interest in what lay beyond Europe and the Mediterranean
coast. But the journeys were made more in the spirit of
adventure than in the spirit of research, and even the
Franciscan Brother John, once outside Christian territories,
feels himself in fairyland: 'As we travelled through the land
of the black Kitai, we came to a sea of moderate size, whose
name remained unknown to us because we failed to ask about
it. On the shores of this sea there was a small hill which had
a hole in it, out of which in winter time such fierce winds blew
that no one could go past without the gravest danger. In the
summer, however, only a light wind came out of the hole,
although the local people said one could always hear the sound
of it.'[21] This is the language of fairyland surely enough, but
meanwhile the sea has been found, and the 'small hill' and
the wind, which indeed makes a continuous noise there, blowing in from the desert past the caves in the hillside. Many of
Brother John's details reappear in the reports of other travellers,
such as Marco Polo twenty-five years later, who went to the
East with his uncle and won the favour of the rich Tartar,
Kublai, who ruled China. Half of his stories were not believed
at home, but experts who followed Marco Polo's tracks and
visited places which for 600 years had not been seen by a
European, were able to identify many features in his journals.[22]
It may well be that other things which cannot now be checked
are equally worthy of credence, such as the organisation of the
vast cities, the fabulous court of the Khan, his banking system
and social welfare and many things that Marco Polo tells us
about Sumatra, Java and India.

The professional scholars (or academics) naturally did not take this sort of experimental science seriously for a moment. It was concerned with what happened on the ground; but no true scholar can make do with less than three dimensions. Therefore he is particularly drawn to astronomy: he studies tirelessly what pagans and Christians have discovered about the planets and their influence on human existence, about the zodiac and the seasons, about eclipses of sun and moon, about the music of the spheres, about the seven heavens and their significance. Thus he has reached the goal: Astronomy has become *the handmaid of theology*.

It does not seem as if this final stage of astronomy interested the Italians particularly. Italy's poet will place the crown on the sacred study of the heavens, but important scientific conclusions in this field were achieved rather outside Italy by men like Albert the Great. In Italy most people were content not to ask why an eclipse happened, but only why God sent such a thing and what its practical effect on earth would be. The only contribution of the scholars was therefore the habit of perhaps more accurate descriptions of events.

> Once we were in the city of Arezzo, where we were born and where we actually wrote this book. This city lies near the end of the fifth climate, at a latitude from the equator of forty-two degrees and a third. One Friday, at the sixth hour, with the sun standing at twenty degrees in Gemini, in a clear sky, the air began to darken, and we saw the whole body of the sun become covered bit by bit until it was entirely obscured. It was quite dark, and we saw Mercury near the sun, and all the stars appeared which were above the horizon. All the animals were frightened, and they were so bewilderd that a number of people did catch them, because they were lost. And we saw the whole sun covered for as long as it takes to walk a good two hundred and fifty paces. And the ground quickly began to cool off. . . .[23]

Those who concern themselves only with gathering facts usually make a mockery of those who evolve theories, and the story of Thales looking so intently at the sky that he fell into a pit was told once again in the *Novellino*.[24] There is another story in the same collection that is typical. One day in Paris the most learned astrologers were discussing the seven heavens, and in particular the highest of all, the Empyraeum, where the throne of God is. 'And while they were disputing, a simpleton came up to them and said, "And above the head of the Lord, gentlemen, what is there?" One of them answered joking, "A hat, of course." So the simpleton passed on. Then one of the wise men said, "Do you think we really answered that simpleton? Aren't we the simpletons? Aren't we looking for the answer ourselves? What is there above the Lord?" And they all applied their learning to this problem but could find no answer. And they said to another, "We are fools to have such exalted thoughts, fools again to try and explain things, and out of our minds to try and know God's mind!" '25

Here again astronomy and theology are meeting as they do so elaborately in the *Commedia*, where each of the seven heavens has its proper place, as does Jerusalem under the one hemisphere and Purgatory at the antipodes under the other, both equally spaced from the equator.26 The fact that so much of the earth was still undiscovered left more room for speculation.

After the *artes liberales* the next steps in a course of study were medicine, law and theology. We have already mentioned the oldest medical school at Salerno, the peaceful little town with its broad blue bay, which lay within the Arabic sphere of influence; and all medical knowledge in Italy at the time came from the Greeks or the Saracens, for Christian scholars mistrusted the body. Constantine from Africa, after many wanderings, became a monk at Monte Cassino and translated for the students at Salerno a number of old Greek texts which had been preserved in Arabic, so that Galen became the textbook for all Italian doctors and every student had to learn by heart the ten books of Ali Abbas's *Pantechne* in the edition prepared by Constantine. There were indeed some distinguished doctors in the thirteenth century, such as Mauro of Salerno, Salicetti of Piacenza and the surgeon Capelluti of Parma. But in general there was no great progress in the art of healing. When the famous Arnald of Villanova wrote his Parables and Remedies about 1300, there was some advance on the old magical formulas, but the knowledge of anatomy and general therapy was still in its infancy. According to an account of Bonvesin da Riva,[27] the brothers who ran the hospitals had little more than a purge to offer as treatment for worms, ulcers or dysentery. But it could hardly be otherwise, when the body was regarded as a curse, given us for our punishment. Many people looked upon the body, in the words of a French ascetic, as a mere 'sack of dung'. St Francis put it in his own way, when he spoke of 'Brother Ass', but Dante returns to the other image, when he speaks of the 'triste sacco'.[28]

Jacopone da Todi goes further and regards as blessed those who suffer any physical infirmity:

O Signor per cortesia   O Lord, do me the courtesy
mandami la malsania.[29]   To send to me infirmity.

He cries out and begs for quartan and tertian fever, dropsy, toothache, headache, stomach ache and so on, even epilepsy; and blind, deaf and dumb to go the grave, which is the only end. What was the art of medicine to do with that sort of thing? Perhaps it is not surprising that medical students were few.

Much more esteemed were legal studies. Bologna called herself 'Legum nutrix' and, in fact, the majority of her students were students of utrumque jus, both civil and canon law. A love of legal problems is an Italian characteristic even today, and it was the same in the thirteenth century. Whether judgement was always given according to the law was another matter,[30] especially in those days of feuds and vengeance, and the academic lawyers seemed to have been chiefly concerned with compilations and commentaries, and sometimes with the philosophical basis of law. The grammarian Boncompagno complained that the lawyers were masters in the art of making the crooked look straight and the straight look crooked, and demonstrating the certain to be doubtful and the logical to be absurd.[31]

Civil law was a conglomeration of Roman, Byzantine and Germanic legal customs accumulated during at least twelve centuries, and it operated in every place in a different way; but canon law, since its codification by the Camaldolese monk Gratian at Bologna in the mid-twelfth century had become a fairly coherent and up-to-date system. One who knew the book was called a 'decretist' and one who also knew all the supplements and commentaries was called a 'decretalist'. Several popes were famous canonists, but the most renowned canonist of Bologna was the Spanish Dominican Saint, Raymond of Peñafort, though he is perhaps better known to many people as a saint than as a canonist. He was a great light of his time and had many distinguished colleagues, such as William Durandus, the Provençal who taught at Modena and Bologna and became papal legate in Romagna, Azzo and Tancred of Bologna and Messer Bagarotto, who wrote the celebrated treatise *De precibus et instantia*. Then there was the great Florentine, Accursius, and his *Glossa ordinaria*, and his learned son Francesco; there was Master Odofred of Bologna, Bonaguida of Arezzo, Giovanni Fasolo of Bologna, Roffredo of Benevento, the pride of Naples and the friend of the Emperor Frederick; distinguished names in the world of canon law.

We have already suggested that the *Duecento* was a period of reassessment, and nowhere is this so evident as in the field of theology, as well as in philosophy, since the two still went hand in hand. This reassessment came at the right time, since the various opinions and systems, though all presumably directed at the same object, were finding themselves in ever more serious conflict. Here indeed order was necessary and the man who more than any in the *Duecento* was to achieve it was a saint, and one who achieved it not so much by inspiration as by his outstanding intellectual acumen. This was Thomas of Aquino, the youngest son of a noble Ghibelline family who were related to the Hohenstaufen. He was born in the ancestral castle at Rocca Sicca, and at one time it was hoped he would become Abbot of Monte Cassino (which was not far from his home), for in those days of Benedictine feudalism this would have been an important worldly career also. But the young student was not attracted by this and he became a Dominican, going in 1245 to Cologne and then to Paris. In Paris he developed his own remarkable capacity for objectivity, amidst so many storms of theories and opinions: *saevis tranquillus in undis*. From now on he became a leader, chiefly through his gift for ordering ideas and co-ordinating them. Order is a special characteristic of his genius, and he sees disorder, or a departure from proper order, as the root of evil and sin.[32] An important element in his task was to attempt to bring order into the theological thought of his time, with its two main streams of neo-Platonic Augustinianism on the one hand and the Arabic Aristotelianism, under the guidance of Averroes, on the other. With the Augustinians the emphasis was on the supernatural element of the great truths of revelation, while the Aristotelians were exalting the autonomy of reason, sometimes to the near exclusion of the supernatural. Thomas's synthesis, with its clear demarcation of reason and revelation, of the natural and the supernatural, and of the realms of philosophy and theology, had, in fact, a profound influence on the subsequent developments of both streams of thought. Yet in everyday piety it was often not philosophy that counted, and frequently it was a matter of temperament whether a medieval Christian continued in the mystical tradition of Augustine or turned to the new linking of this mysticism with Aristotelian rationalism. Ultimately they were two aspects of Christian thought, and this explains why the greatest philosophers on both sides often arrived by widely different means at conclusions which were remarkably close; it also explains why the teaching of Aquinas, in itself so lucid and having energetic papal support, at first sometimes met with a cold reception even among his compatriots and brethren. The Italians are a famously practical people, but in their piety they are often strongly swayed by emotional factors, which may explain why many of them were out of sympathy with the straight reasoning of the quiet man from Naples, who had been called 'the dumb ox from Sicily', and indeed within twelve years of his death some of his own Dominicans had to be called to task 'for speaking disrespectfully and improperly of his writings'.[33] Apart from this there was a kind of resentment in certain quarters against scholasticism in general: 'Scholasticism is wrong, because it is always right about everything.'[34] And there were not wanting those of an ecstatic temperament, out of sympathy with systematic scholastic theology and philosophy, who felt that the Thomist pundits thought too much and believed too little. Thus Jacopone lamented that 'Paris has destroyed Assisi',[35] and that all this dialectic was making an end of religion. He repeatedly found a release for his feelings in animosity against the academic dialectitians who—in his opinion—obscured the clear speech of Christ:

Scienza è cosa assai divina,	Knowledge is divine (or nearly),
dove el bono oro si affina,	Best of gold refining clearly,
ma molti ha messo in ruina	Till the theologians merely
sofistica teologia.	Bring sophistications.
Io vi lasso i sillogismi,	Let them have their syllogistic,
gl'insolubili e i sofismi,	Enthymemic and sophistic,
Ippocrate e gli aforismi	Hippocratic, aphoristic,
e sottil calcularia.	Subtle speculations.
Gridar lasso Sorte e Plato,	Let them shout about Socratic
consumare el vostro fiato,	Plato's questions problematic,
arguendo d'omne lato	Wasting breath from floor to attic,
e provar una imbrattaria.	Proving nought at all, though.
Lasso a voi la gentil arte,	Let them go on gently fighting
che Aristotil scrisse in carte,	Over Aristotle's writing,
e le platoniche carte,	Finding Plato needed righting,
che la più son eresia.[36]	Heretic withal, though.

This reaction was nothing new: a thousand years before, Tertullian had already called heresy no more than a branch of philosophy, and this mistrust of scientific theology had existed all the time, though for the most part among the less educated. This mistrust is more likely to be found among the Augustinians than among Thomists. Among the simpler folk the reaction was against systematic theology in general and not against any particular school; Jacopone, for instance, was not attacking one school or the other, any more than was the rhymster we quoted at the beginning of this chapter.

Then there was the problem of the hangers-on of each school, who bandied about the old textbooks, the *Logica vetus* of Aristotle (in the inaccurate translation by Boethius), or the *Adagia* of Anselm, or the *Sentences* of Peter the Lombard, without fully understanding or developing their thought. Their opponents castigated their arrogance, their behaviour 'as if they were the sons of an emperor, when their father was only a cobbler'.[37]

Among the Franciscans especially there was a genuine horror of what they considered theological arrogance, the behaviour of a kind of intellectual *nouveaux riches* and useless hair-splitting. In this, their spirit of simplicity found a sympathy with the Augustinian mystical approach, of which they soon began to be the champions and to have a profound influence on the piety of Italy, which was already orientated in that direction. The wise old Brother Giles felt obliged to remind the great Bonaventure, a true Augustinian, that an illiterate woman could love God more than a learned master. But Bonaventure was the last man to doubt this: with all his learning he wrote things that went straight to the heart of the people. His poems and his treatises provided the staple spiritual fare of thousands of religious, and his *Meditations on the Life of Christ* (at least in part written by him)[38] had a great influence on popular devotion than even the *Legenda aurea*.

When we come to compare St Thomas with St Bonaventure —who was born in 1220 near Bolsena, called Giovanni Fidanza and cured by St Francis as a child—we find that the philosophical differences between the two friends are in the main differences of approach and of temperament. Thomas is essentially a thinker, Bonaventure is a poet: yet it was Thomas who is said to have composed the graceful liturgy for the new eucharistic feast; while a mass of prosaic pedagogic material came from the pen of Bonaventure, or of his secretaries. Similarly Jacopone, who had inveighed against systematic theology, when he comes to write of the eucharist, uses a dogmatic precision that has little to yield to the *Lauda Sion*.[39] Again, when Bonaventure sets out to explain the mystical marriage of the soul with our Lord, his treatment is entirely in terms of the usual scholastic method. But philosophy for him becomes spiritual guidance; for in his whole character Bonaventure is more a pastor of souls than intellectual.

We should do well therefore—since in this respect he is so typical of the *Duecento*—to look more closely at his briefer works. The titles of some of his writings sound so poetical that the inexperienced reader is surprised to find that the *Way of the Spirit to God*, or the *Mystical Vine*, or *Of the six Wings of the Seraph* or the *Threefold Way* are, in fact, straightforward textbooks which would have much duller titles today. Bonaventure's writings are above all practical guides to the spiritual life; they are written not for those who only want to read about mysticism, but specially for those wanting to practise it. The material of the *Threefold Way* is by no means new: already the Pseudo-Denis and Richard of St Victor[40] had taught that the soul has a threefold path to union with Christ. But what is new is the easy clarity with which this learned man can teach these things to people who are so much less learned. His work is like a lens which many generations have polished and which is so focused by him that even his short-sighted contemporaries can see eternity in it.

ST BONAVENTURE: DE TRIPLICI VIA
(THE THREEFOLD WAY)

(i.e. the soul mounts to the threefold God by a threefold way)

I. THE PURGATIVE WAY

1. BY MEDITATION:

The Blade of Conscience
must be

shaped by remembrance of sins	sharpened by the thought of	used on weak places by virtuous acts to combat
a) carelessness (3 x 3 notions)	a) my own death (3 notions)	a) carelessness (in 3 ways)
b) evil desire (3 x 3 notions)	b) the blood shed for me (3 reasons)	b) evil desire (in 3 ways)
c) evil doing (3 x 3 notions)	c) the divine judge (3 notions)	c) evil doing (in 3 ways)

2. BY PRAYING:

To lament my own misery

in distress (at our 3 denials)	in shame (at our 3 relapses)	in fear (at our condemnation on 3 counts)

3. BY CONTEMPLATION:

To mount by 7 stages to the Quiet of Peace
(with 4 meditations at every stage)

The Quiet of Peace

Sanctification

Self-conquest

Asking God's help

Distress at my sinfulness

Fear of the judgement

Shame at my weakness

II. THE ILLUMINATIVE WAY

1. BY MEDITATION:

The Ray of Understanding
will show up

my sins	God's gift to me	God's goodness in the future life
a) which God permitted and forgave me	a) according to nature (3 x 3 kinds)	a) all evil being removed
b) which I would have committed, had not God prevented me	b) according to grace (3 x 3 kinds)	b) the company of the saints
	c) supernatural (3 x 3 kinds)	c) the fulfilment of all desire

2. BY PRAYING:

Asking for God's mercy

with great desire, received through the Holy Ghost (in 3 ways)	with complete trust, springing from Christ (in 3 ways)	with the help of the Saints in heaven (in 3 categories)

3. BY CONTEMPLATION:

To mount by 7 stages to the understanding of Truth

The understanding
of God's truth,
revealed in the
Cross

Desire to suffer
with Christ

Zeal to become Christ-like

To forget self

Wonder

Compassion at the Cross

Preparation of the mind

III. THE UNITIVE WAY

1. BY MEDITATION:

The Light of Wisdom shows me my ultimate end
by

guiding me to God,
and freeing me from
attachment to crea-
tures (in 3 ways)

firing me with the
love of God alone,
and stilling my
earthly desires
(in 3 ways)

raising me above
things of
a) sense
b) imagination
c) the mind

2. BY PRAYING:

My heart is bowed in adoration before God
in that
it will be

moved to adore God
as
a) Father (because of
his 3 gifts to me)
b) Lord (because in 3
ways he comes as
Redeemer)
c) Judge (because in
3 ways he shows
his gentleness)

penetrated by
God's will
(in 3 ways)

able to find its
only satisfaction
in God (in 3 ways)

3. BY CONTEMPLATION:

To mount by 7 stages to the sweetness of Love

Union with God

Joy in God

Only satisfaction in God

Being taken out of myself

Holy Desire

Complete Trust

Readiness for God

10

The Aesthetes

Con gran disio pensando
    lungamente:
Amor che cosa sia,
E donde, e come prende
    movimento?

My anxious thoughts have
    long been wondering:
What is true love,
And whence it comes, and
    how it comes to move.

Guido Guinicelli[1]

WE ARE accustomed to think of art in Christian Europe as divided into sacred and profane, and indeed since the Renaissance the division has been true enough. But it would be a mistake to take this distinction back to the *Duecento*, although the division was beginning to be discernible even then. Other divisions were also to come into being, and certain arts which hitherto had never appeared except in company were beginning to assert their independence. An obvious example is that of poetry and music; and the time of rhymed sayings under the frescoes and miniatures, which far surpassed the illuminated texts in range and significance, is passed forever.

In the *Duecento* the process had not gone so far; the troubadours were equally musicians and poets, the mystery plays were still sung and the ballads were performed with dance. The secular and sacred arts were still very closely linked and the one idiom still frequently served both worlds. The sacred builders, who left us their cathedrals, felt no embarrassment at placing ordinary mortals among the saints, and even monsters; the sacred singers saw nothing strange in including both psalmody and merry jingles in their motets; and the *Vagantes* hardly thought it profane to change the hymns of the breviary into drinking songs or love songs. It is only a later age which finds this shocking. The preachers may have thundered about the transitory nature of material things, but everybody knew they were God's creatures, and that the Church herself was defending this truth against the heretics who were denying it. As the end of the Middle Ages drew on this love of created things grew stronger, and gradually the balance shifted away from the love of things because they are God's creatures to the love of them because they are themselves, because 'it is good to be alive', the *joie de vivre* of the Renaissance.

All this makes the study of art in the thirteenth century particularly difficult. There is so much variety of expression that one is bound to divide the material in some way, but since the divisions were themselves not yet explicit there is a danger of doing violence to the artistic whole. Nevertheless, with the above observations and reservations in mind, we shall distinguish the artists of this epoch into aesthetes, the singers of earthly things and the singers of heavenly according to their emphasis on the art form itself, on the joys of this world, and on the joys of eternity.

How much truth is there in the common phrase, 'the dark Middle Ages'? When we are in Italy, looking for ancient monuments, we are at once aware of the near 700 years that divide Roman architecture from Romanesque. Roman crypts and catacombs sometimes survived, protected by some vast pagan ruin above them; but once the Church was able to come out above ground the buildings they put up almost everywhere succumbed to the attacks of wind, weather and war, and when they fell down a new generation would hurriedly rebuild them in their own style, and so they would remain until they were thrown down again. From the fourth to the eleventh centuries many of these new generations, and consequently their rebuildings, were of foreign origin and sometimes their work has remained. There are, for instance, the Byzantine buildings at Ravenna; sometimes in a remote place one comes across the

ruins of a Merovingian abbey church, or a rough little chapel
put up by pilgrims, which has remained either by some chance
or simply because it had become a holy place. Often enough in
the apse of some Roman basilica one still finds a mosaic expressing the *devotio* of an earlier age, which contrasts with the
baroque rebuilding of the rest.

By the year 1000 the buildings that went up were more
solidly constructed and more permanent than what had gone
before. Almost all Italian medieval construction dates from
1050 to 1350, with the greater part of it belonging to the
thirteenth and early fourteenth centuries. The number of
extant churches of the *Duecento* is quite considerable: one only
has to think of those in Venice, Vicenza, Bologna, Lucca,
Padua, Florence, Siena and Orvieto, at Assisi and Arezzo, at
Foligno and Viterbo. And then there are all the castles and
fortresses built in the south by the Emperor Frederick, the
municipal buildings that the cities built at the time of their
development, at Todi in 1213, Orvieto in 1216, the Bargello in
Florence in 1255, those at Pistoia in 1259, Viterbo in 1264,
Perugia in 1284, at Siena and San Gimignano in 1288, and
many more, before the Palazzo Vecchio of 1298 and the
Doge's Palace with all its Oriental refinement of 1314, and
then the typical city fountains, many of which belong to the
Duecento. Often the whole piazza is an eloquent monument of
the art of the time, with its splashing fountain in the middle
and massive stones of the town hall on one side and cathedral
with its pointed façade on the other. The new mendicant
orders built hundreds of new churches all over the country
north of Rome: simple and spacious buildings accommodating
large crowds, the most glorious of all being the double basilica
of Assisi.[2] Towards the end of the century we find churches
with small white marble bell turrets and tall pointed windows
in the choir: the Florentine type of S. Croce 19th-century Santa
Maria Novella, linked with the name of Master Arnolfo di
Cambio, which for want of a better word is usually called
'gothic'. This kind of church is so typical of the new age that
the masterpieces of Donatello and Della Robbia seem perfectly

in place there, while in one of the old Romanesque churches with their rough walls they would look as out of place as Greek gods. In those old churches one has to search diligently for the treasures of their own period, little reliefs sometimes hidden away on the side panels of an ambo, on the capitals of a cloister, or the tympanum of a blocked-up doorway. There they are, their stiff little archaic figures with large heads and stylised drapery, with their fixed staring eyes mourning Christ's Passion till the end of the world, undisturbed by the visitors who do not know they are there, because they think Italian sculpture begins with Niccolò Pisano. Niccolò Pisano worked in the second half of the *Duecento* and adorned many pulpits and fountains with Biblical figures, which are carved with a rhythmic suppleness plainly derived from classical Greece. His son Giovanni is already almost baroque; he did the dramatic scene of the Massacre of the Innocents on the famous pulpit at Pistoia.

Niccolò, the father, is said to have come to Pisa from the south; if this is so it would explain his classical style, for Frederick of Hohenstaufen was a great collector of works of art and had assembled there many works of classical antiquity, as Napoleon also did in his turn. In this way he gave an entirely new turn to the art of the south and produced an amalgam which has no parallel in the history of European art. Where else but in Sicily is it possible to find an agreeable harmony of Norman tower, Arabic domes and Byzantine mosaics in a single building? Yet there it is, in the cathedral of Monreale, above the golden Bay of Palermo and its lemon gardens; the brilliant colours of the mosaics that cover the huge interior walls portray the history of the Old and New Testament, all directed towards the gigantic head of Christ which fills the apse, represented more like a formidale Arab Emir, in a way that no European would ever have thought of. And all those Biblical figures, beneath the Lord's sovereign gaze, mark the end of a Byzantine tradition and are more full of vitality than in any other Italian mosaic, such as those of Torcello, Ravenna or Rome, or even in the slightly less Oriental pictures at Cefalù or in the chapel of the palace at Palermo near by. Here at Monreale, 'Mount Royal', two centuries and three cultures blend in a way that the circumstances of history never permitted elsewhere.

When the Emperor Frederick made Apulia his residence that age was already past and there were no more Oriental buildings, except perhaps at Lucera, though here the men of Anjou wrecked most of what remained. Apulia became the treasury of Romanesque cathedrals: almost every little town has its cathedral, a good 800 years old, but they are rarely visited and have received little attention from the historians. Between the remote Troia in the hills and Otranto at the end of that hot coast there are so many that it is hard to say which is the best: Barletta or Molfetta, Bitonto, Trani or Besceglie, Melfi, Andria or Giovinazzo, perhaps best of all Ruvo for the slender grace of its grey outline, or San Nicola at Bari with its arcade and its gateway flanked with those terrible lions, the work of some German or Lombard far from home.[3]

All these astonishing creations of the eleventh, twelfth and thirteenth centuries lie within a ring of fortifications with which Frederick surrounded his beloved kingdom. All along the coast there are remains of his castles, all heavy, Germanic, severe and threatening. Probably they represent both his ideal of architectural massiveness and the requirements of defence, even when no defence was necessary; this he had inherited from his father. There is something of his personality embodied in that remote hunting lodge of his on its lonely hill of the 'Murgie', the Castel del Monte.

Far from any town or battlefield, the Castel del Monte has withstood the centuries. Only the dense woods which in Frederick's time covered the whole area and provided the game for hunting have disappeared. The castle stands alone upon its bare hill, visible for miles around along the road from Andria or from Corato, with only a few thin almond and olive trees for company. A gigantic block of stone, apparently more designed for war and government than for hunting and pleasure; an eight-cornered building, with as many corner towers pierced with embrasures, a central chamber dominating the whole. It seemed to be made for observing bird-migration—one wonders whether the *Ars venandi* was written here. But it is unlikely that the castle was quite finished in Frederick's lifetime, though it did probably serve as an unhappy prison for his grandchildren, the unfortunate children of Manfred, who grew up there in chains and died there. The whole place speaks of Frederick's personality, as one wanders through the empty rooms arranged in two floors round a sunny internal court. Everywhere there are columns and capitals with classical reliefs, and from the flat roof, where the wind always blows, one can look out, as Frederick doubtless did over the tops of the trees, upon Apulia, 'the apple of his eye', as far as the sea, with the dim shape of Monte Gargano on the horizon.

Just as the art of the south was cosmopolitan and enterprising, so the art of Rome remained strictly traditional. In the mosaics of Rome in the titular churches the figures never move, their drapery is stiff and still; they are not like the busy figures of Monreale, but they pose as they had for centuries. Jacopo Torriti only shows himself a child of his age by introducing into the apse-mosaics an occasional modern saint: a little Francis to the left and a little Anthony to the right. Much more original are the mosaics in the baptistery in Florence, where a rougher stone had been used for a century and where the most realistic grimaces of the damned, or of the negress holding the shade over Herodias, show a vigorous break away from traditional forms. It was not so in Rome, where the past dominated the present. The talent of Jacopo Torriti had just the right mixture of conservatism and enterprise to recommend him to the curia, but his colleague Pietro Cavallini had a more emotional style, which was welcome in Umbria, where we shall meet him again.

About the same time we find the first paintings on wood in Rome, although they are still heavily stylised in the Byzantine manner—Byzantium may have been conquered and plundered, but Rome, her rival, was still bound to her style: the

Roman ikons with their golden backgrounds and stereotyped gaze are in marked contrast to the new utterly human Madonnas of Tuscany and Umbria.

Rome's contribution to the art of the *Duecento* lay in a different area: the large-scale work was entirely tied to its traditions, but it was not so with the details of decoration, for here Rome had a colourful triumph. There is a special delight to be found in the pierced columns or balustrades of a cloister, the back of an episcopal throne or the shaft of a paschal candlestick, marble work with delicate carving, studded with coloured stones of gold, black, red and green. This was the work of the Cosmati. Little is known about them, whether they were a gifted family or a larger group working under this name. Their output was enormous and doubtless the classical ruins must have provided much material for this most ancient of *terrazzo* work. And lovely work it is, with every column and every shaft given individual treatment and its own range of colour; perhaps the very lack of symmetry is one of its greatest charms. Throughout the Lazio we come across their gay patterns and arabesques: on an ambo where one cannot but sing, on a pulpit where eloquence cannot be restrained, in a cloister where peace cannot be destroyed.

The artists who produced their mosaics in the apses had, of course, their counterparts in others who worked on the mosaics of notes within the framework of the traditional Gregorian chants. The ancient, half-Oriental Christian chants still held the field in certain circles: monks in their quiet abbeys were still composing hymns and proses, most of which, however, show a greater gift for erudition than for music. The flourishing age of the Gregorian chant already lay some centuries before; the new world in the West set up its own laws in place of those from the East according to which the old antiphons were constructed. For some time interest in the traditional unison had been waning. Naturally, the old offices were still sung in the monastic houses, but a kind of impatience had set in and there was general cry for shortening and simplification of the many psalms and spiritual canticles, especially in the summer, 'when the fleas bite, the nights are short, and the heat is unbearable'.[4] Early in the century a monk praised Abbot Joachim for never sleeping, 'not even in choir',[5] and the Devil himself admitted in the *Legenda aurea* that he found the easiest time to attack the brethren was during office in choir.[6] There are many indications that the older contemplative orders with their traditions were losing ground before a much more vigorous religious attitude, which was also less interested in art. With these moderns Church music in Italy was also in a poor way. New chants were required for the new feasts and offices, as, for example, for Corpus Christi, but most of these chants were third-rate plainsong, being little more than pastiches of the past, and the fact that the modern patterns of the new hymns and sequences are derived from contemporary French sources does little to redeem their quality.

The French canon, Adam of St Victor, exercised an important influence on Italy, as indeed elsewhere in Europe, towards the end of the twelfth century, through his innumerable easy, smooth and rather intellectual verses and melodies. No one in Italy, however, could equal him, though he had many imitators. Four out of five sequences which are now in the Church's liturgy came from Italy, but in all four of these it is the text that is valuable, not the music. The *Stabat Mater*, attributed to Jacopone da Todi, had no satisfactory tune assigned to it; and the music which Thomas of Celano took such trouble to fit to his monumental *Dies Irae* is as surely borrowed from Adam of St Victor, as is the music used by Julian of Speyer for his elegant rhymed office of St Francis.[7] The celebrated *Lauda Sion* of Aquinas rightly receives more praise for its text than for its music. Only the Whitsun sequence *Veni Sancte Spiritus* possesses a musical beauty of its own; with its depth of feeling surpassing national boundaries it can really pass for the work of Pope Innocent III, to whom it is ascribed. But how much rougher and more exuberant, and how much more Italian, is the sequence which Gregory IX wrote in honour of his friend St Francis! Of course, he uses apocalyptic phrases. and he begins with a long *jubilus* on the first syllable, which belongs to neither the Gregorian nor the French style. It could well be Gregory's own work:[8]

According to contemporary sources many Italian musicians of this time were composing pieces for several voices, but next to nothing of these has been preserved,[9] though the descriptions and the texts which they set show us plainly enough that they were on the French pattern. Salimbene tells about two of the most famous: Master Henry of Pisa and Brother Vita of Lucca. The Pisan master composed motets and other pieces upon texts of the Chancellor Philip, typical examples of the school of Notre-Dame in Paris, and his friend Vita would write counterpoints to his monodic melody. Vita seems to have been an early example of the authentic Italian tenor; people would do anything for him because of his wonderful voice, even the nightingale would stop singing when he began and one day a nun who heard him sing threw herself out of a window to follow him, 'but did not get very far, because she broke her leg when she fell.'[10]

The language of these songs and poems during the whole century is almost exclusively Latin, and this fact links them with the academics. Latin was still the usual medium among educated people, the language of manifestos and formal treatises, of letters and poems of a learned kind. Very many people still understood it, but by now there were few who could speak it grammatically. Many of the dialects of the thirteenth century were still very close to Latin, and, in fact, the transition from 'Vulgar Latin' to a proper language of the people came about only slowly and at a late date. Yet the new language, called *lingua rustica* by the arrogant townsfolk, was already sufficiently developed by 1200 to have become a written language: a monk of Monte Cassino had already written a clumsy moralising poem in the vernacular,[11] and at the imperial court the first Italian love songs were being sung. When Francis composed his *Canticle of the Sun* in Umbria he was, in fact, starting a new tradition, for in the north for many years the vernacular had only been used for addressing the common people for their instruction or edification, and generally it was only towards the end of the century that it became fashionable for anything in the nature of true poetry or literature to be written in Italian. For some time literary men had felt that Latin was too prosaic and inflexible for the expression of their dynamic ideas, and they began by turning to the *langue d'oc* and the *langue d'œil*, so that in this field also France gave a lead. Alongside the work of Adam of St Victor and the polyphonic school of Notre-Dame we begin to notice the influx of French singers and story-tellers into Italy.[12] The nobility spoke Provençal better than they spoke Italian, and everyone had been for some time quite familiar with King Arthur and Charlemagne and his glorious knights; already in the twelfth century those most Latin people of Nepi uttered their condemnation of perjury in terms of the fate of Ganelon,[13] and as far away as the district of Otranto one finds a 'Grave of Roland'. Small wonder therefore that Messer Brunetto Latini wrote his *Livres dou Trésor* in a kind of French, however imperfect, as being *'la parleüre plus délitable et plus comune à toutes gens'*. It seems obvious that this ambitious Florentine diplomat felt that the circle of readers he could reach with his Italian *Tesoretto* was much too small and that by writing in French he would be able to impart his somewhat pedantic information to a larger audience. Whether his *Livres dou Trésor* was ever a best-seller we do not know, but he certainly earned by means of it the thanks of Dante, which he offered to him when he met him in the Inferno.[14]

There were also occasional excursions into the vernacular on the part of prose writers, one or two chronicles or special treatises. The earliest examples are clearly experiments in which the author simply wrote as he spoke, with no attempts at style. Gradually, however, the language was taking shape, and some moralists were writing after the manner of Seneca; there was a certain balance and rhythm in their writing, but it was little more than translated Latin. About the same time there arose a fashion among the more educated people for the circulation of short stories, called 'Novels', the actual anecdotes of which had for the most part been known for centuries. About the year 1300 a hundred of these short stories were assembled in a fine volume under the title of the *Novellino* or else the *Libro di novelle e di bel parlar gentile*. It was thus something of a conscious exercise in graceful language. The stories are concerned with noble and learned people from every age and every land, without the sharp and often crude humour of Boccaccio a century later, not as gripping as Boccaccio's *Decameron*, but with a humour of their own, and more distinguished. The *Novellino*, and likewise other similar collections of the *Duecento* such as the *Fiori e vita di filosafi ed altri savii ed imperadori*, do not so much reflect the way of thinking of medieval people as their new way of expressing themselves. Almost all the anecdotes contain dialogues with marked turns of phrase, suggesting a growing love of the use of words, and sometimes the story or description seems to be frankly sacrificed for the sake of the words, or even of word play.

There are enchanting stories in the *Novellino* and, wherever they may have originally come from, there is a certain similarity about them all. There is the wisdom of a Greek prince who visited first a most worthy merchant and then a most worthless tyrant who had been deposed, and to the latter he gave a rich present, for 'I only give to someone who can teach me something. I had nothing to learn from the good merchant, so I did not feel indebted to him; but the other man was just like me, only he had already been deposed for his wickedness, and he taught me so much, that nobody is going to depose me now. Compared to the value of what I learned from him, my gift was as nothing.'[15] Then there is the gentle wit of the philosopher, who remained silent when he was reproved: 'I do not answer, for I hear nothing that pleases me',[16] and the story of the three rings, which has been told so often again down to the time of Lessing's *Nathan der Weise*.[17] Many stories come from the East, one of the pleasantest being that about the cook who brought a poor man to court for having consumed through his nose the smell of his exquisite cooking, without having paid for it; the judge ordered the poor man to pay for the smell by clinking his coins to the cook.[18]

Of purely Italian origin seems to be the anecdote of the story-teller of Azzolino, that is, Ezzelino da Romano.[19]

> The Lord Azzolino had a story-teller among his servants, whom he employed to tell him stories during the long winter evenings. One night the story-teller would have preferred to go to bed, but Azzolino ordered him to go on. So he began the story of a certain peasant who went to the market with a hundred pieces of gold, to buy some sheep. For every piece of gold he got two sheep. As he took his flock home, he had to cross a river; but there had been a rain storm and the river was greatly swollen. While he stood on the bank, he saw a poor fisherman nearby with such a very small boat that it would only hold one man and one sheep at a time. He agreed with the man about the crossing, and pushed off in the boat with one sheep. He began to row. It took a long time, as the river was very broad, but he rowed hard and got across. . . . The story-teller paused. Azzolino said, Go on! The story-teller said, Let him first get all the sheep across, and then I will tell you what happened afterwards; but this might take about a year, and in the mean-time it would be so nice to get a bit of sleep.

As the writers' skill in the vernacular developed they began to turn from prose to poetry, and a great deal of verse was turned out by the generation before Dante. It is useless to deny that the main value of these verses is as period pieces and not as poetry; for the most part there is little genuine poetic feeling in the dull civilities of the Sicilians, the artificial sonnets of Guittone, Arezzo's 'Merry Friar', the rhyming dialectic of the Bolognese pundits, or the clumsy commonplaces of the moralising preachers. Yet here and there in all this slow struggle towards expression there are moments when the poetic richness of the Italian language begins to be explored. One is surprised to find in the course of a rather dull *tenzone* by one Orlanduccio Orafo the following lines, which possess a certain untranslatable greatness:

> O tu, che sei errante cavaliero
> de l'arme fero e de la mente saggio. [20]

> O thou who art a travelled chevalier,
> In armour fierce, in spirit yet so wise.

That is an *acclamatio*, a form which did not achieve true rhythmic grace until we come to Farinata's cry to Dante in hell:

> O Tosco che per la città del foco
> vivo ten vai, così parlando onesto. [21]

> O Tuscan, walking through this place of fire
> Alive, and speaking words of reverence.

Chiaro Davanzati is another among those poets, who though they never reached the heights, yet possessed moments of genuine charm:

> Ai, dolce e gaia terra fiorentina,
> fontana di valor e di piacenza,
> fior de li altri, Fiorenza,
> qualunque ha più saver, ti tien reina! [22]

> How gay the country round sweet Florence is,
>   The source of strength and every pleasing scene,
> The flower of all flowers is what Florence is:
>   And those who know acknowledge her the queen!

Chiaro was writing for *qualunque ha più saver*—those who know—and was among the first to use the polished style which Dante with approval named the *dolce stil nuovo*. The new style was born under the prison windows of King Enzio and among the scholars with their endless legal disputes, and the new writers were at first mainly concerned with demonstrating their ingenuity with the new medium, so that the style would more rightly be called '*dotto*' than '*dolce*'. But after the jejune and artificial verse of their predecessors, the new group were beginning to achieve a certain rhythmic elegance and sense of the beautiful, which justifies Dante's phrase. Two men both called Guido stand out among them: Guido Guinicelli, '*il dottor*', was born in 1240 at Bologna and was much addicted to scholastic distinctions in his love songs, so that, for instance, he can spend much time discussing which are the properties of the everlasting God of love which adorn the heart of his beloved.[23] A little later there is Dante's friend Guido Cavalcanti, who was an arrogant and rather unattractive Florentine with an absurd confidence in his own skill and an equal sureness about the stupidity of the masses:

> Tu poi sicuramente gir, canzone,
> là've ti piace, ch'io t'ò sì adornata
> ch'assai laudata sarà tua ragione
> da le persone ch'anno intendimento.
> Di star con l'altre tu non ài talento.[24]

> Depart, my song, and safely go thy ways,
> Where'er thou wilt, for I adorned thee so,
> That it is thine by right to merit praise
> From people with a proper wit endow'd.
> Not thine to stand among the common crowd.

What has happened here? Is it Guido who is a bore, or is it we who have somehow got out of sympathy? Or must we admit that tastes change with the centuries? For there is no question that among the predecessors and contemporaries of Dante, Guido Cavalcanti holds a place of special esteem. Like many a Florentine he entered politics, and like many of them he went into exile when his political fortune changed. His *Ballata*, which he wrote near the end of his life, a lonely exile feeling the approach of death, is among the loveliest things of the period. Admittedly the poem is still cramped by the framework of the traditional *courtoisie* and bound by Guido's limited vocabulary; but it has something of a genuine human document, and this quality will give it immortality. Here, then, is the famous *Ballatetta*: 'Little ballad, go for me . . .':

Perchè io no spero di tornar
　giammai
Ballatetta, in Toscana,
Va' tu, leggiera e piana
dritta alla Donna mia
che per sua cortesia
ti farà molto onore.

All my hope is left behind

　Of return to Tuscany:
　Little ballad, go for me,
Go my Lady sweet to find,
She is courteous, she is kind,
　She will surely welcome
　　thee.

Tu porterai novelli de'
　sospiri
piene di doglia e di molta
　paura;
ma guarda che persona non
　ti miri,
che sia nimica di gentil
　natura;
chè certo per la mia
　disavventura
tu saresti contesa,
tanto da lei ripresa,
che mi sarebbe angoscia;

dopo la morte poscia
pianto e novel dolore.

Go to tell her of my woe,

　Every fear and every sigh,

Watch that gentleness's foe

　Halt thee not from drawing
　　nigh;
Cruel is my fate to me,

　Surely it will thee pursue,
Cruel it would be to thee,
　Bringing me to anguish
　　too;
Even if I buried be,
　This would bring me
　　sorrows new.

Tu senti, Ballatetta, che la
　morte
mi stringe sì, che vita
　m'abandona,

Little ballad, tell her how

　Life is failing, seized by
　　death,

e senti come 'l cor si sbatte
    forte
per quel che ciascun spirito
    ragiona;
tant' è distrutta già la mia
    persona,
ch'io non posso soffrire;
se tu mi vuoi servire,
mena l'anima teco
(molto di ciò ten preco)
quando uscirà del core.[25]

How my heart, scarce beating
    now,
Fights for every fleeting
    breath;
How I lie in such distress,

Suffering is meaningless;
When my spirit shall depart,
    If thou wilt my servant be,
(This I beg with all my heart)
Take away my soul with
    thee.

It is not difficult in these early struggles for expression to recognise the world in which Dante grew up. As a young man he lived among those who were cultivating '*gentilezza*', the new nobility which was ousting nobility of birth or wealth; but while his contemporaries remained at this stage his own genius enabled him to grow into something far greater. Yet we must admit that in his minor works his style and diction hardly outstrip those of his companions: his ecstatic veneration of Beatrice in the *Vita Nuova* bears the stamp more of a contemporary literary device than of a mystical experience. Even Cavalcanti speaks in such exalted terms of his beloved that the words sound more like a praise of our Lady:

Chi è questa che ven, ch'ogni uom la mira,
che fa tremar di claritate l'a're
e mena seco Amor, sì che parlare
uomo non può, ma ciascun ne sospira?[26]

Who is she that captures all men's eyes,
Sets the whole air trembling with her light,
Bringing Love with her; to speak aright
No man can, but utter silent sighs.

This is the language of the Song of Songs indeed, but so is that of Dante's famous sonnet, when at the passage of My Lady 'every tongue with trembling becomes mute', and it seemed as if a breath came from her lips, commanding silence.[27]

It is almost impossible now to distinguish symbol and reality in the poets of the *dolce stil nuovo*, and it is equally impossible to know whether their contemporaries made the distinction. At any rate they have not left us any indication. With regard to the *Vita Nuova*, most people have always taken it literally as the description of a youthful love, never uttered but never forgotten since the early death of the beloved. Yet the fact remains that the story contains so many evident symbolic features which utterly confuse any literal interpretation, and for this reason the more recent theory cannot be dismissed, according to which the whole love story is symbolic. Then Beatrice appears, freed from all considerations of earthly love. Could she stand for the Lady Theology, of whom the poet says in the *Convivio* that she had been excluded from his life by the two loves of philosophy and poetry? Then she might be the Beatrice of both the *Vita Nuova* and the *Divina Commedia*, too.[28]

A symbolic interpretation of Beatrice at once places Dante in a completely different world from that of his predecessors. No longer can he be thought of in terms of their mannered compositions, but only in terms of the greatest of the heavenly lovers.

33. This fresco portrait of St Francis in the Sacro Speco or Holy Grotto at Subiaco dates from 1228 and is thus the oldest surviving likeness of the saint.

34. This gabled Pisan altarpiece shows St Francis flanked by scenes from his life. Note the Byzantine domes in the small scenes in which the lively narrative sets off the ascetic austerity of the central image.

35. In this simple room in the Convent of San Damiano just outside Assisi, St Clare, the friend and helper of St Francis, died in 1253.

36. The severe façade of the Cathedral of San Rufino in Assisi (1144–1228) is divided into three storeys by the arcaded loggia and flat cornice. Behind stands the rectangular mass of the campanile.

38. Begun in 1228, two years after St Francis's death, the Basilica of San Francesco in Assisi actually comprises two churches, one above the other. The porch fronting the entrance to the lower church can be seen on the left.

39. The relief of Christ as Judge surrounded by angels was made in the late eleventh century for the doors of San Zeno in Verona. Part of the earliest surviving Italian exercise in the art of bronze relief, the primitive immediacy and expressiveness of the scene seem to take us to the very springs of pictorial art. (See plate 27)

40. The very ancient theme of a powerful beast holding its prey is common in Italian romanesque art. Here the roaring lion at the entrance to the Cathedral of Modena serves as a symbolic warning to malevolent forces that might seek to profane the church.

41. This ornate rose window of the Cathedral of Troja in Apulia is noteworthy for its enclosing sculptural band and for the pierced panels between the spokes, which serve to filter the bright southern sunlight into the interior.

42. With their timeless serenity the bare clay hills of the Umbrian landscape outside Assisi form a particularly appropriate setting for St Francis's formative years.

43. The paired columns of the cloister of St Paul's without-the-walls in Rome, many of them twisted and encrusted with variegated mosaic, are typical of the work of the Cosmati, a central-Italian family of sculptors and decorators active in the twelfth and thirteenth centuries.

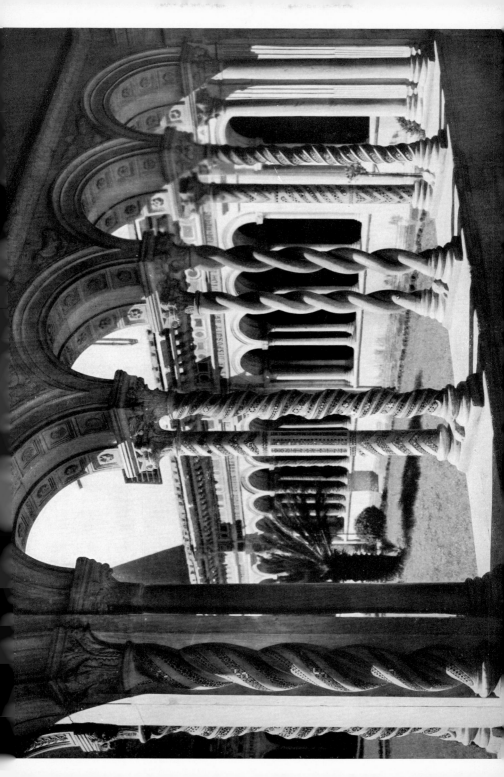

44. While St Francis prayed before this cross in San Damiano in Assisi, he was answered by a voice that said 'Go, Francis, and repair my house'. The Saviour, victorious over death, is flanked by the Virgin, saints and angels.

45. The late twelfth-century mosaic in the half dome of the apse of Monreale Cathedral in Sicily represents Christ as Ruler of the Universe (Pantocrator). The powerful conception of the figure is purely Byzantine. In the open book the parallel Greek and Latin inscriptions from St John's Gospel (8 : 12) symbolise the essential unity of the eastern and western traditions.

47. This crucifix in San Domenico in Orvieto shows how Gothic sculptors evolved a new artistic concept of the suffering Saviour that could be endowed with an almost unbearable pathos.

48 (overleaf). Cimabue's great panel of the Madonna in Majesty in the Uffizi Museum in Florence is unique in its combination of expressive delicacy and monumental design. The figures of the angels, with their tender concern, derive from the tradition of Byzantine art.

11

The Earthly Lovers

Partite, amor, adeo!	Begone, my love, farewell!
Chè troppo çe se' stato:	Too long has been thy stay:
lo maitino è sonato,	There sounds the matins bell,
çorno me par che sia.	And dawns another day.

'Alba', from the *Memoriale* of Bologna[1]

SINCE THE days of Ovid's *Ars amandi* the Italians have been a nation of lovers. But a glance at the calendar of the Roman Church with its multitude of Italian saints shows that Italy is capable of a twofold love, a love of heaven and a love of earth, and both of them sublime.

In history there seems to be an alternating rhythm of predominance, now of the love of transient things and now of things eternal. It is obvious that the Italian late Middle Ages belong for the most part to the second category, for however practical and hard-headed the north Italian city people were—and their chronicles and business dealings make this clear enough—the whole culture of the *Duecento* was religious. Religion lay very close below the surface of the obvious practicality, closer perhaps than anyone would consider 'healthy' today. Almost all the art that is concerned with transient things comes from abroad, while nearly all the truly native art, when at its best, is ultimately concerned with heaven. This is significant.

Although earthly love was overshadowed, it did produce its blossoms. Small wildflowers they were perhaps during the *Duecento*, but in the next century they were strenuously cultivated and became important. Their importance here is to see the origins, however insignificant they may have seemed. Of secular music of the *Duecento* nothing has been preserved, except the fact that it existed. We know that a great deal was sung and played outside the churches and chapels, and all the chroniclers show us that almost every civic event was accompanied by music, but the songs and dances of the people have not so far been discovered in any manuscript and it is unlikely that they ever will be, for probably they were always performed from memory. In the field of painting there is hardly any evidence of the treatment of secular subjects. If we search for Italy's secular literature, we shall reach our goal only beyond the frontiers, in France, for here also the *Duecento* depended on the *esprit gaulois*. Just as the manuscripts of church music came from the Île de France into the monasteries and cathedral libraries of Italy, so also the Provençal poets and singers went the rounds from one castle to another, to entertain the nobles with their *gaya scienza*, their witty dialogue and their charming songs. Among the common people French strolling players, jesters and story-tellers moved from town to town and gathered the townsfolk to watch their tricks and listen to their recitals. There was a sharp division between the common folk in the towns and the nobles in their castles, which remotely dominated the scene everywhere, especially in Lombardy. A nobleman with no particular political ambition was apt to lead a secluded life: the busy, crowded streets beyond his castle gates were to him almost like a distant village, and his life was entirely concerned with his family and his retainers. A visit from a strolling singer provided a genuine diversion, from the moment when he stood before the gates and blew upon his horn until he waved the young lady good-bye on the gallery of the tower. These things were common scenes all over western Europe. In Lombardy especially it was Provençals who provided these merry interludes, but even if they were not Provençals it would hardly have been noticeable, for the Italian troubadours spoke Provençal. The troubadours were as a rule at least in earlier times, of good family. Their elegant verses they left to a junior minstrel in their group to sing aloud, while they occupied themselves with the young ladies of the house or encouraged their host to try his hand at writing verse. Some have thought that these Provençal troubadours were actually Albigensians, refugees from their homes and sent to spread their beliefs in Italy. But although there was perhaps a connexion between the heretics and the troubadours, it seems certain that in Italy at any rate the troubadours were more concerned with entertainment than with preaching. They were always welcome at the various courts, in the more important of which life was by no means secluded and the arts were vigorously pursued, and often practised by the princes, with considerable rivalry among them. The castle of Monferrato still maintained its reputation for poetry, and here Raimbaut de Vaqueiras, Peire Vidal and Gaucelm Faidit competed with one another in singing the praises of the prudent Beatrice. To the north lay the half-French court of the Savoy; but he who would try his talent farther south would go to Genoa, or better still to Ferrara to the court of the d'Este. Here also there was a Beatrice, to whom Aimeric de Peguilhan lost his heart and to whom he wrote poems likening her to an angel when she entered a convent.[2] Perhaps Dante's and Aimeric's Beatrice are not too far apart. Various distinguished Italians followed in the footsteps of the Provençals, such as the Marchese Manfredo Lancia, the Marchese Alberto Malaspina, and the Bolognese Buvalelli who afterwards became the mayor of Milan. A few of their verses have been preserved: a well-turned declaration of love or a rhyming account of rival lovers—all plainly derived from French patterns. The lives of some of these poets were full of troubles:[3] Lanfranc Cigala was murdered, Sordel of Mantua, much esteemed by Dante,[4] was driven from Ezzelino's court because of his love for Cunizza da Romano, took to drink and led a rough life among the common strolling players. Later, we are told, he was given a property near Naples by the Anjou. Although the lives of the *trovatori* have provided ample material for subsequent romances, their own poems are for the most part dull and artificial; very occasionally there are original turns of phrase, but generally they belong to the generation of cliché poetry of the later French troubadours.

In southern Italy, however, at the imperial court a genuine poetic movement was developing at the time, and however international the court may have been there is no doubt about the Italian character of their work. There are, of course, traces of French influence, and perhaps of Eastern lyricism, but there is a purity of language, with only very rare elements of Sicilian dialect; this must be ascribed to the policy of the Hohenstaufen of achieving political unity in the kingdom by means of unity of language.

The princes gave a lead to their court poets in the matter of writing poetry. Of the Emperor Frederick it is stated that he 'knew how to read, write, sing, and compose songs and verses'.[5] A few poems are traditionally ascribed to him; they are sharp, quick dialogues, the kind of recreation one would expect of him,[6] and there is a similar tradition about Conrad IV.[7] The most gifted of Frederick's sons was certainly his favourite son, Manfred. Handsome like his father, but more sensual, he could play several instruments and could sing well, he enjoyed the company of minstrels and beautiful women, and always went dressed in green.[8] If anyone was in trouble it was known that he would receive royal favour if an approach was made through the *trovatori*. The chronicler Ottokar of Austria mentions by name no less than seventeen troubadours at Manfred's court,[9] and it is curious that most of these were Germans, born in Zittau, Würzburg, Erfurt and elsewhere; but the Sicilian writers mention none of these, and the only poems from the Hohenstaufen court that remain are pure Italian.

The traveller on the road from Catania to Syracuse, not far from Frederick's colony of Augusta, comes upon a small town called Lentini, overlooking its lake. One has to stretch the imagination to realise that this is the birthplace of one of the earliest Italian poets, Jacopo of Lentini, who died before 1250. On his own evidence he was a notary by profession, a fact which is borne out by the orderliness of his poems. The invention of the sonnet form is attributed to him, and maybe this exact and exacting form is again characteristic of the precision of his mind. At the same time he occasionally produced some attractive poems in a free and almost playful metre:

Dal cor mi vene
che lgli ochi mi tene,
   rosata.

Red my heart has burn'd,
My eyes are turn'd
   Red.

Spesso m'adivene
che la ciera ò bene
   bangnata,

Shed my tears are now
Upon my brow
   Shed.

quando mi sovene
di mia bona speme
   c' ò data

Said my hope for thee
May once more be
   Said:

in voi, amorosa
bonaventurosa.[10]

Long my love express'd,
Thou heaven-blest.

To the same period belongs the work of Pier della Vigna, the *logotheta* of the Emperor Frederick, and also that of a certain Giacomo of Apulia, who in the year 1246 was struck down by the evil power whom he had accused in a poem long before:

Mortte, perchè m' ài fatta sì gran guerra,
che m' ài tolta madonna, ond' io mi dolglio?
la fiore de le belleze mort' ài in terra;
perchè lo mondo non amo nè volglio . . .[11]

O death, why hast thou made this war on me?
My lady thou hast taken, and I weep;
The flower of loveliness lies in the ground,
And I this empty world can love no more.

The most important of the poets at the Sicilian court was Rinaldo d'Aquino, who belonged to the same gifted family that produced the great theologian. He served the Hohenstaufen first, and then the Anjou; he died in 1280. Rinaldo has left us the lament of a woman, left behind as she watched her beloved leave for a crusade. They are neat and compact verses, and although there are many hackneyed phrases of the time, a genuine human feeling can be discerned:

Gia mai non mi conforto
nè mi volglio ralegrare:
le navi son giunte al porto
e volgliono colare.

For me there is no comfort,
I can no more be gay,
The ships down in the harbour
Will soon be under way.

Vassene lo più giente
in terra d'oltra mare,
ed io, oi mè lassa, dolente,
come degio fare?

The warriors are embarking,
For lands across the blue
But I, alas, left grieving—
For what ought I to do?

Vassene in altra contrata
e no lo mi manda a dire
ed io rimangno ingannata,
tanti sono li sospiri,

They go to distant countries,
From which one never hears,
And I, betrayed, must stay here
To sigh amid my tears:

che mi ffanno grande guerra
la notte co la dia;
nè 'in cielo ned in terra
non mi pare ch' io sia.

For this is my great battle,
The night as much as day
Whether in earth or heaven,
I find it hard to say.

Santus, santus Deo,
che ne la Vergine venisti,
tu salva e guarda l'amor meo,
poi che da me lo dipartisti.

O holy God, I pray thee,
Of purest Virgin born,
Do thou protect my loved one
Who leaves me here forlorn.

Oit alta potestate,
temuta e dottata,
il dolze mi' amore
ti sia raccomandata.

Almighty God in heaven,
My humble prayer I send,
My sweet and own beloved
To thee I recommend.

La crocie salva la giente,
e me facie disviare,
la crocie mi fa dolente
e non mi vale Dio pregare.

The cross may save the pagans,
But me it leads astray,
The cross to me is torment:
To God I cannot pray.

Oi me, crocie pellegrina,
perchè m' ài così distrutta?
oi me, lassa tapina,
ch' io ardo e 'nciendo tutta.

O cross of the crusaders,
What hast thou done to me?
Alas for me, sad woman,
On fire with agony.

Lo 'mperadore com pacie
tutto 'l mondo mantene
ed a me guerra facie
chè m' a tolto la mia speme.

The emperor is maintaining
In all the world his peace,
To me he has done violence,
And made my hoping cease.

Oit alta potestate,
temuta e dottata,
lo mio dolze amore
ti sia raccomandata.

Almighty God in heaven,
    My humble prayer I send,
My own and sweet beloved
    To thee I recommend.

Quando la crocie pilgliao,
cierto no lo mi pensai,
quelli che tanto m' amao
ed i' llui tanto amai,

But when he turned crusader,
    He thought of me no more,
Although I know how sweetly
    To each our love we bore,

Ch' i' ne fui batuta
e messa in presgionia
ed incielata tenuta
per la vita mia.

And now I am in torture,
    As if to prison sent,
And cast into a dungeon
    Until my life is spent.

Le navi sono a le colle,
im bon' ora possan andare
e lo mio amor con elle,
e la giente che v' à andare.

The ship is set for sailing,
    An hour and she will go:
My love is going with her,
    With those who also go.

Padre criatore,
a santo porto le conducie,
che vanno a servidore

de la santa crocie.

O Father, my creator,
    See voyage safe is made,
For they have gone to serve
        thee
    Upon the great crusade.

Però ti priego, dolcietto,
che ssai la pena mia,
che me ne facie un sonetto
e mandilo in Soria,

And now I ask my darling,
    Who knows of all my pain,
To send a little sonnet
    From Syria o'er the main,

ch' io nom posso abentare
notte né dia:
in terra d' oltre mare
istà la vita mia.[12]

For both by day and darkness
    No peace is here for me,
For all that all my life is
    Is there across the sea.

We can only guess at the melodies that must have gone with many of the Sicilian poems. It is probable that they were as cosmopolitan as the poems, and like the Sicilian folk songs of today, which include echoes of Spanish, Greek and Oriental elements. It is probable also that Frederick, with all his love of Oriental decoration, would have included Oriental music. Indeed, with the movements of crusaders and merchants in northern Italy there came also Eastern music. We learn from the chronicler Salimbene something of the impression it made on Western listeners. One day he and another of his brethren were engaged on the quest at the seaport of Pisa, and they chanced to be in the inner court of one of the city houses. He tells us that

> there we saw leopards and other animals from beyond the sea. There were also girls and boys, in the full bloom of youth, well dressed and pleasant to look at. They all held fiddles and zithers in their hands, and other instruments besides, playing most sweetly and providing suitable gestures also. . . . Their song was unusual and beautiful, both in the words and in the arrangement of the voices and in the melody, so much so, in fact, that our hearts were unusually elated. They said nothing to us and we said nothing to them, but all the time we were there, their music did not cease, both vocal and instrumental, and we stayed a long time and with difficulty took ourselves away. I do not know—only God knows—how it is that anything could produce such happiness, for we had never seen such a thing before, nor were we likely ever to see the like again.[13]

What Brother Salimbene heard on that occasion was most likely a serenade held in the courtyard of some rich house: what was heard on the streets was of a lower order altogether, singers of popular songs, people of the fairs and ordinary clowns who were often enough allied with the thieves in making money out of their audiences. No doubt the good friar would not have had such kind words for them.

These *joculatores* were a problem. They gave as much trouble to the authorities as they gave fun to the people; their influence was immense and it was rare that a sermon could counteract a song—in fact, the preachers themselves fell victims to the frivolous ways of the clowns. Over and over again councils and synods forbade clerics to go to concerts and plays or to associate with players and singers of popular songs; the very frequency with which these decrees were repeated suggests that perhaps they were often not too scrupulously observed. There must have been occasional clerical students who found

pleasant company among the strolling players and ended up
by joining them. The reverse also happened and more than one
popular singer became a saint: St Raynerius of Pisa began life
in the twelfth century among the popular musicians. A Pisan
song book says of him:

Hom era disviato	He was a wayward man,
et era sonatore,	A street musician too,
non gl' er' altro a gradire.	Who liked no other thing,
Sonando uditte re vei	Till, while he played one day,
l'angelo che passa:	He saw an angel pass:
la rotta adesso lassa	He left the evil way
seguillo volentieri.[14]	And followed in his path.

Another man who felt music was his vocation was the celebrated
singer whom the Emperor Frederick crowned as the 'poet-
king', but whom we only know under his name in the cloister:
Brother Pacificus.[15] It was not an angel that he met, but St
Francis, whom he heard preaching in the district of Ancona.
The heart of one artist spoke to that of the other, and the man's
life was suddenly changed. He threw himself at the saint's feet
with words that sound strange on the lips of the 'poet-king':
'Why do we talk so much? Let us get down to business. Take
me away from men and give me to the Great Emperor.'[16] In
all his subsequent life he remained true to his ideal, and even
if in several anecdotes he seems still to be the elegant actor
which he must have been before,[17] he seems also to have been
one of St Francis's favourite disciples.[18] But not all such con-
verts were so persevering. The character of the minstrels was
one to be easily stirred and visions and conversions followed
quickly, but the conversions were seldom permanent and more
than one chronicler laments about ex-actors who leapt out of
the cloister as quickly as they had leapt in.[19] The attraction of
the free life of the road was too strong for them and they
would return to it, hard though it often was, with little protection from the weather and still less from the hatred and
insult that was sometimes their lot. The players usually got
the necessities of life, and mostly even without resorting to

robbery or murder. For a little cash, a drink or a garment they were always ready to perform, or if required to compose comic verses about the local *podestà*, or the bishop, or a whole abbey or a political party.[20] They were to be found everywhere. Bishop Bonfiglio of Siena issued an order that 'none of the clergy shall permit any street musicians to play in their churches during services, and moreover that they must not eat at the same table with such persons'.[21] That may have been the rule, but at the same time the Cardinal Archbishop of Ostia made this interesting remark to an importunate player: 'You can eat as much as you like in my house, but as to singing and playing the fiddle—I can do that as well as you!'[22] The Devil, however, seems to have taken the stricter view, if we are to believe Jacopone. The Devil was making his accusations in the heavenly court of a sinner whom he claimed as his own, and this was one point in his favour:

Quanno era assembiamento	When the noble girls and boys
de donne e de donzelli,	Went into a gathering,
andava con stromento	He would take his instrument
con soi canti novelli.[23]	All his latest songs to sing.

In Cortona the same Devil tried to lead the penitent Margherita astray by means of 'the most disgraceful songs, which he invited the Servant of God quite shamelessly to join him in singing'.[24]

The Church had had her say, but now the secular powers also had their objections to the *joculatores*: they were distracting the people from what really mattered, namely from business. The city council of Bologna therefore expressly ordered that 'French players shall in no circumstances be allowed to sing in the squares of the city'.[25] Respectable citizens disapproved of these *saltatores, balatores, thymelici, nugatores, scurrae, bufones, gladiatores, praestigatores, palestritae*, or whatever else they called these people who made a living by amusing the masses.[26] Three of them once called on Count Guido Guerra asking for lodging and a tip in exchange for a performance. But the Count was not amused—at least

not in the way they expected, for he had his own rough kind
of humour. The first was called 'The Magpie' because of his
propensity for stealing, and the Count made him flap about
like a bird; the second, who was called 'Malanotte', the Count
took literally and put him out on the roof for a night in the
rain; and the third, 'Maldecorpo' or 'Pain in the Body'—
'Pain in the Neck' as we might say—he obliged to stand so
close to the fire that he got roasted. That was the way to deal
with these fellows.[27] Salimbene was proud of his musical
uncle: 'a friendly and sociable man, a connoisseur of wine,
and a fine singer and string-player—*non tamen joculator*'[28]—he
was no strolling player! Yet only fifty years before, St Francis
had not hesitated to call himself the *joculator Domini*, 'the
Lord's clown'; but times had changed since then.

What exactly the songs of the *joculatores* contained, apart
from a very few quotations from them, almost entirely eludes
us, since no one ever bothered to write them down. But it is
fairly certain that most of it was pretty vulgar stuff. Rough
humour appeals to the masses in every age, and it may be
supposed that it was even more coarse in the Middle Ages than
it is today. The kind of thing is perhaps illustrated in a so-called
sonnet by the Florentine Filippo Rustico, which, however, we
must remember was 'refined' compared to the humour of the
strolling players. The writer is mocking at the appearance of a
fellow citizen, who was known as '*Messerino*' or the 'Little
Mister':

> Quando Dio messere Messerino fecie,
> bene si credette fare grande maravilglia,
> ch' uciello e bestia ed uomo ne sodisfecie,
> c' a ciascheduna natura s'apilglia.
>
> Chè nel gozzo anigrottolo contrafecie,
> e ne le reni giraffa s'asomilglia,
> ed uomo seria, secondo che si dicie,
> ne la piagiente sua ciera vermilglia.
>
> Ancora riscembra corbo nel cantare,
> ed è diritta bestia nel savere,
> ed uomo è sumilgliato al vestimento.

Quando Dio il fece, poco avea che fare,
ma volle dimostrare lo suo potere:
si strana cosa fare ebe in talento. [29]

When Messer Messerino was by God Almighty made,
    That here there was a marvel sprang to every mind,
That bird and beast and human in one should be displayed,
    And every kind of creature in one should be combined.

When he made his neck, then, a duck has been portrayed,
    But then he's quite giraffe-like, if looked at from behind;
His face is nearly human, if it's true what has been said,
    And scarlet in its colouring, but pleasant of its kind.

And when you hear him singing, it reminds you of a crow,
    And then he has the wisdom of the livestock on a farm;
        But when he puts his clothes on, he looks quite like a man.

For God at his creation had time to spare, and so
    To show just what he could do, would not do any harm.
        And can he make a joke too? Yes, of course he can.

This man Filippo Rustico came from the common people:
his father belonged to the silk workers' guild, and he is one of
small and sturdy group of poets who represent the atmosphere
of the north Italian cities much better than do the court poets
or the refined adherents of the *dolce stil nuovo*. They stood for a
kind of reaction, with a deliberate roughness, against the
highbrows and the polished style of the poetic aristocracy that
had come into being. The most important of them is Cecco
Angiolieri of Siena, of whose life we only know the seamy side:
runaways, revolts, prison, escapes and so forth, until a little
after 1300, when he died. He was in love with Becchina, the
shoemaker's daughter, but this was not the strongest passion in
his heart, which was his hatred of his father which developed
into a hatred of the world in general. Then suddenly he discovered that he could give vent to his feelings in verse and
that he could tell the truth in rhyme just as well as other people
uttered their flatteries. Cecco threw all restraint to the winds
and became an Italian version—and these were rare—of

the completely uninhibited vagrants north of the Alps. No one
was to have any illusions about him:

Da la cima del capo 'infin al   From the top of my head to
   suolo   my soles
Cosa non regna 'in me che   Nought there is of good in
   bona sia.   me.

Nor need anybody think that he had any desire for a respectable
citizen's life; his desires were of a different kind:

> Tre cose solamente mi son in grado,
> le quali posso non ben ben fornire:
> ciò è la donna, la taverna e 'l dado:
> queste mi fanno 'l cuor lieto sentire.[31]

> Three things alone my pleasure can advance,
>   Of which there never are enough for me,
> And these are women, drink and games of chance:
>   With these alone my heart can merry be.

Whenever the old man Angiolieri made any difficulties about
his ne'er-do-well son's realisation of his desires, Cecco went
wild with rage. But these outbreaks of versified rage were not
entirely new. Girardo Pateg, the rhetorician, in his *Book of
Boredom*, had many violent things to say of his contemporaries:

> Si me noja, non so che mi facia![32]
> If anyone bores me, I know not what I do!

Cino da Pistoia also had his bad moods:

> E piacemi veder colpi di spada
> altrui nel viso, e navi andare al fondo,
> e piacemi veder Neron secondo
> e che ogni bella donna fosse lada.[33]

> I like to see a swinging sword cut deep
> Across a human face; and ships go down.
> I wish another Nero on the world,
> And ugliness on every pretty girl.

Cecco Angiolieri is more suggestive in his use of words, and sometimes a certain primitive terror is evoked:

> S' io fossi fuoco, arderei lo mondo,
> s' io fossi vento, io 'l tempesterei,
> s' io fossi acqua, io l'allagherei,
> s' io fossi Iddio, lo mander' in profondo.
>
> S' io fossi Papa, allor sare' giocondo
> chè tutti i Cristian tribolerei,
> s' io fossi Imperador, sai che farei?
> A tutti mosserei lo capo a tondo.
>
> S' io fossi Morte, io n' andre' da mio padre,
> s' io fossi Vita, non stare' con lui,
> e similmente farei a mia madre.
>
> S' io fossi Cecco, com' io sono e fui,
> torrei per me le giovane leggiadre,
> e brutt' e vecchie lascerei altrui.[34]

> If I were fire, the whole world I would burn,
> If I were wind, I'd be a hurricane,
> If I were water, bring the flood again,
> If I were God, the world to hell I'd turn.
>
> If I were Pope, I'd make it my concern
> To see the whole of Christendom in pain,
> If I were Emperor, what would be my gain?
> I'd cut off everybody's head in turn.
>
> If I were Death, I'd soon my father meet,
> If I were Life, I'd quickly come away,
> My mother in the same way I would treat.
>
> If I were Cecco, as I am today,
> I'd capture every woman young and sweet,
> And leave the ugly ones to take who may.

In the *Duecento* there were also a few women who wrote poetry. There must have been some among the many graceful ladies courted by the Provençals, and there was certainly the young 'Compiuta' in Florence, who wrote a few sonnets of genuine feeling, hoping that her father would not forbid her to leave this evil world. What the reaction of the men was to her writing is not known, but poetry was not generally regarded as a feminine accomplishment. A certain Master Torrigiano, a teacher in Bologna, pays somewhat oblique compliments to certain women poets: first he addresses them with no less a title than that of '*divina Sibilla*', but then adds that a woman writing poetry is a rare thing, as rare as a horse that plays the lyre. . . .[35]

As the century drew to a close there begins to appear something like genuine folk songs and folk poetry. In the documents drawn up by a notary of Bologna in the '80s we find repeatedly verses and dancing songs scribbled in the margins. This is the famous *Memoriale* of Bologna. It is evident that the people, since the French singers had been expressly excluded, were producing their own popular ballads and satires. They must surely be of a higher quality than the pieces produced by the *ioculatores*, their form has a certain refinement and their language is more or less fluent. In contrast to the mannered sonnets of Filippo Rustico and Cecco Angiolieri the *Memoriale* of Bologna shows some spontaneous poetry, which doubtless was sung and often danced. There are love songs, dialogues, especially between mother and daughter about the choice of a husband, laments of deserted wives and so on, in fact the perennial themes. There is a special charm about the little song about the nightingale which flew away:

For de la bella gaiba fuge lo lusignolo.	From out the cage so comely Flew the nightingale.
Plange lo fantino, perochè non trova lo so osilino ne la gaiba nova, e dice cum dolo,	The little boy is weeping Because he cannot find In the cage so comely His little bird confined, And speaking through his weeping,
chi gli avrì l'usolo?	He asked, where can he be?

For de la bella gaiba
fuge lo lusignolo.

For from the cage so comely
Had flown his nightingale.

E in un boschetto
se mise ad andare,
sentì l'osoletto
sì dolce cantare.
Oi bel lusignolo
torna nel mio broylo.

But one day in the spinney
When passing by he heard
A-singing oh so sweetly
There his little bird.
O nightingale my lovely,
Come back now to me.

For de la bella gaiba
fuge lo lusignolo.[36]

But from the cage so comely
Had gone the nightingale.

These are the first small fruits of the mighty harvest that the next century would bring, and indeed they hardly belong any more to the *Duecento*: their pattern shows the beginning of the new generation. The song books of the *Trecento* are full of such songs with their quick rhythms and returning rhymes. But maybe they are a sign not merely of the loss of a nightingale but of the loss of the medieval spirit.

12

The Heavenly Lovers

Amor dolce senza pare—

se' tu Christo per amare.

In this sweet love beyond compare
Christ himself through love is there.

Hymn from Cortona[1]

IF WE would understand something of the songs of heavenly love of the *Duecento* we must go back to a certain Christmas night in the hills above Rieti. We must follow the little group of ragged men, toiling barefoot up the narrow path between the rocks. It is Francis and his friends; long ago they have left the valley below, where the people are celebrating the feast in an earthy way. They are going up to spend Christmas in the wild solitude of the caves of Greccio.

At Greccio there is a little hermitage, roughly cut out of the wall of rock and commanding a magnificent view over the Appenine country, to one side towards Lazio with all the remembrances of the classical world, and on the other side Umbria of the mystics. It is symbolic of the *Duecento*, with both the classics and the mystics in its view.

St Francis loved Greccio and perhaps the fact that the ideal of poverty survived in this hermitage is due to its privileged position as a favourite retreat of the holy founder. For when the troubles came after his death and the purity of the ideal was threatened it was to this little hermitage that the best elements of the 'spiritual' party fled, the *'tres socii'*, the 'three friends' of the saint, Ruffino, Angelo and Leo, who were being thrust aside during the troubles, as well as the minister-general John of Parma, who had been removed because of his Joachite ideas. Greccio must also have been the scene of the moving legend of Francis's marriage to Lady Poverty.[2] When she arrived (the legend runs) the brethren received her with great honours, offered her water in a broken dish to wash her hands and one of their habits to dry them on, for at Greccio there was no dish that was intact, nor any towels. When she sat down at the little stone table the brethren went out to collect a few herbs to give more taste to the dry bread of the wedding feast, and at night the only bed they could prepare was a clearing on the bare ground. This was a welcome after Lady Poverty's heart. When in the morning she was about to leave she asked if she might see their friary. They took her out of the cave and stood with her on the hillside overlooking the hills and valleys: 'This is our cloister-garth, my lady,' they said.[3]

This, then, is Greccio, and here on that Christmas night, only a few years before the death of Francis, the little group of ragged friends arrived after toiling barefoot up the narrow path. Here Francis saw the cave of Greccio as if it were the cave of Bethlehem, which he had recently visited, and here he put up a crib for the Child Jesus—the beginning of the romance of Christmas which has become the heritage of Europe, not perhaps the first Christmas crib ever made, but certainly the one that fired Europe's imagination.[4] The rest of the legend is well known: the brethren sang the night office of Christmas and 'as their voices rang through the silent woods, the rocks joined in their rejoicing by echoing the sound. The brethren were singing God's praises and the night was filled with song. The holy man put on his deacon's vestments (for this was his part in tonight's High Mass) and sang the

Christmas gospel with wonderful devotion: his voice was strong and sweet and clear, and summoned everyone to join him in praise . . .'[5] Then he preached, and every time he uttered the name of Jesus he appeared overwhelmed with love and seemed to savour the sweet sound upon his lips. Everyone then saw him turn towards the crib, and there in the crib lay a little boy, asleep. Francis bent down and took him in his arms. The little boy woke up, looked at Francis and smiled . . .

The intimacy of this event remained hovering over the whole century. It is there in Jacopone's famous *Laude* on the Nativity:

L'amor m' encende tanto,	Fired is my heart by his love,
ch' en carne me s' è dato;	To earth he came to save me;
terrollome abracciato,	I hold him in close embrace,
ch' è fatto mio fratello,	Who has become my brother,
o dolce garzoncello,	O sweet my little brother,
en cor t' ho conceputo.[6]	In love my heart conceived thee.

Here is the first ecstasy of the Italian Christmas carol. We find it again in the carol book of Cortona:

Christ took birth upon this earth
To save our human kin,
When all our race was lost to grace
By our first parents' sin.[7]

The same ecstasy is found in the frescoes of Giotto and his school when they depict Christmas, be it at Bethlehem or at Greccio. The originality of this Franciscan view of Christmas is the emphasis upon the Child of Bethlehem as one of us, 'my little brother', lying there between the ox and the ass. For all his heavenly majesty in the old ikons and mosaics, he is now our 'little brother', be it at Bethlehem or Greccio. The new emphasis is on the humanity of our divine Saviour and this is first shown among works of art in the crucifixes of Umbria and Tuscany.

The crucifix that spoke to St Francis is still to be seen at San Damiano: the stylised figure of Christ stands rather than hangs upon the cross; the cross itself is bright with colours and there is room for the figures of saints chattering peacefully; Christ stands there, a tranquil figure, with the wide still eyes of the Lombard tradition. But scarcely had this crucifix uttered the command to Francis, 'Go and rebuild my house', when Francis and his friars went out and brought a new piety into the hearts of the faithful, with a new and dynamic emotion, and at once the crucifixes become different: the divine tranquillity becomes overshadowed by the human pain. There is a desperate harshness about the Franciscan crucifixes of the *Duecento*, which sometimes offends the eyes of those of us brought up with the crucifixes of the late Renaissance. Here it is the Son of Man, looking like any lean workman of the Appenines, but stretched and racked in the struggle with death. The primitive anatomy of the naked body is still a heritage of romanesque sculpture, but what is new is the movement, the twisted torment, the desperation. 'There is no beauty in him, nor comeliness.' This was how the people of the *Duecento*, so often scourged by war and pestilence, so often oppressed and full of anxious dread, the world of the flagellants, saw their Saviour and found consolation.

Giunta Pisano, who worked round 1235, is the most important painter of crucifixes at this time. In his compositions there is still a certain tranquillity, which shows him as the fellow citizen of Niccolò Pisano; but at the same time there is a dramatic quality which made him the favourite painter of Umbria. These things make him one of the most characteristic painters of the period before Cimabue. But as the century moved on the straight lines of the old crucifixes became too stiff for the newer and more emotional painters; the outstretched arms are raised and the whole body is tensed as with a cry of pain. But this is a Franciscan posture: thus stood Francis as he received the stigmata, and thus his children stand when they recite their 'cross prayers' with uplifted arms.

Pictures of the Madonna were also becoming more natural. There was at the beginning still something of the stylised Byzantine manner, but gradually there appears a motherly quality that at first seems strange to them. With Florentine painters our Lady strokes the little foot of the Child, who is now no longer a hieratic little king, but is a real lovable child; or she points out to him a little bird; though we still see her looking majestically towards the faithful. Yet after the events at Greccio, our Lady herself becomes more one of us; she is given youthful grace and the painters were beginning to give her all that their ideal of womanly beauty could provide. This way of painting our Lady has remained with us ever since.

Next to our Lady and her Child we now find among the accompanying saints a new figure: that of St Francis. He appears for the first time at the Sacro Speco of the Benedictines at Subiaco; he is portrayed without stigmata or halo. It is possible that this picture was painted in his lifetime and there are those who think that in this young man with fair hair and a shy expression we have an authentic portrait of the saint. But we have to admit that the picture, obviously by the same artist and only a few feet away, representing the lusty Pope Gregory IX, is so similar that we are forced to suppose that lifelike portraiture is not to be found here, and indeed is hardly to be expected in the *Duecento*. That it is Francis here we know only through the inscription; in all later pictures the stigmata become the indentifying symbols of the saint, however he may otherwise be represented, even looking like a Greek patriarch. In the pictures he always shows the stigmata, as much as in real life he tried to hide them. His picture is often surrounded by small scenes from his life, how he preached to the birds, or drove out evil spirits, or received the wounds from a seraph.

Throughout the century there were various lesser masters who did paintings of saints. The names of most of them are unknown, though as painting became more consciously a profession they did begin to sign their work. Thus we have the Florentine Coppo di Marcovaldo and his son Salerno, and a fellow from Pisa known as the '*prete insalato*', then there is Guido of Siena, the Berlinghieri, a family of painters, and one of the first painters of St Francis, Margaritone of Arezzo. At Spoleto a certain Renaldictus was copying the manner of Giunta Pisano, while at Subiaco Master Conxulos was painting such lively figures that they looked as if they would leap off the walls.[8] These minor masters are in general more typical of the art of the northern cities than are the three giants who together show the whole genius of the century: Cavallini at first, then Cimabue, and finally Giotto.

In the work of the first two of these there is still evidence of a reaction: Cavallini came from Rome, where tradition was inflexible, and in reaction to this he was more supple than the dispassionate Cimabue from turbulent Florence. At Santa Maria in Trastevere in about 1290 he made his mosaic of the three Kings, rather shy-looking, and the Child eagerly stretching out his hands to the gold, frankincense and myrrh. When he turned to painting, at first in Rome and then at Assisi, his figures become much more free, as with the apostles for instance, or Esau deceiving his father, when he makes special use of the flash of the white of the eyes; his Rebecca in the upper basilica at Assisi is one of the most tense figures of a woman ever painted. The other great master, Cenno di Pepo, called Cimabue, is really still within the Byzantine tradition. His Madonnas indeed have the dark almond-shaped eyes of Umbria and Tuscany, but there is something impersonal about their glance; the Child is never quite childlike, and the angels, arranged in careful patterns, are really little more than decorations. The enormous *Deesis* in the cathedral at Pisa, which he must have done during the last years of his life, although it is less oriental than the Christ at Monreale, is more abstract. A whole school was to pursue his stylised ideal, with Duccio di Buoninsegna being perhaps the most important member. But the generation that followed was already transferring its favour from the hieratic style of Cimabue to the lively rhythms of Giotto:

> Credette Cimabue ne la pintura
> tener lo campo, e ora ha Giotto il grido,
> sì che la fama di colui è scura.[9]

> In painting Cimabue made a claim
> to hold the field, but Giotto's name is now
> the cry, and faded is the former fame.

With Giotto di Bondone comes finally the achievement of uniting the classical *majestas* with the simplicity of the Franciscan spirit. On the walls of Assisi, Padua and Florence he painted his wonderful blue skies as a background for his gentle figures with their rich, soft lines and smoothly blending tones. Angels and saints assume a kind of Florentine grace, and their figures hitherto bound to rigid conventions assume a fresh individuality: Mary, the great Lady, absorbed in gazing at her little Son, or Judas, the depraved miscreant, busy kissing his Master. All this, however, occurs on the threshold of the new century, when only too soon Francis the beggar-man will be turned into the delicate aristocrat of Gozzoli and Della Robbia. Giotto stands at the end of an age, that was also the beginning of a new; but he was still in the tradition of Greccio.

At Greccio, Francis sang the Christmas gospel in the ancient Latin of the liturgy, but he also began something new: the love song of heavenly love. Francis has been called a troubadour, a minstrel, for throughout his life he was uttering poems and singing songs. He certainly began as a troubadour, but after his conversion from rich young man to beggar he equally deliberately descended the social scale, and from being a genuine troubadour he became a common strolling player: *'joculator Domini'* he called himself, 'God's clown'. Did he not sing in the piazza at Assisi when he begged for stones to rebuild San Damiano?

> Qui mihi dederit unum lapidem, unum habebit mercedem;
> Qui mihi dederit duos, duos habebit.[10]

> Whoever gives me one stone, will get just one reward;
> Whoever gives me two—gets two.

God's fool, indeed. Nevertheless, his love for the *gaya scienza* retained its pure chivalrous character right to the end. The stories of chivalry, the true minstrels' stock in trade, were often on his lips and he frequently speaks their language:

> Tanto è il bene ch' io   So great the heavenly joy I
>   m'aspetto,   see,
> che ogni pena m' è diletto.[11]   That earthly pain is sweet
>   to me.

That is in the tradition of the serenade, the love song of the troubadours and there is a little-known chapter of the *Fioretti*, perhaps more characteristic than authentic, where he speaks in the tradition of chivalry in praise of *la cortesia*: 'Courtesy,' he says, 'is a property of God, who gives his sunshine and his rain to good and bad alike, because he is courteous; and courtesy is the sister of charity, because it prevents hatred and preserves love.'[12] It was probably on account of his love for this tradition of chivalry that he preferred to speak Provençal to the end of his life—or was it the *langue d'oeil?*—even though his biographers tell us that he did not speak it perfectly.[13] He also sang French songs when he first set out to live as a beggar[14] and again when he began the rebuilding of the ruined chapel.[15] Later, when the fire of love burned so fiercely within him that he was compelled to give expression to it in song, Thomas of Celano tells us that 'the sweet music of the Holy Spirit that was singing within him would frequently break forth from him in French'.[16] It was also said of him that when he was in ecstasy he sometimes seized a piece of stick from the ground and began to wield it as if he were playing the viol, but, Thomas adds at once, 'most of those merry dances usually ended in tears'.[17] There was also the great occasion when 'suddenly an angel appeared to him in great splendour, and he had a viol in his left hand and a bow in his right. Francis stood there and watched with astonishment. Then the angel placed the tip of his bow on the strings and began to play, whereupon such was the sweetness of the melody that overwhelmed the spirit of Francis that he was rapt away from bodily sensation; and, as he himself afterwards told his friends, he thought that if the angel had bowed the down-stroke also, the sweetness would have been so unbearable as to sever his soul from his body.'[18] On another occasion another unearthly musician played to Francis on the zither as he lay ill one night at Rieti, and one of the brethren, afraid to make a noise, had refused to play to him: 'there was no one to be seen, but from the sound of the music one could easily distinguish the movements of the musician as he went up and down'.[19] It is a matter for theologians and philosophers to decide how far the special character of the visions of a mystic are in harmony with his own nature. But the fact remains that such musical manifestations are claimed for few saints as much as they are for this singer of Umbria, who began in the Provençal tradition of song, and who sang of 'Sister Death' at the end.[20] How else should he die but singing a psalm?[21] Meanwhile, above the little hut the larks were singing in the sky, and 'while they sang, they formed a circle as for a dance'.[22]

For Francis music was not just a pastime: it was an apostolate. He explains to three of his companions, the ex-troubadour Pacificus among them, that he was sending them out to win men's souls by song, for 'what are God's servants if not his musicians, sent to raise men's hearts to heavenly joy?'[23]

When a man is a saint and an artist who sees his mission in this way we might expect many songs of him. Perhaps there were indeed many, and a later biographer tells us of many such compositions that Francis himself is supposed to have written;[24]

Jncipiūt laudes creaturarū qs fecit beat[us]
fra̅ciscus. ad laude z honore dei. cū eet i firmit apud
scm damianū. +

Canticū frı̅s solis

Altissimu onnipotente bonsignore. tue

sole laude la gloria el honore z onne
Ad te solo altissimo se
Konfano. z nullu homo
ene dignu te mētouare
benedictione.

Laudato sie mısıgnore cū tucte le tue crea
ture. spetialmēte messor lo frē sole. loqua
le iorno z allumini noi p loi. Et ellu ebella
eradiante cū grande splendore. de te altiss
mo porta significatiōe. Laudato sı mısıgnore
p sora luna ele stelle. in celu lai formate
clarite z ptiose z belle. Laudato sı mısıgre
p frē uēto z aere z nubilo z sereno z onne
tēpo. p loquale ale tue creature dai sustēta
mēto. Laudato sı mısıgnore p sor aqua. la
quale emulto utile z humile z ptiosa z casta.
Laudato sı mısıgnore p frē focu. p loquale
ennallumini la nocte. edello ebello z iucūdo
z robustoso z forte. Laudato sı mısıgnore p
sora mā matre tra. la quale ne sustenta
z gouerna. z pduce diusi fructi cō coloriti
flori z herba. Laudato sı mısıgnore p quelli
Ke pdonano p lo tuo amore. z sostengo in
firmitate z tribulatione. beati quelli Ke
sosterrano ipace. Ka da te altissimo sirano
incoronati. Laudato sı mısıgnore p sora
nostra morte corpale. da la quale nullu
bō uiuēte poskappare. guai acquelli Ke
morrano ne le pcrata mortali. beati quel
li Ke trouarano le tue stissime uolūtati.
Ka la morte secūda nol farra male. Lau
date z bndicete mısıgnore z rēgratiate
z seruiate li cū grande humilitate.

Most high, omnipotent, good Lord,
Thine are praise, glory, honour and every blessing,
To thee alone, most high, do they belong,
And no man is worthy to speak thy name.

Praise to thee, my Lord, with all thy creatures,
Especially Sir Brother Sun,
Who brings the day, through whom thou bringest light,
Who is beautiful and radiant with great splendour;
Of thee, most high, he is a sign.

Praise to thee, my Lord, for Sister Moon and the stars,
In the sky thou hast formed them, bright and precious and beautiful.

Praise to thee, my Lord, for Brother Wind,
And for the air and cloud, clear sky and every weather,
By which thou givest sustenance to all thy creatures.

Praise to thee, my Lord, for Sister Water,
Who is most useful, humble, precious and chaste.

Praise to thee, my Lord, for Brother Fire,
By whom thou dost illuminate the night,
And he is beautiful and merry, robust and strong.

Praise to thee, my Lord, for our sister, Mother Earth,
Who sustains and keeps us,
And produces divers fruits with coloured flowers and grass.

Praise to thee, my Lord, for those who forgive for love of thee,
And who bear infirmity and trouble;
Blest are those who will in peace abide,
For by thee, most high, they shall be crowned.

Praise to thee, my Lord, for our Sister Death, in this body,
From whom no living man can find escape;
Woe to them who die in mortal sin,
Blest are they who are found in thy most holy will,
For the second death shall do to them no harm.

Praise and bless my Lord and give him thanks,
And serve him with great humility.   Amen.

in fact, some Latin *laudi*, in the style of the Psalms, have been preserved. But of the semi-improvised hymns in the French or Italian vernacular, such as we might expect from a *joculator Domini*, only one has been handed down and this is the famous *Cantico del Sole*, the *Canticle of the Sun*.[25]

There is now not much doubt that the 'Canticle of Brother Sun', or the *Laudes creaturarum*, the 'Praise of all Creation', as it is also called, is an authentic work of St Francis. There is still discussion among the experts about the original form of the poem and about its Biblical themes. But what is more important is that we have not got the melody to which the saint sang it. That there was a melody is certain and the oldest manuscript is a witness to this, for at the top there are the lines of a musical staff, alas with no notes written in.[26] Without its tune it is only half a song; even so it is a precious heritage and a document of the Franciscan spirit. Francis sang the song a year before his death, after a night of joy and pain at San Damiano. We must not forget that this rejoicing over the sun and moon, and wind and water, was that of a sick man, almost blind, and confined by infirmity between the narrow walls of a little garden, with just the view over the valley which he could hardly see.

The *Canticle of the Sun* is the first echo of Greccio. It faded out; but one thing is certain, that without Francis the poetry and music of that dark *Duecento* would not have been so full.

First, there are the moralists. They used the vernacular because they wanted to reach the masses, to whom they offered their advice in jingling rhymes. They were a kind of pious rhetoricians, and the series begins with the gloomy Girardo Pateg, who utters warnings against earthly love, without ever, it seems, giving a thought to the heavenly:

E questo ben saçatelo,	Now gentlemen, listen,
segnori veramente:	This well you must know:
qi de cor ama femena,	If you're off with a woman,
molto tardo se pente.[27]	Repentance is slow.

Rhymsters such as Pietro Barsegapè were fond of edifying simple folk with benign platitudes:

No è cosa in sto mundo,	There is one thing in this world
tal è lla mia credença,	I'm a great believer in,
ki se possa fenir,	That there's nothing you can finish,
se la no se comença.[28]	Unless you first begin.

To the same group belongs Brother Bonvesin da Riva, of the Humiliati, whose verses we have already quoted. His most important work is a devout epic, interesting mainly because it is a description of a journey through hell and heaven, and in that sense is a predecessor of the *Divina Commedia*. There the likeness stops abruptly, for Bonvesin was no visionary, had no understanding of symbolism at all, and was certainly not a poet: he was a preacher in verse. But he enjoyed his preaching, and particularly in his 'Black Scripture' or description of hell he possessed a kind of crude humour, of which this account of Beelzebub's kitchen, where the damned were roasted, is an example:

Ke lo meto a rostir com' un bel porco al fogo,
en un gran spe de fer per farlo tosto cosro,
e po prendo acqua e sal e caluçem e vin
e fel e forte aseo, tosego e venin . . .[29]

So I put him like pork on a good iron spit,
And in front of the fire I then roast him a bit,
And then salt and water and calcium rub in,
Adding poison and vinegar, wine and toxin. . . .

After this it is pleasant to reach Paradise, where all is golden and fragrant. Bonvesin had a colleague, the Franciscan Jacomino of Verona, who uses the same theme in a similar way. But every now and then he rises to a level of poetry which is beyond the usual capacity of his milieu:

El par ke tut' el celo, le aere e le contrae,
sia plene de strumenti con voxe melodiae.[30]

> All the land and air and heaven seemed to be
> Full of instruments with voice of melody.

But it was not these moralists who were to point the way to the solitary summit later reached by Dante. We must seek the thirteenth-century preparation for his coming elsewhere. Moralising rarely achieves grandeur; still more seldom does it touch poetry. The beginnings of sacred poetry are to be discerned elsewhere, in that period of panic among the common people in the middle of the century when a genuine poetic spirit appears in simple guise among the simple folk.

It is quite remarkable how within a period of about fifty years the whole land became seized with poetry and song. The poets and the composers are unknown, and the singers even as they sang remained anonymous; but there are the songs, on the vellum of the local hymn books, presenting a quality that no Italian musician of a later age could have bettered. The songs are about the saints, about the life of our Lord, and about the love of God, and they often show a true poetic feeling. Is this authentic folk song? There were, of course, the songs that were sung in the fields and in the farmhouse, but these are not the *Laudes* of the *Duecento*; the latter almost always have a precise form and their content reveals a theological basis. It is more probable that many of them were written by local chaplains of confraternities where they were sung, or sometimes by some better-read citizen, such as Garço Dottore, the notary of Cortona, whom some claim to be the great-grandfather of Petrarca. At the same time the *laudi* have not the refinement of the Sicilian minstrels, nor that of the *dolce stil nuovo*; rhythm and metre are not developed, the choice of words is stereotyped and the Biblical quotations are garbled. Moreover, the language itself was still very unstable, on the one hand falling back into vulgar Latin and on the other hand slipping into clumsy dialect. But all through there is the restlessness of a people torn between the gentleness of Francis and the severity of the flagellants:

Praised be holy Francis,
Who appeared crucified
Like to our Redeemer.[31]

And at the opposite pole:

I pray you all,
Do penance here;
Before the judgement
Live in fear.[32]

The *laudi* can certainly be regarded as folk song and among the best folk songs of Europe. From the hill country of Urbino a lament has been preserved, which can be placed alongside the *Canticle of the Sun*. Like the canticle (and hundreds of others) no tune has come down to us, but also like the canticle the lament of Urbino has a feeling for the universality of nature and is a call to all creation to join not in rejoicing but in mourning at the death of Christ:

Planga la terra, planga lo mare,	Weep o earth, and weep o sea,
planga lo pesce che sa notare,	Weep o fish that swim in thee,
plangan le bestie nel pascolare,	Weep o beasts that grazing be,
plangan l'aucelli nel lor volare.	Weep o birds that fly so free.
Plangano flumi e rigarelli,	Weep o rivers, weep o screes,
plangano pietre e arvoscelli,	Weep o brooks, and weep o trees,
tucti faççamo planti novelli,	Let us make new melodies,
edd io dolente più ke kivelli.	I have greater pain than these.
Planga lo sole, planga la luna,	Weep o moon, and weep o sun,
planga planeta onenessuna,	Weep o planets every one,
l'aire, lo foco cum façça bruna	Air and fire, be not outdone,
siano a lo planto ke ss' araduna.	Join the weeping now begun.
Planga lo bene, planga lo male,	Weep o sad, and weep o gay,
planga la gente tucta ad uguale,	Weep o folk of everyday,
mort' è lo rege celestiale	Heaven's King in mortal fray
e no de morte sua naturale.[33]	Violently has passed away.

It is not surprising that this century, which had so prolonged a Gethsemani and Golgotha itself, should experience its deepest feelings at Passiontide. It is the hymns of the Passion that are

the greatest treasures of the Cortona hymn book, a special
virtue of which is that the melodies are given throughout.[34]
Margherita, who was the central figure of the piety of
Cortona, lived entirely by the Passion of Christ, and in her
visions followed the Way of the Cross in its every phase. The
power of such experience cannot fail to have touched the
brethren of the Third Order, from whose midst came the
Laudesi di Santa Maria in San Francesco. Among their
Passion hymns is one which with its emotional refrain and its
lines of Gregorian recitative is not surpassed by any of the
abundant Italian cantatas of later centuries:

At the cruel death of our Saviour
All men bitter lament shall make him.

When the Jews came to Christ and found him,
Then on ev'ry side they surround him,
And by his hands they firmly bound him,
As a common robber they take him.[35]

It is as if a miracle had occurred in that little town of Cortona
on its hilltop; forty-five jewels of melody were collected there
and sung until the manuscript was worn out. In the next
century the manuscript was lost, until in 1875 a librarian found
it among the peat and firewood in a cupboard under the stairs
in the municipal library. But another fifty years were to pass
before the melodies were gradually deciphered from the
tattered pages, transcribed and published. In 1934 an official
edition appeared which although not perfect is a valuable
contribution to our knowledge of Italian culture of the time.[36]

It is difficult to decide which of all the melodies of the
Cortona manuscript are most typical of thirteenth-century
music. There is the charming Invitatory in honour of our
Lady:

O come and sing the praises,
Which a loving voice raises,
To our own beloved Virgin Mary.[37]

And there is the song of Magdalene, which nowadays looks
more an instrumental than a vocal line:

Magda—lena degna da laudare

sempre degge Dio per noi pregare.

> Magdalena, thou our praises leading,
> Always for us to God interceding.[38]

Gradually the poetry of the *laudesi* was becoming more personal and emotional. At the beginning of the fourteenth century the Pisa manuscript was put together and is now kept in Paris.[39] Once more the musical staves at the headings are empty and we shall never know the tunes which made these ecstatic poems comprehensible, or at least acceptable to the businessmen of Pisa as they stood round the lectern singing out of this large book. The anonymous poet—some think it was Jacopone da Todi[40] who here pours out his love in song, is so carried away that song is not enough: he must dance, too:

Nollo pensai gia mai,	I never thought before,
Ihesu, di dansar alla dansa,	My Jesus, I should dance,
ma la tua innamoranza,	But you gave me the chance
Ihesu, si llo mi fece fare.	To dance for love of you.
Non vi meravigliate,	You will not feel surprise
s' io alla dansa dansai,	If dancing I should go,
alli dolci miei frati	Amid my brothers rise
si mmi mossi et andai;	And caper to and fro;
poi dissi 'nnamorati:	So lovers I advise
Or dansate oramai.	To go and dance also.
Gia non mi ricordai,	I now can think no more
si fu intrato alla dansa,	When I began to dance:
tutti senti allegransa,	O happy circumstance,
Ihesu, non si poria contare.[41]	I danced so long for you.

It must be admitted that the still young Italian language was not yet capable of expressing fully the poet's feeling, and it would be difficult to put such a piece down as folk song. The same applies to the following verse of a *laude* from Pisa, exalting the difficulty of the Christian vocation:

Et chi è illustrato,	Whoever walks in light,
si porti la croce,	If he carries his cross,
sera condennato	May yet be condemned
se non rende luce;	If he doesn't *shine* his light;
chi a questo stato	And whoever reaches this state,
Cristo lo conduce	Brought by Chirst,
metta sì gran voce	Should shout so loudly
che muoia d'amore.[42]	Of his love, as to die of it.

Among all these singers of heavenly love the final place of honour must go to one who has been many times quoted: Jacopone da Todi.[43]

Seven years after the great year of the flagellants there was a disaster at Todi: during a wedding feast a gallery in the hall collapsed. Amid the shouting and confusion of the escaping guests, there was a piercing cry of distress. It was the cry of a young man who found that the one victim who lay dead among the debris was his wife. Until that day he had been known as Jacomo Benedetti, the advocate. From now on he became Jacopone, the ne'er-do-well.

There is a picture of him in the cathedral at Prato, a man who looks crazed with grief, with wasted features and eyes burning in their sunken sockets, holding a book of his poems, open at the passage:

> Ke farai, Frate Japone?
> Hor se' giunto al paraone.[44]
>
> What will you do, Fra Jacopone?
> Now you have come to the trial.

Ke farai? After the disaster of the wedding feast he never did know; and henceforth his life revolved round the contradiction of man's helpless ignorance and God's almighty wisdom. At one stroke the confident pride of the rich intellectual in the simple little country town was destroyed. This is all that we know about him. And his wife? In none of his poems does he even mention her in a single word; the story of the collapse of the gallery might be a legend composed by an unreliable biographer a century and a half after his death. In reality we do not need any motive to explain the conversion of the gifted, sensual man educated in Bologna. Was he not an Umbrian? The way to madness was more natural to him than the cheap, golden mean. But he pursued this way so passionately that even his own fellow-countrymen were horrified. One day he was rich and respectable and the next day he was coursing through the town in a rough tunic wailing and lamenting; he not only gave up his wealth, he literally threw it at his friends who had come to reason with him. Once in order to bring home to people the transitory nature of all wordly things he walked into a banquet all tarred and feathered, and another time he crawled across the piazza on all fours wearing the harness of a donkey. The townsfolk may be forgiven for having thought all this was strange. But in all his craziness he had found himself as a poet:

Quando jubilo se scalda,	When joy is kindled,
si fa l'uomo cantare,	And makes a man sing,
e la lengua barbaglia,	When the tongue gets tangled,
e non so que parlare,	And can't say anything,
dentro non pò celare	Then he still cannot hide
tanto è grande el dolzore.[45]	Such a sweetness within.

This 'holy folly' of his 'song within' drove him on to write his poems, first during his silent years of penance in the friaries and hermitages of the Third Order and then the First Order of St Francis; than during those wild years of the manifesto on behalf of the Colonna, whom he actively supported against Pope Boniface VIII; still during the dark years in the dungeon, where the victorious Pope had thrust him, excommunicated; and finally during his last years, after the death of his opponent, when he was allowed to retire to a quiet friary near Todi.

The extraordinary popularity of this Franciscan rebel is a

remarkable thing, and is perhaps to be explained by the circumstance that he appears to stand alone in giving voice to a spiritual outlook among the simple people of Italy which remained theirs through several centuries—during which his poems were read everywhere—until the new spirituality of the Jesuit and baroque age displaced it. There is also the further fact that apart from the love laments of his last years nearly all his work was addressed to the simple people, who somehow at once recognised themselves in him and knew that he was sincere:

Venite gente a odire	Come o people, come to me,
e stupite del vedere:	Marvel at what here you see:
enferno era l'anema heri,	Then a soul was hell, and burned,
en paradiso oggi è tornata.[46]	Now to heaven is returned.

No one could resist such a confession for everyone knew that this was how the prosperous lawyer had turned into a beggar. He had a great following and a profound spiritual effect upon the people. With his bitter satires on false mystics and unworthy dignitaries, his theological poems which show a fine under-standing, his allegorical teaching of the virtues, he drew the people after him and stripped them naked before their own consciences, and naked therefore before God. A recurrent theme in his poems is death. One of his *laudi* is an imaginary dialogue with a skeleton invited to come out of its tomb, to show how things of this world pass away. Where are your clothes, he asks, your fine blond hair? Your lovely eyes have been eaten by worms, and you could not prevent what they have done to your nose. Your lips have gone, your teeth are bare:

Or ov' è la lingua tanto tagliente?	Where is that tongue with wit so rare?
Apre la bocca: non hai niente![47]	Open your mouth—there's nothing there!

It is a kind of *danse macabre*, which was after all a favourite medieval theme. 'We're galloping all to the same dark tomb,' he tells us,[48] and there is no escape for anyone, knights, women, boys, nuns, priests, whoever they may be. And yet with Jacopone it is not a matter of morbid imagery: his is the voice of a prophet. The year 1260 was indeed past, but Jacopone remains a spiritual son of the Abbot Joachim.

When Jacopone terrifies the people he does not withhold from them God's consolation. From being a herald of doom he becomes a minstrel and then the poet 'Frate Japone' is at his best: he sings of God and all his saints, of our Lady in heaven, and of heaven itself where all the blessed dance to the music of Isaiah, who has assumed the role of a *joculator*. Finally he sings of what he loves best: the love that binds together God and all his creatures. The theme of the love of God is the theme of the Bible, of St Francis, of the theologians, of St Bonaventure with his 'threefold way' and of every mystic; but with Jacopone it becomes a spiritual transport of joy, which he would share with the whole of creation:

> Voglio invitar tutto 'l mondo ad amare,
> le valli e i monti e le gente a cantare,
> l'abisso e i cieli e tutte acque del mare,
> che faccian versi davanti al mio Amore.[49]

All the world I would invite to come and share my love,
The valleys and the mountains and the men to share my song,
The abyss and the heavens; all the waters of the sea,
I would they all would come with me to sing to my Beloved.

This again is the cosmic view which is characteristic of the sacred poets of the *Duecento*. But at the summit of ecstasy Jacopone inevitably stands alone. His love leads him to where words will come no more:

Clama la lengua e 'l core,	My tongue, my heart, are crying,
Amore! Amore! Amore!	My love! My love! My love!
Chi tace el tuo dolzore	If I should cease my sighing,
Lo cor li sia crepato.[50]	My heart will split. My love!

There was still a last battle with Christ: his earthly nature was still fighting back. 'I flee from the Cross that consumes me,'[51] he tries desperately to ward off the fiery arrows of love, but in vain: 'En foco amor mi mise! En foco amor mi mise,'[52]—'Love has set me on fire! Love has set me on fire!' Finally his body surrendered, and sank down to the 'sleep of peace', and his spirit was free. Jacopone's last cries seem to come from eternity:

Amor, non so o' me sia,	My love, where am I now?
Jesù, speranza mia,	Jesus, my hope art thou,
abissame en amore. . . .[53]	Enfold me in thy love. . . .

Some people thinking of Jacopone think at once of the *Stabat Mater*, but it is very unlikely that it is his work:[54] neither the Latin nor the stylised form is at all in his style. Jacopone's own *laude* on the same theme, the *Donna del Paradiso*, is much more important even from a purely literary point of view. In this astonishing poem we can see the transition from the lyric to dramatic dialogue; it has become a passion play in which Mary, the Magdalen, the Jews, the dying Christ, each in turn cry out their strongly dramatic lines.

With this the song of the heavenly lovers, the spiritual *Minnesänger* (minstrels) or troubadours, is turning into something new, something that belongs to the next century. The old community songs were becoming too simple for the new cult of the *bel canto*, and the plain prayer songs of the *Duecento* give place to the *bravura*, virtuoso style of aria, which fill the books of *laudi* of fourteenth-century Florence.[55] But on the other hand, the music became a serious handicap to the actors; so it was given up and the simple rhymes disappeared; more elaborate patterns were devised until the Italian mystery play, the *devozione*, came into being.[56] Poetry adopted a different style, with much more emotion and sentiment, so that in the *devozioni* of the fourteenth century in Umbria that have been preserved[57] kissing and weeping and lamenting are normal devices; at every new event of the Passion 'Mary falls to the ground and remains there for a time'. This exaggerated drama on the one hand and the sheer virtuosity of the song on the other hand destroyed the balance that the *Duecento* knew so well how to hold. For the art of the common people in the last decades of the *Duecento* had reached a summit. It remained for one poet to gather together the thoughts and prayers of those hundred years, and with the sure touch of his Florentine refinement together with the humanism of the new age to bring together the heritage of the saints and thinkers, the poets and painters of the century into the one 'divine comedy'.

Epilogue

WHEN THE men of the Renaissance looked back on the *Duecento* they saw it as a period of darkness, unhappiness and ignorance, when men struggled and failed to express themselves, partly through lack of feeling and partly through lack of developed forms. But it easily happens, and it still happens today, that we misjudge an age simply because it is remote from our own and very great changes have come in between. Yet when we look back at an age with tenderness, with a love of its people and an understanding of its problems, every age is found to have its lovable qualities.

This is what we have tried to do. We have tried to see the Italian *Duecento* as a struggle between heaven and hell, a great living mystery play, that was not a play but a history, with real living people playing their parts in one of Europe's greatest dramas.

Principal Abbreviations used in the Notes

Acta SS: Acta Sanctorum of the Bollandists, 2nd ed. 1854 ff.

I Celano: *S. Francisci Assisiensis Vita I*, by Thomas of Celano (the first of two lives written by Thomas of Celano).

II Celano: *Vita II* (the second of the two lives by Thomas of Celano).

Crestomazia: Monaci, *Crestomazia italiana dei primi secoli* (Città di Castello 1897). [See note in Biblio.]

Dav.: Davidsohn, *Geschichte von Florenz*, vols I and II (Berlin 1908).

Ferri: *Le Laude di Fra Jacopone da Todi secondo la stampa fiorentina del 1490*, a cura di Giuseppe Ferri (Bari 1915). [See note in Biblio. s.v. Jacopone.]

Greg.: Gregorovius, *Geschichte der Stadt Rom im Mittelalter*, vol. V (Stuttgart 3rd ed. 1878).

Kant.: Kantorowicz, *Kaiser Friedrich der Zweite*, two vols (Berlin 1927).

Liuzzi: Liuzzi, *La lauda e i primordi della melodia italiana*, two vols (Rome XIII E.F. [1934]).

M. G. SS.: *Monumenta Germaniae Historica Scriptores*, ed. Pertz and others (Leipzig 1826 ff.).

Migne PL: Migne, *Patrologia Latina* (Paris 1844 ff.).

RIS: *Rerum Italicarum Scriptores*, ed. Muratori (Milan 1723–51).

Sal.: *Cronica Fratris Salimbene de Adam*, ed. Holder-Egger in M. G. SS., XXXII. [See note in Biblio.]

Schnürer: Schnürer, *Kirche und Kultur im Mittelalter*, vol. II.

Tresatti: *Laudi del b.Fra Jacopone da Todi*, ed. F. Tresatti (Venice 1617).

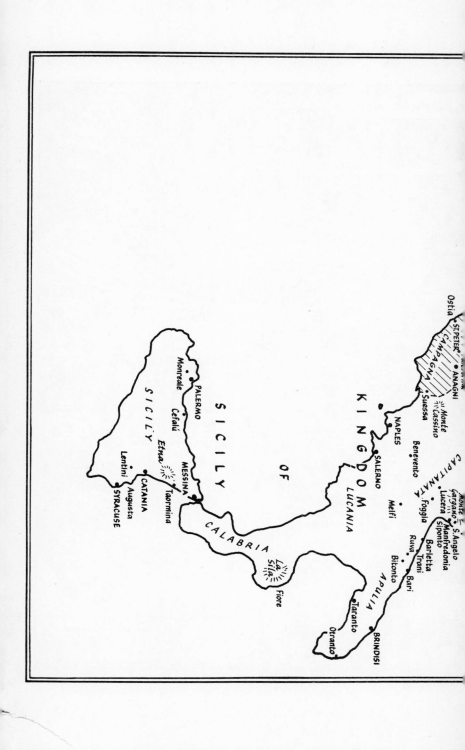

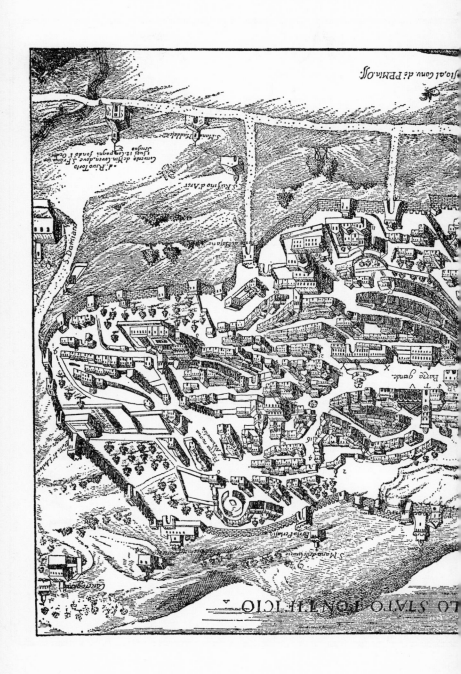

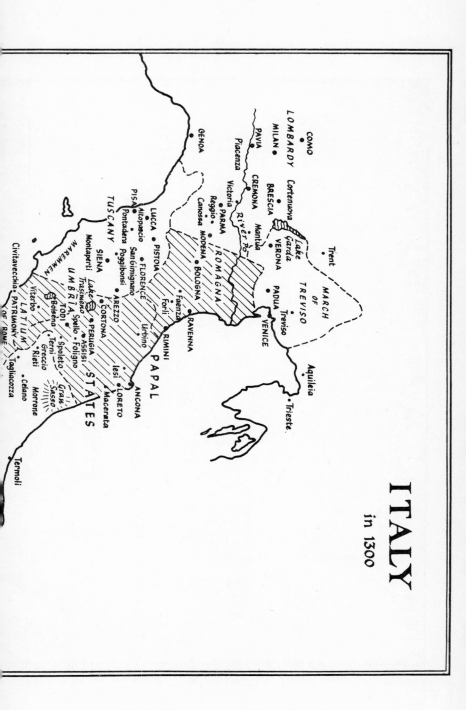

ITALY
in 1300

Notes and Excursus

INTRODUCTION

1 *Le Laude di Fra Jacopone da Todi secondo la stampa florentina del 1490*, a cura di Giuseppe Ferri, Bari 1915. Lauda LXXI (Omo que vol parlare). New critical edition: *Laudi, trattato e detti*, a cura di Franca Ageno, Florence 1953. Only those poems of Jacopone, selected by Bonaccorsi and published in 1490, can be considered certainly authentic. Our quotations are mainly taken from this collection, which we shall indicate by the editor's name, Ferri; but occasionally we have quoted from the less reliable collection of P. Francesco Tresatti, Venice 1617 (quoted as Tresatti).

2 A modern example of unscientific enthusiasm for the Middle Ages is J. Walsh, *The thirteenth, greatest of centuries*, which has been republished many times since it appeared in America in 1924.

3 J. Huizinga, *Geschonden Wereld* (Haarlem 1945), p. 47.

4 *Inferno*, 32,9: the grim world of the ninth circle of hell is not easily described by a 'lingua che chiami mamma e babbo'.

5 Cf. the registers of Cardinal Hugolino of Ostia (*Fonti per la storia d'Italia*, Rome 1900), *passim*.

6 F. Gregorovius, *Geschichte der Stadt Rom im Mittelalter*, V (Stuttgart 1878²), p. 116. We shall often make use of this great work (quoted as Greg.), without entering into the objections which can certainly be made against it. In so far as its author brings the past to life by his wealth of anecdotal detail, his method coincides with our own, and he thereby provides a richer material than most historians of Rome before or after him.

CHAPTER ONE

Normans and Germans in South Italy

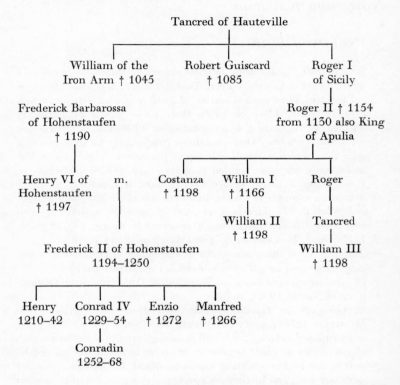

During the minority of Frederick II, Philip of Swabia (1198–1208) and Otto of Saxony (1198–1215) were struggling for ascendancy in Germany and Italy. Otto was crowned as Emperor by Pope Innocent III in 1209, but was excommunicated in 1210 and threatened by the young Frederick in 1211. The latter postponed the crusade, to which he was bound at his coronation in 1220, so long that he also was excommunicated. He undertook it eventually in 1228, and in 1229 conquered Jerusalem and other holy places. In 1230 he ended his conflict with the Pope at the Peace of San

Germano; but it reopened and he was again excommunicated, and was declared deposed by the Council of Lyons in 1245.

1250–4 Conrad IV.

1256–66 Manfred King of Sicily.

1265 Charles of Anjou crowned in Rome as King of Sicily.

1266 Manfred defeated by Charles of Anjou, and killed on the 'Field of Roses' at Benevento.

1268 Conradin of Hohenstaufen defeated by the Anjou at Tagliacozzo, and beheaded at Naples.

1282 The 'Sicilian Vespers', Sicily liberated from the Anjou.

1283 Peter of Aragon King of Sicily.

1 Monaci, *Crestomazia italiana dei primi secoli* (Città di Castello 1897), p. 517. For Cecco Angiolieri, see below, chapter 11, p. 184.

2 For these and other remarkable details in Bishop Conrad's account, cf. Arnold of Lübeck, *Chronica Slavorum*, Book V, chapter 19, in M. G. SS., XXI, p. 194.

3 Princess Anna Komnena in her *Alexias* (Migne, P.G.131, 133–4).

4 *Chronica regia coloniensis* (in *Scriptores rerum germanicarum in usum scholarium*, Hanover 1880), p. 159.

5 E.g. in Malespini, in *Rerum italicarum scriptores* (abbreviated RIS), ed. Muratori (1723–51), vol. VIII, p. 939.

6 According to Brother Salimbene of Parma in his *Cronaca* (M. G. SS., XXXII), p. 358. This chronicle, from which much material is taken, will be quoted as Sal.

7 Malespini, loc.cit.

8 Sal., pp. 42 f.

9 Cf. E. Kantorowicz, *Kaiser Friedrich der Zweite* (Berlin 1927–31), vol. II, p. 15. In recent years there has been nearly as much difference of opinion about this biographer as about the Kaiser himself, to mention only the *a priori* criticism of Brackmann, *Kaiser Friedrich II in 'mythischer Schau'* (in *Hist. Zeitschr.* 1929, pp. 534 ff.) and the more positive assessment of Hampe, *Das neueste Lebensbild Kaiser Friedrichs II* (ibid., 1932, pp. 441 ff.). While it may not be possible to share Kantorowicz's hero-worship, his use and evaluation of sources, and the picture of the Kaiser and his time which he brings out of them, make the work a masterly biography. It will be frequently used, and quoted as Kant.

10 Amari, *Altre narrazioni del vespro siciliano* (Milan 1887), p. 23. Frederick spoke nine languages and wrote seven.

11 In a letter to his son-in-law Prince Vatatzes. Huillard-Bréholles, *Historia diplomatica Frederici II* (6 vols, Paris 1852–61), vol. VI, p. 685.

12 Amari, *Biblioteca arabo-sicula* II (Italian text, Turin-Rome 1880 ff.), p. 210. Another, admittedly unfriendly, contemporary speaks of the harsh glance of the Kaiser, which he likens to that of a snake, though there is no mention of a squint (Amari, *Altre narrazioni* . . ., p. 23).

13 Kant, I., p. 176.

14 E.g. the answer of the famous Moroccan Ibu Sabin. Cf. A. Mehren, *Journal asiatique*, series VIII, vol. XIV (1879), pp. 341 ff. and 357 ff.

15 Cf. Renan, *Averroës et l'Averroisme* (Paris 1869), pp. 254, 291.

16 Kant., I, p. 177.

17 Amari, *Altre narrazioni* . . ., p. 29.

16 M. G. SS., II, p. 178. Other gifts were a precious Indian lute, and a tree made of silver, on which birds sang when the wind blew (Amari, *Altre narrazioni* . . ., p. 27). One of Frederick's gifts in return was a polar bear, which to the astonishment of the Arabs would only eat fish (Amari, Appendix to *Bibl. arabo-sicula*, p. 20).

19 Cf. the Austrian chronicle in rhyme of Ottokar in MGH, *Deutsche Chroniken*, I, p. 422.

20 Huillard-Bréholles, *Hist. dipl.*, V, p. 603.

21 *Il Novellino: le ciento novelle antiche, secondo l'edizione del 1525* (many subsequent editions), Nov. XC.

22 *De Arte venandi cum avibus*, according to the edition of Schneider (Leipzig 1788–9). C. H. Haskins, *Studies in the History of medieval science* (Cambridge, Mass., U.S.A. 1924) examines this and other aspects of the Hohenstaufen court. He thinks, among other things, that the *Ars venandi* originally had a much wider scope (*op.cit.*, p. 309). Vatican MS Pal.Lat.1071 is the oldest illustrated manuscript of Frederick's book about falconry that is known to us, and it belongs to the second half of the thirteenth century. There is good reason to suppose that it is a copy of an older manuscript illustrated by the Emperor's own observations and perhaps even by his own sketches. Cf. Erbach-Fürstenau, *Die Manfredbibel* (Leipzig 1910), pp. 47 ff.

23 Ed. Schneider, p. 2.

24 According to MGH, *Deutsche Chroniken*, III, 1, p. 572.

25 Chronicle of Franc. Pipinus (RIS IX, p. 669).

26 *De arte venandi*, II, c. 2 (ed. Schneider, p. 73).

27 'Quod ergo Aristoteles dicit libro animalium aves uncorum unguium idem sunt quod aves rapaces non sic se habet' (Schneider, p. 43).

28 Sal., p. 350.

29 'O quot dii ex hoc frumento suo tempore conficientur': John of Winterthur, *Scriptores rerum germanicarum*, new series, vol. III (Berlin 1924), p. 9.

30 Sal., p. 351.

31 Cf. Michael Scotus in the preface to his *Encyclopaedia*, which was apparently compiled at the suggestion of Frederick (cf. Kant., I, p. 324).

32 Kant., I, p. 437.

33 According to the account of Nicholas de Carbio, published by Pagnotti, *Archivio della Società romana*, XXI, p. 102 (ch. 29).

34 The church of Altamura in the Murgie in Apulia, rebuilt in the sixteenth century. Cf. Haseloff, *Die Bauten der Hohenstaufen in Unteritalien* (Leipzig 1920), pp. 26 f.

35 MGH, Constitutiones II, no. 219, p. 304.

36 Cf. E. Müller, 'Peter von Prezza', *Heidelb. Abhandl.*, XXXVII (1913), p. 113.

37 Huillard-Bréholles, *Hist.diplom.*, VI, p. 126.

38 *Inferno* 13, 58 f.: 'Io sono colui che tenni ambo le chiavi del cor di Federigo . . .' (Peter de Vinea appears among the suicides.)

39 *Liber augustalis* (Constit. regum regni utriusque Siciliae . . .) publ. by C. Carcani (Naples, 1786), I, pp. 95, 98.

40 Gregory IX in MGH *Epist. Pontif.*, I, no. 750, p. 648.

41 Huillard-Bréholles, *Hist. diplom.*, IV, p. 253.

42 The finest chapter of Kantorowicz's biography, 'Tyrann von Sizilien' (I, pp. 195 ff.), deals with his political theory. We feel compelled to agree with the opinion that his interpretation of the well-known but none too lucid *Proœmium* is far too materialistic (Averroistic?), while Brackmann (op. cit.) explains the Kaiser's thought in too traditional and Augustinian a manner. Only H. Niese seems to have pointed out clearly the contradiction in the *Proœmium*: 'Indeed we find here a combination of the traditional theory of the Church and an as yet incomplete view, which perhaps stems from the Arabic Aristotelianism which was influencing the court: the prince's power comes not only *divina*

providentia, but also *ipsa necessitate cogente*' ('Zur Geschichte des geistlichen Lebens am Hofe Kaiser Friedrichs II, *Histor. Zeitschrift*, 1912, p. 537).

43 *De Arte venandi*, I, c. 23 (Schneider, p. 27).

44 *Liber augustalis*, I, 4 (ed. Carcani, p. 6).

45 Sal., p. 330.

46 Sal., p. 335. Cf. Z. Schiffer, *Markgraf Hubert Pallavicini* (Leipzig 1910), p. 42.

47 Sal., p. 364. Alberic died in 1260, his brother Ezzelino in 1259.

48 Chronicle of Ant. Godus in RIS, VIII, p. 83. Cf. Herodotus, *Hist.*, V, 92! F. Stieve wrote a monograph *Ezzelino von Romano* (Leipzig 1909).

49 Chronicle of Laurentius de Monachis, in RIS VIII, pp. 146 f. Nearly all the men were killed, and the cries of the tortured filled the towns, no one dared to go to church any more; 'ingens erat clamor lugentium et dicentium Vae, Vae'.

50 Chronicle of Jac. Malvecius in RIS XIV, p. 935: 'Mulierum hostis crudelissimus adeo ut eum nunquam cum muliere concubuisse credatur.'

51 Kant., I, p. 571; for the gallows ibid., p. 191.

52 Kantorowicz (I, p. 628) attaches importance to the fact that Luther's Reformation began exactly 267 years after Frederick's death.

53 E. Davidsohn, *Geschichte von Florenz* (Berlin 1908), II, 1, p. 375.

54 According to Eccleston, M. G. SS., XXVIII, p. 568.

55 Kant., I, p. 628.

56 Huillard-Bréholles, op. cit., VI, p. 738.

57 RIS VII, p. 1095.

58 RIS VII, p. 1093.

59 Greg., p. 351.

60 The chronicler's 'French' leaves nothing to be desired: 'Alles idit moi ale Sultan de Nocere hoggi meterai lui en emfern, ò il metrà moi em paradis', *Chronicle of Villani*, VII, 5.

61 RIS VIII, p. 1030. On p. 1032 is the jingle that was circulating:

> Deh, com' egli è gran pietade
> delle donne di Messina,
> veggiendo iscapigliate
> portando pietre e calcina.

62 RIS IX, p. 933.

CHAPTER TWO

The popes of the thirteenth century

Innocent III	1198–1216
Honorius III	1217–27
Gregory IX	1227–41
Celestine IV	1241
(Twenty months *sedisvacatio*)	
Innocent IV	1243–54
Alexander IV	1254–61
Urban IV	1261–4
Clement IV	1265–8
(Two years *sedisvacatio*)	
Gregory X	1271–6
Innocent V	1276
Hadrian V	1276
John XXI	1276–7
Nicholas III	1277–80
Martin IV	1281–5
Honorius IV	1285–7
(Thirteen months *sedisvacatio*)	
Nicholas IV	1288–92
(Two years and three months *sedisvacatio*)	
Celestine V	1294
Boniface VIII	1294–1303

1215 Fourth Lateran Council
1245 First Council of Lyons
1274 Second Council of Lyons

(1252–8 Brancaleone degli Andalò, Senator of Rome)

1 Melody according to F. Ludwig in Adler's *Handbuch der Musik-geschichte* (Berlin 1930), I, p. 161.
2 Gregorovius (op. cit., pp. 37 ff., 44 ff.) gives a gripping account of the feuds among the Roman nobility; less valuable, because not objective, is his characterisation of the various popes.
3 Böhmer, *Regesta imperii*, V (Innsbruck 1892–1901), 3–5, 9482.
4 Quoted from Kant., I, p. 390.

5 Huillard-Bréholles, op. cit., V, p. 1077.

6 Quoted from Schnürer, *Kirche und Kultur im Mittelalter*, II.

7 Cf. the valuable study of P. Lehmann, *Die Parodie im Mittelalter* (Munich 1922), pp. 43 ff.

8 *Inferno*, 19, 90 ff.

> Deh, or mi dì: quanto tesoro volle
> Nostro Segnore in prima da san Pietro
> ch' ei ponesse le chiavi in sua balìa?

9 Innocent III died convinced that the right of appointing the prefects of the city belonged for ever to the Holy See; yet his successors were rarely able to exercise this right. In the second half of the century, when there were no more Hohenstaufen to interfere and no Chauvinism to restrain the Quirites from appointing even foreign princes as senators, such as the Anjou or the Spanish Infante, it was also easier for the popes to have an influence in the senate. They, in fact, usually appointed relatives, who were also most to be relied upon.

10 Clement IV to Charles of Anjou (Martène, *Thesaurus epistolarum Clementis IV*, Ep. 105 from Perugia; quoted by Gregorovius, p. 358).

11 According to the surviving *ordines romani*, fully described by Gregorovius, op. cit., pp. 9 ff.

12 The mysterious figure of Genesis 14:18, 'Melchisedech the King of Salem, bringing forth bread and wine, for he was the priest of the most high God,' has from earliest Christian times been seen as a type of Christ, through Hebrews ch. 7 using Ps. 109 (110). In the writings of Innocent III this priest-king represents the unity of spiritual and temporal sovereignty.

13 For Frederick's political theory, see the previous chapter, and note 49.

14 MGH, *Epist. Pontificum*, I, no. 750, pp. 646 ff.; cf. also Matthew Paris in M. G. SS., XXVIII, p. 169.

15 M. G. SS., XVIII, p. 483.

16 Greg., p. 224.

17 M. G. SS., XVIII, p. 215. For the ride across the Maremma, when Innocent IV 'took off the pope and put on old Senebaldo Fieschi again', see Matthew Paris, M. G. SS., XXVIII, p. 431.

18 RIS, XI, p. 528.

CHAPTER THREE

The events of a selected period of ten years, taken from the chronological table of Salvatorelli (*Storia d'Italia* IV: *l'Italia communale*, Milan n.d., p. 878), give an impression of the wars and political activities of the citizens of the century.

1250 Cremona and the emigrants from Parma defeat the army of Parma. The legate Pietro Capocci defeated by the imperial troops at Cingola. Revolution of the Primo Popolo in Florence. Parma goes over to the Emperor. December 13th: death of Frederick.

1251 Genoa takes possession of Savona. Aldobrandeschi makes an agreement with Orvieto and later with Florence. Innocent IV returns to Italy; Conrad IV and the towns on the imperial side, such as Cremona, Pavia, etc., are excommunicated. Siena, Pistoia and Pisa make a treaty at Pontedera; Florence, Genoa and Lucca are also allied. The party of the Uberti is driven from Florence. Conrad IV in Italy.

1252 The Lombard alliance becomes active again. Uberto Pallavicini makes a treaty with Ezzelino da Romano. Peter of Verona is murdered near Como. Florence defeats Pisa and Siena near Pontedera. Brancaleone becomes Senator of Rome. Florence attacks her emigrants at Figline.

1253 Capua yields to Conrad IV, followed by Naples. Peace between Milan and Cremona. Unsuccessful conspiracy against Ezzelino. Siena appoint a *capitano*.

1254 Treaty between Florence and Pistoia. Uberto Pallavicini becomes *podestà* of Cremona, Vicenza, Pavia and Vercelli. Innocent IV excommunicates Florence. Death of Conrad IV. Peace between Florence and Siena. The army directed against Ezzelino enters Padua. Florence turns against Poggibonsi. Cervia surrenders to Bologna. Innocent marches into the Empire, but is defeated near Foggia and dies.

1255 War between Venice and Genoa. Manfred is excommunicated by Alexander IV. Arezzo surrenders to Florence. Brancaleone is imprisoned in Rome.

1256 Florence, Lucca and Genoa allied against Pisa. Unsuccessful plot of Ezzelino against Padua. Brancaleone freed in Rome. Pisa makes peace with Florence and Lucca. Thomas II of

Savoy occupies Chieri, but falls in the hands of the Turinese and is captured at Asti. The Ghibelline party returns to Genoa. Manfred takes Sicily.

1257 Alberic and Ezzelino join forces. Pallavicini is driven out of Piacenza and Pavia. Armistice between nobles and people in Milan. Giovanni Boccanegra becomes *capitano* at Genoa. Treaty between Venice and Pisa. Bonaventure becomes General of the Franciscans.

1258 Treaty between nobles and people in Milan. Battle between Venice and Genoa near Acri. Ezzelino and Pallavicini defeat the papal troops. Brescia falls to Ezzelino. The Ghibellines are driven from Florence. Death of Brancaleone d'Andalò.

1259 Great struggle between artisans and merchants in Milan. Pallavicini allies himself with Azzo d'Este. Manfred comes to the help of Siena. In the battle of Cassano d'Adda Ezzelino is taken prisoner and later executed. Siena's victory over the Guelphs near Campagnatico.

1260 War between Florence and Siena. Florence loses the great battle near Montaperti. The Ghibellines return to Florence. Alberic da Romano executed. Ludovico di San Bonifacio driven out of Verona. Empoli has a Ghibelline city council. Peace between Verona and Mantua. The first flagellant processions.

1 Monaci, *Crestomazia italiana dei primi secoli* (Città di Castello 1897), p. 284.[A new and revised edition of this useful book appeared in 1955—Tr.]

2 Sal., p. 375.

3 Sal., p. 482.

4 RIS, VIII, p. 987.

5 Sal., p. 203.

6 M. G. SS., XVIII, p. 675.

7 RIS, IX, p. 796.

8 M. G. SS., loc. cit. The *mala zobia* fell on August 18th, 1250.

9 '*Lo sfiorato fiore*', as Guittone d'Arezzo says in a poem, in D'Ancona, *Manuale della letteratura italiana* (Florence 1925), I, p. 80; and similarly Chiaro Davanzati, in op. cit., p. 98.

10 The *carroccio* seems not to have been used in Rome, cf. Greg., p. 182, note 1.

11 Pertile, *Storia del diritto pubblico* (Turin 1896), II, p. 120.

12 Davidsohn, *Geschichte von Florenz* (henceforth quoted as Dav.), II, 1, p. 169.

13 Cf. Dav., loc. cit.

14 RIS, VII, pp. 844 f.

15 RIS, VIII, p. 576.

16 According to an item in the archives at Todi, quoted by Greg., p. 130, note 1.

17 RIS, VIII, p. 1151; Sal., p. 510.

18 Huillard-Bréholles, *Hist. diplom.*, IV, p. 310.

19 In particular Verona, Piacenza, Todi, Padua, Turin and Bologna.

20 M. G. SS., XXVIII, p. 134: Frederick gathered an army 'ut Italicos insolentes expugnaret'.

21 Cf. Kant., I, p. 387.

22 Kant., I, p. 325.

23 Thus Greg. and Kant. *passim.*

24 RIS, VIII, p. 1110.

25 M. G. SS., XVIII, p. 496.

26 *Annales Placentini*, ed. Huillard-Bréholles (Paris 1856). p. 215.

27 Thus at Padua, RIS, VIII, p. 225. There is a valuable account by the chronicler Rolandus Patavinus of the reception which the citizens of Padua prepared for the Emperor in 1239: they made a great show with all their instruments; distinguished ladies paraded before him and came to greet him. The Kaiser provided food and games, and took part in their Easter services in the most engaging way, so that the people were surprised and distressed when they heard that he had been excommunicated on Maundy Thursday.

28 Dav., II, p. 178.

29 *Annales Placentini*, p. 174.

30 The building of a temporary town of this kind was not unusual. The Lombards in 1168 had built such a city for Pope Alexander III against Barbarossa, and this is Alessandria today. Frederick as a repressive measure in Sicily destroyed an old town and then built a new one on the site: this is Augusta, not far from Syracuse, built in 1232.

31 Sal., pp. 195 f., 203.

32 Dante, *Epistle*, VI, 19: 'Nam et hi, quamquam de Victoria victoriam sint adepti, nihilominus ibi sunt de dolore dolorem memorabiliter consecuti.'

33 RIS, VIII, p. 787: '. . . formae geminae mulierum super Tusciam in aere nubigero comparuerunt, humanis obtutibus, pendentes ut nebula super terram . . .'

34 M. G. SS., XVIII, p. 718.

35 Cf. Volpe, *Movimenti religiosi e setti ereticali nella società medievale italiana* (Florence 1922), pp. 83 ff., 125.

36 Dav., II, 1, p. 301.

37 Pertile, *Diritto pubblico*, II, p. 59.

38 Sal., pp. 158 ff.

39 Kant., I, p. 262.

40 Pertile, *Storia del diritto privato* (Turin 1894), p. 65.

41 Dav., II, 1, p. 409.

42 Details in Salvatorelli, op. cit., p. 585.

43 Bonvesin will reappear in chapters 9 and 12.

44 RIS, XVI, p. 680.

45 Villani, *Storia fiorentina*, VI, 39; examined by Dav. II, p. 384, and by Luchaire, *Les démocraties italiennes* (Paris 1915), p. 110. [An ell is 45 inches.]

46 Dav., II, 1, p. 333.

47 A thorough study of the office of *podestà* in Pertile, *Storia del diritto pubblico*, II, pp. 29 ff.

48 Salzer, *Über die Anfänge der Signorie in Oberitalien* (Berlin 1900), pp. 61 f.

49 Pertile, *Dir. pubbl.*, II, p. 40.

50 Pertile, loc. cit.

51 Luchaire, *Démocraties* . . ., p. 133.

52 Statuti di Bologna, II, p. 277, *Monumenti istorici pertinenti alle provincie della Romagna*, 1st series.

53 Luchaire, *Démocraties*, pp. 95 ff.

54 Thus in the formula used at Alessandria for the house of Anjou (cf. Salzer, op. cit., p. 55).

CHAPTER FOUR

1 M. G. SS., XVIII, p. 715. The invitation, 'Exite foras, canes de Cremona, exite foras, garrule, et venite ad prelium', is indeed a classic example of the boyish escapade that they called 'war'.

2 E.g., at Reggio in 1233; Sal., p. 59.

3 According to John of Winterthur (op. cit., p. 10); and cf. Anecdote XXIII in the *Novellino*, in which Frederick gave a large gift to a tramp, because he kept his drinking cup so clean ('per la nettezza di colui, li donò molto riccamente').

4 Villani, VI, 26.

5 Dav., II, 2, p. 511.

6 Salimbene (p. 642) describes such a house: the home of the wine grower Albareto.

7 For the bells at Pavia, cf. RIS, XI, p. 29; and also Mancini, *Cortona nel medio evo* (Florence 1897), p. 171, where it is indicated that the arrangement of the bells at Pavia was also followed in central Italy, with evidence for this from *De laudibus Papiae* in RIS, IX. A further enquiry into the use of bells and trumpets in the cities of the *Duecento* may be seen in the present author's study: *De oudste melodiek van Italië* (Utrecht 1948—a dissertation), pp. 19 f.

8 RIS, VIII, p. 289.

9 RIS, VIII, p. 1120.

10 According to Anecdote LII of the *Novellino*, this bell was hung by Jean de Brienne, King of Jerusalem (1210–25). In time, however, the bell rope became worn out, and it was replaced by a vine tendril. 'Now you must know', the story continues, 'that a certain knight had a horse that was very noble, but also so old that it could not work any more. So, in order to save buying fodder, he let the old horse run free and graze where it pleased. One day the horse, driven by hunger, began to eat the vine tendril, and so the bell began to ring. The judges all arrived and saw what was happening and supposed that the horse was claiming his right to be heard. So the matter was investigated, and the court decided that the knight who had used the horse in its youth was now bound to provide for its old age; and the king kept him to this with threats of dire punishment if he disobeyed'.

11 Sal., p. 634.

12 Villani, VI, 46.

13 Sal., pp. 634, 14.

14 E.g., RIS, IX, pp. 791, 796.

15 Muratori, *Dissertazioni sopra le antichità italiane* (Milan 1836–7), 37, IV, 22.

16 Dav., II, 2, p. 283.

17 Dante, *Inferno*, 26, 1:

> Godi, Fiorenza, poi che se' si grande,
> che per mare e per terra batti l'ali,
> e per lo 'nferno tuo nome si spande!

18 Villani, VIII, 36.

19 Villani, VI, 53.

20 Thus particularly in a trade agreement with Faenza in 1204, cf. Dav., I, p. 669, note 1.

21 Sal., p. 341.

22 Laude *Udite una pazzia* (ed. Tresatti), stanza 23.

23 The Florentines also knew all about usury, though it had no evil repute there. Yet the learned law professor Accursius made a lot of money out of his more penurious students by making loans to them. Even so respectable a citizen as Folco Portinari, the father of Dante's Beatrice, made much of the money with which he founded the hospital of Santa Maria Nuova out of his money-lending transactions (cf. Dav., II, 2, p. 426). In Paris it was otherwise: the people rejoiced openly when in 1277 and 1291 the King put a whole lot of Italian moneylenders into prison.

24 Sal., p. 391.

25 The sharp distinctions laid down by Lombard law between the different degrees of serfdom (near-free *aldiones*, duty-bound domestics, and the tied *coloni*) were still valid during the thirteenth century. Yet one has the impression that the ideas were being obliterated, especially since Christian slavery was officially being abandoned at this time. The Church had for long been struggling for the freedom of the serfs, but she had to wait until economic reasons for its abandonment came to reinforce the moral ones (cf. Pertile, *Diritto privato*, pp. 13 ff.). It was for economic reasons, probably, that the first cities officially to abolish slavery were the smaller communities (Pistoia in 1205, Assisi in 1210), while the greater cities only followed suit later (Bologna in 1256 and Florence not till 1299).

26 Böhmer, *Regesta Imperii*, V, 2146a.

27 Greg., op. cit., pp. 13 f.

28 Kant., I, p. 246. Cf. R. Strauss, 'Die Juden im Königreich Sizilien unter Normannen und Staufern', *Heidelberger Abhandlungen*, Heft 30 (1910).

29 Pertile, *Diritto privato*, p. 56.

30 Pertile, *Diritto pubblico*, II, pp. 129 ff.

31 Every now and then the chroniclers give us a picture of great prosperity in the smaller communities. The *podestà* tells Salimbene that in his town nobody can possibly be hungry: a dish of salt, full to the brim, costs only one dinar, and that is the price at an inn for twelve boiled eggs; in the season anyone can buy a wild duck, as fat as butter, for four dinars; and someone who plucks ten ducks is entitled to keep five for himself (Sal., p. 482).

32 RIS, IX, p. 814.

33 RIS, IX, p. 191.

34 Sal., pp. 586 f.

35 Sal., p. 169.

36 Sal., loc cit. Cf. Dante's strictures on the 'sfacciate donne fiorentine' in the *Purgatorio*, 23, 101 ff. From the old legend of Margherita of Cortona (*Antica leggenda della vita e de' miracoli di Santa Margherita di Cortona, scritta dal confessore di lei, Fr. Giunta Bevegnati*, published at Siena in 1897) we learn that beauty queens were already known in the *Duecento*: they were chosen with great ceremony by the *podestà* in the town hall.

37 Biondelli, *Studi linguistici* (Milan 1856), p. 145.

38 Dav., II, 1, p. 43.

39 Cf. above, p. 42.

40 On almost every page the chronicles include stories like that of the four pirates who were hanged at Genoa: two of them survived and afterwards said that St John the Baptist had appeared to them; they were pardoned, loaded with favours and set free (RIS, IX, p. 46).

41 Pertile, *Storia della procedura* (Turin 1901), pp. 91 f.

42 Ferri, Laudi 54–59, especially 54, 'Che farai, Fra Jacopone'. In his underground dungeon there ran a sewer, 'which was not with fragrance scented'; the warder had to confess it as a sin if he spoke to him; the prisoner wore chains on his feet like a hunting-hawk; whoever went past his prison heard dance music within, but it was only the music of his chain as he stumbled about inside; he had to pay his warder for his food with many a Paternoster, and it was difficult for him to eat it, because he was shivering with cold.

> Iaci, iaci en esta stia,
> come porco di grassia!

43 Dav., I, p. 664.

44 Pertile, *Procedura*, p. 145.

45 Pertile, *Storia del diritto procedurale* (Turin 1892), p. 75.

46 Account by Collenuccio, quoted from Güterbock, 'Eine Biographie Friedrichs des Zweiten', *Neues Archiv*, XXX, p. 66.

47 Pertile, *Diritto privato*, p. 80. The lot of distinguished exiles seems from the material point of view not to have been too bad: everywhere there were fellow party members who were prepared to help. Dante himself declared that he was not utterly ruined: 'Nonne solis astrorumque specula ubique conspiciam? Nonne dulcissimas veritates potero speculari ubique sub caelo, ni prius inglorium, ymo ignominiosum populo Florentineque civitati me reddam? Quippe nec panis deficiet' (Conclusion of Epist. XII [IX]). But what he really resented breaks out elsewhere in a cry of anger against the perfidy of his fellow citizens: 'A, Tuscorum vanissimi, tam natura quam vitio insensati!' (Epist. VI), and a whole hell would be peopled with his enemies before the insult would be avenged.

48 RIS VIII, pp. 623 f., 1104.

49 M. G. SS., XIX, p. 364.

50 RIS, VIII, p. 1083.

51 Sal., p. 639.

52 E.g. at Verona: RIS, VIII, p. 632.

53 RIS, XI, p. 663.

54 RIS, VIII, p. 842.

55 Account book of John Makiel (published by Gaillard, *Arch. du Conseil de Flandre*, quoted by Dav., II, 2, pp. 69 f.)

56 RIS, VIII, p. 1006.

57 Thus in Parma, RIS, IX, p. 841.

58 RIS, VIII, p. 1039; Villani, VII, 98.

59 RIS, VIII, p. 180.

60 Folgore da San Gimignano, one of the first poets of the *fêtes galantes*, quoted from d'Ancona, *Manuale*, I, p. 126.

61 Dav., II, 1, p. 93.

62 Dav., II, 2, p. 64.

63 M. G. SS., XVIII, p. 571: all the household things were of gold, and the bedroom was studded with precious stones!

64 RIS, IX, p. 730.

65 This occurred, apparently, on Mont Canigou in the Pyrenees: Sal., p. 598.

66 For these identifications, cf. Marco Polo: *Travels* (English text of Ricci, 1931, pp. 139, 189 f.) [Ref. by Tr.]

67 Cf. the moralising *Bestiario* which a rhymster of Gubbio composed out of sixty-four bad sonnets (Monaci, *Crestomazia*, pp. 315 ff.). The reader learns not only of the evil of the salamander but also of the foolishness of the tiger: hunters who steal tiger cubs leave mirrors in their place, so that the tiger looks at the mirror and thinks he is looking at his young; so also we in our folly look in the mirror of Satan . . . etc.

68 Marco Polo, *Travels*, Eng. ed. Ricci, p. 44.

69 For the *Vecchio del Monte* cf. RIS, IX, pp. 407 f., 706 f. Jacques de Vitry also speaks of him in ch. 15 of his *Historia orientalis* (Douai 1597).

70 For the Tartar Father John a Plano Carpini, cf. Muller, *Voorlopers en navolgers van Marco Polo* (Leiden 1944). We shall refer again to this traveller in chapter 9.

71 From a letter of Brunetto Latini to Guido Cavalcanti; cf. Schück, 'Gedanken über die Zeit der ersten Benutzung des Kompasses', Archiv für Geschichte der Naturwissenschaft, III (1910), p. 138.

CHAPTER FIVE

1182 Francis di Pietro born at Assisi.

1202 Abbot Joachim of Flora dies at the Abbey of Pietrafitta in Calabria.

c. 1206 The crucifix at San Damiano speaks to Francis.

1210 Innocent III gives (verbal?) approbation to the rule.

1212 Clare leaves the world. (Dies 1253, Abbess of San Damiano.)

1220 Cardinal Hugolino (afterwards Pope Gregory IX) becomes Cardinal Protector of the Order.

1223 The final rule is accepted by Honorius III. The Christmas at Greccio.

1224 Francis receives the stigmata at La Verna.

1225 Francis composes the Canticle of the Sun at San Damiano.

1226 Francis dies at the Portiuncula.

1170 (or 1172) Dominic de Guzman born at Caleruega in Castile.

1206–7 Convent for convert heretic women established at Prouille.

1216 Rule of the Dominicans, based on the Rule of St Augustine, is approved by Honorius III.

1221 Dominic dies at Bologna.

1195 Ferdinand born in Lisbon.

1220 At Coimbra he leaves the Augustinians and joins the Franciscans, taking the name of Anthony.

c. 1222 His first appearance as a popular preacher. (Most dates in his life are very uncertain.)

c. 1224–7 perhaps in France.

1231 His death at Padua.

1 Lauda 41 from the Cortona song book (ed. F. Liuzzi, *La Lauda e i primordi della melodia italiana*, Roma Anno XIII E. F. [1934], part 1, p. 448).

2 Cf. the spiritual and suggestive, but somewhat subjective, biography by E. Aegerter, *Joachim de Flore, l'Evangile éternel* (Paris 1928), part I, p. 86. The second part includes a selection from Joachim's work.

3 Aegerter, I, p. 75.

4 *Liber Concordantiae Veteris et Novi Testamenti*, cf. Aegerter II, p. 31.

5 *Liber Concord.*, ch. 91–92; cf. Aegerter II, p. 71.

6 Aegerter, II, pp. 65 ff.

7 *Liber Concord.*, V, 22, 71 b, quoted by Grundmann, *Studien über Joachim von Floris* (Leipzig 1927), p. 57.

8 Details from Gratien, *Histoire de la fondation et de l'évolution de l'Ordre des Frères Mineurs au XIIIe siècle* (Paris 1925), p. 527.

9 The oldest manuscript of the *Fioretti* dates from 1396. The *Fioretti* go back to a cycle of stories which is essentially older: the so-called *Actus B. Francisci et sociorum eius*, which are always attributed to Ugolino da Monte Giorgio, who lived from 1262 to 1348 and was Bishop of the Abruzzi until the reign of Boniface VIII. But this attribution is uncertain, as are also the sources which are used. In any case the author, who certainly belonged to the 'spiritual' party, probably depended more upon oral traditions already in circulation than upon any written sources.

10 *Fioretti di San Francesco*, ch. 7.

11 *Fioretti*, ch. 13.

12 *Fioretti*, ch. 8.

13 Goethe, *Italienische Reise* 25 (October 1786).

14 *Fioretti*, ch. 15.

15 Text in *Opuscula b.p.n. Francisci* (Quaracchi 1904), pp. 77 ff.

16 *Portug. Monumenta historica*, Script. I (Lisbon 1856), p. 118.

17 *Summa theologica*, II–II, q. 188, a. 7.
18 *Fioretti*, ch. 18.

CHAPTER SIX

Elias was received into the order by St Francis in 1211 or 1212, perhaps at Cortona. He spent a few years in Germany and in 1221 became head of the order. His break with the order was in 1239 and he died in 1253.

Several of Francis's most famous companions survived, however much overshadowed, until after 1260: Giles died in 1262, Ruffino in 1270 and Leo in 1271. John of Alverna belonged to the generation nearer to the fourteenth century (†1322), to which also belonged the most important 'spirituals', such as Pier Olivi (†1298) and Angelo Clareno (†1337).

Some other useful *obitus* dates are: Philip Benizi 1285, Juliana Falconieri 1341, Lucchesio c. 1260, Novellone 1280, Guido c. 1250, Pier Pettinaro of Siena 1289, Rose 1254, Angela 1309, Margherita 1297.

1 Jacopone da Todi, *Lauda* 24 (Ferri).
2 The old attitude, which excused Elias nothing, is put forth at its clearest by Lempp, *Frère Elie de Cortone* (Paris 1901). In his defence, though hardly objective either, is Attal, *Frate Elia compagno di San Francesco* (Rome 1936). A more complete estimate is that of van den Borne, 'Antonius en Elias', in *Collectanea franciscana neerlandica*, VII, 2 (Den Bosch 1949). [The most valuable new assessment, through a complete re-examination of the historical sources, is that of Rosalind Brooke, *Early Franciscan Government* (Cambridge 1959), involving considerable revision of previous ideas.—Tr.]
3 Historians whose sympathies lie both with thirteenth-century anti-clericalism and with St Francis sometimes find themselves much entangled. Thus Kantorowicz (I, p. 464) sees in Elias's going over to Frederick 'a secret association of the Ghibelline and the Franciscan movements', without, however, fully adverting to the fact that it was in great part Franciscan preaching which brought about Frederick's decline, and that in consequence they were forbidden his realm.
4 Sal., p. 157.

5 *Disputatio inter zelatorem paupertatis et inimicum domesticum eius* (ed. Salamanca 1506), Tract. III, fol. 201 ff.

6 *Vita B. Aegidii*, in *Acta SS.*, April III, III, 1.237.

7 *Fioretti*, ch. 49.

8 'Arcus tenditur in studio, postea sagittatur in praedicatione': Hugh of St Cher (*Opera omnia*, ed. Venice 1600, I, 13, col. 3).

9 Sal., pp. 240 ff.

10 Sal., pp. 403 ff.

11 Sal., loc cit.

12 *Vita B. Aegidii* (loc. cit.). The story is also the *Chronica XXIV Generalium*, in *Analecta franciscana*, III, pp. 78 f.

13 Sal., p. 501; RIS, IX, p. 791.

14 *Inferno*, 23, 103.

15 A very old pattern for these orders of layfolk may be seen at the abbey of Hirsau, cf. Schnürer. In Italy we find already in the twelfth century the statutes of the confraternity of S. Appiano Valdelsa, and we do not have the impression that it was unique. Cf. Monti, *Le confraternite mediovali dell'alta e media Italia* (2 vols, Venice 1927), I, pp. 70 f. Cf. also Van den Borne, 'Die Anfänge des franziskanerischen dritten Ordens', *Franzisk. Studien*, Beiheft 8 (Münster 1925). It would seem that the importance of the Franciscan Third Order in the thirteenth century has sometimes been exaggerated, and that of the many similar organizations of layfolk neglected, not excluding the *disciplinati*. That the Third Orders outlived the others is chiefly because of the powerful protection of the First Orders.

16 Bonaventure, *Opusculum*, XIII, Part II, Quest. 16, in *Opera omnia* (ed. Quaracchi 1898), VIII, p. 368.

17 *Acta SS.*, April III, pp. 596 f.

18 Cf. Lanzoni, *I primordi dell'Ordine francescano in Faenza* (Faenza 1910), p. 31.

19 *Acta SS.*, June II, p. 602.

20 *Acta SS.*, Sept. II, p. 433.

21 The mystical progress of Angela of Foligno, described by a Friar Minor, 'Frater A.', according to her own statements, was for the first time published in a critical edition by Paul Doncœur: *Le livre de la bienheureuse Angèle de Foligno* (Latin: Toulouse 1925; French tr.: Paris 1926). For Margaret the biography by her confessor, the *Antica leggenda di Santa di Cortona* (ed. Siena 1897), remains the principal source.

22 'Ego diligo te plus quam aliquam quae sit in valle Spoletina,' said the Holy Spirit to Angela 'at the twentieth spiritual step'. And to Margaret Christ declares his love: 'Tu es filia mea, quia mi obedis, tu sponsa mea, quia me solum diligis, tu es mater mea, quia voluntatem Patris mei imples.'

23 *Acta SS.*, Sept. II, ibid.

24 *Acta SS.*, loc. cit.

25 *Acta SS.*, April III, p. 9, 499.

26 *Acta SS.*, March II, p. 236.

27 *Acta SS.*, May IV, pp. 386 ff.

28 *Purgatorio* 6, 17–18: ' . . . quel da Pisa che fè parer lo buon Marzucco forte.'

29 *Novellino* 17.

CHAPTER SEVEN

1 *Purgatorio*, 6, 76–79.

2 *Antica leggenda*, V, 14.

3 Gebhart, *L'Italie mystique* (Paris 1890), p. 9.

4 Sal., p. 227.

5 Quoted by Böhmer, *Analekten zur Geschichte des Franziskus von Assisi* (Tübingen 1904), p. 98.

6 Sal., p. 228.

7 Sal., p. 327.

8 The French version of the letter from hell is in Thomas of Cantimpré, *Liber Apum* (ed. Douai 1597), I, c. 20; the Italian version in Salimbene, p. 419.

9 Ubertino a Casali, *Arbor vitae crucifixae Jesu* (ed. Venice 1485).

10 Cf. Dav., II, 1, p. 327, and II, 2, p. 136.

11 *Inferno*, 10, 120.

12 Sal., p. 518.

13 According to the account of an attendant of the Bishop of Parma, who escaped through the back door of his palace into his sawmill and then by water to take refuge in a friendly monastery (M. G. SS., XVIII, p. 716).

14 Sal., p. 518.

15 Jacques de Vitry, *Historia occidentalis* (ed. Douai 1597), ch. 30.

16 *De contemptu mundi* (Migne PL, 217, col. 701).

17 Dav. II, 2, p. 296.

18 Sal., p. 425.

19 Sal., p. 411.

20 RIS, IX, p. 767.

21 *Inferno*, 30, 148.

22 M. G. SS., XIX, p. 133.

23 M. G. SS., XXVIII, p. 134.

24 Dav., II, 1, p. 303. His account of the trials of heretics in Florence (II, 1, pp. 296 ff., and II, 2, pp. 283 ff.) is very prejudiced.

25 Sal., pp. 256 ff.

26 Haskins, *Studies* . . ., pp. 245 ff., 272 ff.

27 Kant., I, p. 375.

28 Sal., p. 538.

29 Sal., p. 512; RIS, VIII, p. 1153. Cf. Dante, *Inferno*, 20, 115 ff.

> Quell 'altro che ne' fianchi è così poco,
>> Michele Scotto fu, che veramente
>> de le magiche frode seppe il gioco.
> Vedi Guido Bonatti; vedi Asdente,
>> ch' avere inteso al cuoio ed a lo spago
>> ora vorrebbe, ma tardi si pente.

30 Sal., p. 289.

31 Cf. Dav., II, 1, pp. 170 ff.

32 Cf. Jakobsen, *Sienesische Meister des Trecento in der Gemälder-galerie zu Siena* (Strasburg 1907), p. 11.

CHAPTER EIGHT

1 Mazzatinti, Laudi dei Disciplinati di Gubbio', *Il Propugnatore* N.S., II, 1, p. 159.

2 *Purgatorio*, 1, 1–3.

3 For Benedictus de Cornetta, see especially Sal., pp. 71 f.

4 Cf. I. della Giovanna, 'San Francesco Giullare', *Giornale Storico della letteratura italiana*, XXV, p. 16.

5 Florentine MS Mgl. 1, 2, 122, no. XVIII. The structure of this song is much simpler than the other *laudi* in this collection, and it is certainly older. That the remembrance of the 'Alleluia year' remained fresh until the end of the century is shown by the anecdote from Salimbene (p. 595) already quoted. It is also not impossible that this Alleluia song, which also appears (but without its tune) in the second fascicule of Cortona MS 91, which is early

fourteenth century, is a genuine relic of 1233, perhaps with slight alterations. Since this argument is, however, not conclusive, it may still be true that the oldest purely Italian melody is that of the flagellants of 1260, given on p. 119.

6 Thus Gerard of Modena; Sal., pp. 75 ff.; RIS, XI, p. 60.

7 M. G. SS., XIX, p. 370. The mysterious character 'Frater I., vili contectus tegmine tamquam de ordine minorum,' who brought Cassino to penance has by some been identified with the celebrated John of Vicenza. This, however, seems unlikely, since John's field of activity was Lombardy and moreover this man wore a habit like a Franciscan. The opinion of Della Giovanna (loc. cit.), that such abbreviations do not occur in the chronicles and that the I here is a scribe's mistake, is also unconvincing, since though abbreviations are commoner in registers, they are to be found in chronicles, too.

8 Sal., p. 595.

9 Cf. the monograph of von Sutter, *Johann von Vicenza und die italienische Friedensbewegung* (Freiburg i.B. 1891).

10 RIS, VIII, p. 128.

11 Sal., p. 83.

12 M. G. SS., XIX, p. 59.

13 RIS, IX, p. 742. (The passage is from Luke 21: 25–33.)

14 For this and other prophecies, see Holder-Egger, 'Italienische Profetien', in *Neues Archiv*, XV, pp. 143 ff.

15 RIS, XII, p. 347, and XIII, p. 174 (= Villani VI, 30).

16 Conclusion of the *Expositio in Apocalypsin* (cf. Aegerter, II, p. 144).

17 Ferri *Lauda* 50.

18 Sal., p. 465.

19 RIS, VI, p. 527.

20 Kant., I, p. 543.

21 *Inferno*, 1, 31–105.

22 According to the Sienese historian Tizio, quoted by Carducci, *Intorno ad alcune rime dei secoli XIII e XIV*, in his collected works, vol. XVIII, p. 174. The *brigata* is that mentioned by Dante in the *Inferno* 29, 130.

23 Sal., p. 465.

24 Galli, 'I Disciplinati dell 'Umbria', *Giornale storico*, supplem. 9, p. 13. The flagellants started something with their letter from heaven: the German flagellants of the plague years 1348 and 1349

also had their letter from heaven, which according to Pfannens-
chmidt was taken from an Italian thirteenth-century source to
form their *'Vrone Botschaft'*. Cf. his note in Runge, *Lieder und
Melodien der Geissler des Jahres* 1349 (Leipzig, 1900), p. 155.

25 RIS, VIII, pp. 712 ff.
26 RIS, XI, p. 66.
27 RIS, VIII, p. 1121.
28 RIS, XVI, p. 471.
29 RIS, VI, p. 527.
30 RIS, IX, p. 49.
31 Sal., p. 465.
32 Sal., loc. cit., and RIS, VIII, pp. 713 f.
33 Cf. also RIS, IX, p. 134.
34 The music of this song was preserved by the Genoese contemporary, Bartolomeo Scriba, but with a Latin text, which appears
in two forms as follows: version (*a*) being that given by Muratori
(RIS, VI, p. 527), and (*b*) the later version in M. G. SS, XVIII,
p. 241:

(*a*) Domina sancta Maria, (*b*) Domina sancta Maria,
    recipite peccatores   recipite peccatores,
    et rogate Jesum Christum   et rogetis Jesum Christum
    ut nobis parcat.   ut nobis parcere debeat.

About fifteen years later this song was inserted in Italian (which,
of course, was the original) in the well-known song-book MS
Cortona L.IV. In its structure this *laude* is much simpler than the
others. Liuzzi was the first to identify it as the song of the
flagellants (*La Lauda*, I, p. 271). His transcription there into
modern notation is, however, rhythmically unacceptable. Cf. the
present author's own study: *De oudste melodiek van het Duecento*,
p. 39, note 5.
35 For the Italian confraternities, see the already mentioned and
outstanding work of Monti, *Le Confraternite dell'alta e media
Italia*, I, pp. 68 ff.
36 Thus is the Confraternity of St Stephen at Assisi, that remained
until 1810, cf. Cristofani, *Delle storie di Assisi* (Assisi 1866),
p. 224.
37 Monti, 'Gli albori di musica e lirica religiosa italiana', *Arte
pianistica*, VIII (Naples 1921), pp. 9f.
38 Monti, *Confraternite*, I, pp. 146, 193, 285. Many religious
groups founded in 1233 were turned after 1260 into flagellant

societies, only to place the emphasis thirty years later on the less penitential activity of *laudi*.

39 Sal., p. 375.
40 In the story of the seventh day of the *Decamerone*, a Capitano de' Laudesi is introduced.
41 Cristofani, loc. cit.
42 Padovan, 'Gli uffici drammatici dei Disciplinati di Gubbio', *Archivio storico per le Marche e per l'Umbria*, I, p. 2.
43 Monti, *Albori*, p. 8.
44 Ibid., p. 9.
45 Ibid., p. 8.
46 Padovan, op. cit., p. 1.
47 Monti, *Albori*, p. 8.
48 Verse 6 of the *laude* from Cortona *Stomme allegro*, from Liuzzi, *La Lauda*, I, p. 408.
49 Rondoni, 'Laudi drammatici', *Giornale storico*, II, p. 300.
50 Monaci, 'Uffici drammatici dei Disciplinati dell' Umbria', *Riv. di Fil. rom.*, I, p. 242, note 2.
51 Scipioni, '3 Laudi sacre pesaresi', *Giorn. stor.*, VI, p. 216.

CHAPTER NINE

The Rise of the Universities (after Schnürer, vol. II).

Ninth century: Salerno.
End of twelfth century: Bologna (Paris, Oxford).
c. 1200 Modena, Reggio (Montpellier, Cambridge).
1204 Vicenza.
(*c.* 1212 Palencia.)
1222 Padua.
1224 Naples.
1228 Vercelli.
(1229 Toulouse.)
(1243 Salamanca.)
1244 at the Roman Curia.
(1245 Valencia.)
1248 Piacenza.
c. 1250 Arezzo (Orleans, Angers).
(1348 Prague: the oldest university of Germany.)

1221 Bonaventure born.

1243 Goes to study in Paris under Alexander of Hales.

1225 Birth of Thomas Aquinas.

1245 Studies in Paris and Cologne (Albert the Great).

1255 Both of them in Paris resist the attack of William of St Amour on the mendicant orders.

1257 Both are made Masters in Paris; Bonaventure becomes general of his order.

1274 Both die.

1 Genoese popular jingle 'Contra lectores et non factores', from *Crestomazia*, p. 439.

2 *L'art religieux du XIIIme siècle* (Paris⁴ 1931), p. 1.

3 Sal., p. 344.

4 *Legenda aurea*, ch. 101 (*De septem dormientibus*). At the end: 'Quod CCCLXII annis dormiisse dicuntur, dubium esse potest, quia anno Domini CCCCXLVIII surrexerant, Decius autem regnavit uno tantum anno et tribus mensibus, scilicet anno Domini CCLII et ita non dormierunt nisi CXCVI annos.' [Note by Tr: Text says supposed total 372, here 362, which tallies with Caxton's text as given in Butler-Thurston-Attwater's *Lives*; but there Decius's year is given as 270, their awaking as 478, and their sleep therefore as 208.]

5 Sal., pp. 515, 584.

6 Sal., p. 521.

7 The most balanced account is still probably that of Denifle, *Die Entstehung der Universitäten des Mittelalters bis 1400* (Berlin 1885), and cf. also Rashdall, *The Universities of Europe in the Middle Ages* (revised ed., Oxford 1936).

8 Denifle, op. cit., p. 278.

9 Op. cit., p. 429.

10 Op. cit., p. 534.

11 For the University of Naples, cf. Kant., I, pp. 270 ff., and also the excursus 3 in Kant., II (pp. 266 ff.), on the University and its teachers.

12 *Cambridge Medieval History* (Cambridge 1932–43), VI, pp. 580 f.

13 Jacques de Vitry, *Hist. Occident.*, ch. 7 (of the students in Paris): 'Anglicos potatores et caudatos affirmantes; Francigenas superbos, molles et muliebriter compositos asserentes; Theutonicos furi-

bundos et in conviviis suis obscenos dicebantur; Normannos autem inanes et gloriosos; Pictavos proditores et fortune amicos. Hos autem qui de Burgundia erant, brutos et stultos reputabant, Britones autem leves et vagos iudicantes . . . Lombardos avaros, malitiosos et imbelles; Romanos seditiosos, violentes et manus rodentes; Siculos tyrannos et crudeles; Brabantios viros sanguinum, incendiarios, rutarios et raptores; Flandrenses superfluos, prodigos et commessationibus deditos, et more butyri molles et remissos appellabant.' A situation hardly encouraging for the United Nations!

14 Denifle, op. cit., p. 170.

15 *Cambridge Med. Hist.*, loc. cit.

16 Ibid.

17 Sal., pp. 77 f.: 'more Florentinorum trufator maximus,' the chronicler explains.

18 Dante, *De acqua et terra*, ch. 6; cf. Kant., I, p. 361, and Haskins, *Studies . . .*, pp. 266 f., 296 ff.

19 Haskins, op. cit., p. 265.

20 Kant., I, p. 318.

21 Joannes a Plano Carpini: *Historia Mongalorum, quos nos Tartaros appellamus*, ch. 9; cf. Muller, *Voorlopers en navolgers*, p. 17.

22 Muller, *Marco Polo's reizen* (Leiden 1940), p. 12, mentions the expeditions of Wood, who rediscovered in 1838 Marco Polo's plateau of Pamir; and of Prjevalski who in 1871 reached Lop-Nor.

23 Ristoro d'Areço, 'La composizione del Mondo', *Crestomazia*, p. 364.

24 *Novellino*, 38.

25 *Novellino*, 29.

26 *Purgatorio*, 4, 61, and such cosmological ideas are to be found in almost every canto of the *Purgatorio* and *Paradiso*.

27 Bonvesin da Riva, *Vulgare de Eleemosynis*, lines 257 ff., edited by Bekker in the acts of the *Akademie der Wissenschaft zu Berlin* (1850), p. 438.

28 *Inferno*, 28, 26–27: 'e'l triste sacco/che merda fa di quel che si trangugia.'

29 Lauda 48 (Ferri).

30 See above, note 13, p. 242.

31 Cf. Röckinger, 'Der "Cedrus" des Boncompagno', *Quellen zur bayerischen Geschichte*, IX, p. 123; cf. also Dav., I, p. 666.

32 *Summa Theologica*, I–II, q. 21, a. 1.

33 Cf. Bennett, *The early Dominicans* (Cambridge 1937), p. 8.

34 Quoted by G. Truc, in his rather confused booklet *Le retour à la scolastique* (Paris 1919), p. 33.

35 Lauda 31 (Ferri):

> Tale qual' è, tal' è;
> non c' è religione.
> Mal vedemmo Parisi
> ch' hane destrutto Assisi;
> con la lor lettoria
> l' han messo en mala via.

36 Lauda *Udite una pazzia*, verses 17, 19, 20, 21, ed. Tresatti.

37 Lauda 31, last verse (Ferri).

38 On the authorship of the *Meditationes* cf. the studies of Fischer, *Arch. Franciscanum historicum*, XXV (1932), pp. 3 ff., 175 ff., 305 ff.

39 Lauda 46 (Ferri): 'Con gli occhi che aggio nel capo.'

40 Cf. Pseudo-Dionysius, prologue to the *Mystica Theologia* (Migne, PG, 3), and Richard of St Victor in his *Benjamin Major* (*De gratia contemplationis*) in Migne PL, 196. For the text of the *Triplex Via* see Bonaventure's collected works (Vol. VIII), also his *Decem Opuscula* (Quaracchi 1896). [The older editions usually give to the work *De Triplici Via* the title *Incendium Amoris*, and thus it is often referred to.—Tr.]

CHAPTER TEN

1 Guido Guinicelli was born about 1240 at Bologna, and was one of the first exponents of the *dolce stil nuovo*.

2 According to Vasari, the architect of the double basilica was a certain Jacopo Tedesco; but in the earlier records his name is unknown. Then a certain builder-overseer, named Magister Philippus de Campello, is mentioned as working between 1232 and 1235. If the design of the church really was his, it is curious that no one recorded the fact; and it seems wiser to continue to think that he, or another, did no more than to carry out the designs of the real *auctor intellectualis*, namely Elias. For this cf. H. Thode, *Franz von Assisi und die Anfänge der Kunst der Renaissance in Italien* (Vienna 1936), pp. 210 ff.

3 Excellent pictures of the churches of Apulia are provided in Willemsen, *Apulien, Land der Normannen, Land der Staufer* (Leipzig ⁴1944).

4 Sal., p. 31.

5 Gebhart, op. cit., p. 71. Temptations during office in choir were proverbial in most lands. In the *Liber Apum* a certain German prior is praised for his zeal, which was demonstrated by the thick layer of dust on the seat of his place in choir!

6 *Legenda Aurea* 113.

7 On the authenticity and history of the *Dies Irae* see Lampen, 'Intorno al Dies Irae', *Studi francescani*, XIII, p. 1. On the music see the (somewhat inadequate) article by Clop, 'La prose du Dies Irae', *Revue du Chant grégorien*, XVI, pp. 46 ff., and Gastoué, 'Sur les origines du Dies Irae', *Études franciscaines*, XX, pp. 399 ff. For the rhymed office by Julian of Speyer see Bruning, 'Giuliano da Spira e l'officio ritmico di S. Francesco', *Note d'Archivio*, IV, pp. 127 ff. Cf. also the present author's study *De oudste melodiek van Italië*, pp. 30 f.

8 According to Bruning, *Officium ac Missa de festo S.P.N. Francisci* (Rome 1926), p. 114. There follow seven further verses, *durchkomponiert* in pairs. Salimbene (p. 383) expressly names Gregory IX as the author.

9 An exception is an entirely insignificant two-voice *Virelai*, written by a court poet, a certain Bonaiutus of Casentino on the occasion of a blood-letting of Boniface VIII (printed in *Acta musicologica* IX, p. 1).

10 Characteristic is the story of the song which Henry heard a girl sing at Pisa, which ran: E se tu no cure de me
                                                                e no curaro de te,
evidently a simple love song, which the composer turned into a sacred song with the words:
                              Christe Deus, Christe meus,
                              Christe rex et omnium. (cf. Sal., p. 393.)
[Story of the nun in Sal., p. 265, ed. Bernini.—Tr.].

11 The so-called *Ritmo cassinese*, ('Eo, sinjuri, s'eo fabello), in Zonta, *Letteratura italiana* (Turin 1928), I, p. 370, [and Dionisotti and Grayson, *Early Italian Texts* (Oxford 1949), pp. 76–90.—Tr.]

12 Cf. the article by Meyer, 'De l'expansion de la langue française en Italie pendant le moyen âge', *Atti del Congresso internazionale di scienze storiche*, 1903–4, pp. 61 ff.

13 Schnürer, vol. II.
14 *Inferno*, 15, 30 ff. During the conversation Dante held his head bowed in reverence (line 45).
15 *Novellino*, 8.
16 *Novellino*, 27.
17 *Novellino*, 73.
18 *Novellino*, 9.
19 *Novellino*, 31.
20 *Crestomazia*, p. 258.
21 *Inferno*, 10, 22.
22 D'Ancona, *Manuale*, I, p. 97.
23 Op. cit., p. 105.
24 Bertoni, 'Il Duecento', *Storia letteraria d'Italia* (Milan 1910), III, p. 170.
25 D'Ancona, *Manuale*, I, p. 116 (including two more strophes).
26 Op. cit., p. 114.
27 *La Vita Nuova*, Sonnet 15 (in chapter 26).
28 Much has been written on the identity of Beatrice. The identification of her with Theology does not, of course, exclude the possibility of an earthly Beatrice as model for the symbolic Beatrice. Scholastic theology was anyway part of the general heritage of educated people of the time. A particular theory was advocated by Mandonnet, in his *Dante Théologien* (Paris 1935).

CHAPTER ELEVEN

1 *Crestomazia*, p. 292.
2 The Provençal codex (R. 71 sup.) in the Biblioteca ambrosiana at Milan, entirely written in Italy and for Italians, gives an impression of the troubadours in Italy. The following are mentioned: Folquet de Marseille, Bernard de Ventadorn, Gaucelm Faidit, Arnaut de Moroill, Guiraudo lo Ros, Aimeric de Peguillan, Peire Vidal, Peirol, Peire Raimon of Toulouse, Gui d'Uisel, Richard de Berbezill, Perdigo, Raimon de Miraval, Arnaut Daniel, Guillelm de Saint Lédier, Pons de Capdoill and Uc de Saint Circ. The text was edited by Sesini, *Le melodie trobadoriche nel Canzoniere provenzale della Biblioteca Ambrosiana* (Turin 1942).
3 Cf. Schulz, 'Die Lebensverhältnisse der italienischen Trobadors', *Zeitschrift für romanische Philologie*, VII, pp. 175 ff.

4 *Purgatorio*, 6, 58 ff.

5 Sal., p. 348.

6 Sal., p. 329.

7 Bertoni, *I Trovatori d'Italia* (Modena 1915), p. 25.

8 RIS, VIII, p. 978; cf. chapter I above.

9 Ottokar, *Österreichische Reimchronik*, line 277 (MGH Deutsche Chroniken I). They are: Meister Wildunc, Werner von Ruofach, Friderich von Valschenberg, Ramwolt, Meister Pab, Walther von Sittou, Friderich von Wirzpurc, Kuonrât von Rôtenberc, Sibot von Erfurt, Meister Otte, Heinrich von Landeskron, Gebehart, Uolrich von Glesin, Walther von Swinitz, Alberich von Merspurc, Kuonrat von Tyrol, Perthold von Sumerech.

10 *Crestomazia*, p. 47.

11 Op. cit., p. 92.

12 Op. cit., p. 82.

13 Sal., p. 44.

14 Staaf, *Le Laudario di Pisa du Ms. 8521 de la Bibliothèque de l'Arsénal de Paris* (Uppsala 1931), p. 254 (Str. 2).

15 'Erat in Marchia Anconitana saecularis quidam sui oblitus et Dei nescius, qui se totum prostituerat vanitati. Vocabatur nomen eius rex versuum, eo quod princeps foret lasciva cantantium et inventor saecularium cantionum. Ut paucis dicam, usque adeo gloria mundi exulterat hominem, quod ab imperatore fuerat pomposissime coronatus.' Thus the unfavourable account of Thomas of Celano (*Vita II*, ch. 72). Some have seen in this 'rex versuum' a certain Guglielmo Divini, but without any warrant, since we know nothing of the worldly past of Brother Pacificus. Nothing is known of any officially crowned poet in the time of Frederick II, nor even among the Ottos; so that we are compelled to suppose that the Franciscan authors (Bonaventure in his *Legenda major*, 50, as well as Celano) have perhaps exaggerated the worldly glamour of Pacificus. On the whole question, apart from the present author's study *De oudste melodiek van Italië*, pp. 36–38, see Cosmo, 'Frate Pacifico', *Giornale Storico*, XXXVIII (1901), pp. 1 ff., reprinted as 'Il re dei versi', *Con Madonna Povertà* (Bari 1940), pp. 59 ff.

16 'Quid opus plus serere verba? Veniamus ad facta. Tolle me ab hominibus et magno me imperatori restitue!' in Thomas of Celano's *Vita II* (i.e. the second of two Lives of St Francis by Thomas of Celano, usually quoted as I Celano or II Celano), ch. 72.

17 II Celano, ch. 72 and ch. 99.

18 Another converted musician was 'Brother Zither-player' in II Celano, 89.

19 Cf. Hugh of St Victor, *De bestiis et aliis rebus*, ch. 46 (Migne PL 177).

20 E.g., Sal., pp. 160, 175, 628; RIS VIII, p. 1032. The city of Siena gave a new set of clothes to a *joculator* 'quia fecit cantionem de captione Tornielle' in 1255, cf. D'Ancona, *La poesia popolare italiana* (Leghorn 1906), p. 9.

21 Quoted by Della Giovanna, op. cit., p. 23.

22 Sal., p. 323.

23 Jacopone, Lauda 21 (Ferri), verse 8.

24 *Antica leggenda*, VII, 9–10.

25 'Ut cantatores Francigenorum in plateis Communis ad cantandum omnino morare non possint,' quoted by Tamassia in *Atti e memorie della R. Deputazione di Storia patria per le provincie di Romagna* (3rd series), XII (1895), p. 375.

26 No sharp distinction between various forms of public entertainment seems to have been made in the thirteenth century: there is mention of jumpers, runners, actors, fencers, boxers, wrestlers, conjurors, singers, all together. Cf. De Bartholomaeis, *Origini della Poesia drammatica* (Bologna N.D.), I, pp. 26 ff.

27 Dav., I, p. 769.

28 Sal., p. 440.

29 *Crestomazia*, p. 250.

30 Op. cit., p. 513. Cecco lived about 1258 to 1305.

31 Loc. cit.

32 Op. cit., p. 529.

33 Bertoni, *Duecento*, p. 174.

34 Torgioni-Toselli, *Antologia di poesie italiane* (Leghorn 1885), p. 142.

35 *Crestomazia*, p. 281.

36 Op. cit., p. 294.

CHAPTER TWELVE

1 Cortona song book, Lauda 44 (ed. Liuzzi, I, p. 459).

2 The tendentious but very poetical work *Sacrum Commercium b. Francisci cum Domina Paupertate* (ed. Quaracchi 1929), which belongs to the thirteenth century, is often ascribed to John of

Parma. This may indeed be so, especially as the detailed description of the view (such a rare thing at this time) does suggest that the work was actually written at Greccio.

3 *Sacrum Commercium*, ch. 63 (p. 73).

4 Cf. M. Boehme, *Das lateinische Weihnachtsspiel* (Leipzig 1917), p. 5.

5 I Celano, 30.

6 Lauda 65 (Ferri).

7 Cortona song book, Lauda 18 (ed. Liuzzi, I, p. 330).

8 A thorough treatment of the painting of the *Duecento* is the work of R. van Marle, *The development of the Italian Schools of Painting* (The Hague 1923), the first part being devoted to the period 'from the sixth until the end of the thirteenth century,' and this has appeared revised and amplified in Italian as *Le scuole della Pittura italiana* (The Hague and Milan 1932).

9 *Purgatorio*, 11, 94.

10 *Legenda trium Sociorum* (ed. Faloci-Pulignani, Foligno 1898), cap. VII, 21.

11 *Fioretti: Prima considerazione delle sacrosante stimmate.*

12 *Fioretti*, 37.

13 *Tres socii*, cap. I, 10: 'Licet eam recte loqui nesciret.'

14 Cf. the delightful rhymed office by Julian of Speyer, 4th Responsory: 'Dum seminudo corpore laudes decantat gallice'; and cf. I Celano 7.

15 *Tres socii*, cap. IX, 33.

16 II Celano, 90; cf. also the *Speculum perfectionis*, as delightful a book as the *Fioretti*, written probably about 1300, and edited by Sabatier (Paris 1898), ch. 93: 'Dulcissima melodia spiritus intra ipsum ebulliens exterius gallicum dabat sonum.'

17 II Celano, 90.

18 *Fioretti: Seconda considerazione . . .* (near end). In the *Liber Apum* a French canon uses similar words: the music was so beautiful 'quod, nisi Deus aliter ordinasset, fere eius animam extra corpus sine reditu rapuisset.'

19 II Celano, 89: 'Non videbatur aliquis, sed transitus et reditus citharedi, ipsa hinc inde auditus volubilitas innuebat.'

20 *Speculum perfectionis*, ch. 123.

21 II Celano 90. Psalm 141 (142): 'Voce mea ad Dominum clamavi', and for this reason this Psalm is used at the Introit of the Mass of the Stigmata of St Francis (September 17th).

22 'Legenda antiqua', Delorme, *Arch. Franc. Hist.*, XV (1922), no. 110.

23 'Quid enim sunt servi Dei nisi quidam ioculatores eius qui corda hominum erigere debent ad laetitiam spiritualem?' *Speculum perfectionis*, 100.

24 Bartholomaeus Pisanus, 'De conformitate vitae b.p. Francisci ad Vitam D.N. Jesu Christi' (1385), *Analecta franciscana*, IV–V, Conf. II, fr. XI, 2.

25 Monti assembled a bibliography on the Canticle of the Sun in *Bibliofilia* XXI–XXV, but it only goes up to 1909. More useful is the study of Brancaloni, *Il cantico di frate Sole* (Todi 1925, new ed. Milan 1927). Benedetto published *Il cantico di frate Sole* (Flornece 1941), of no great critical importance. The musical problems (did Francis also compose the tune, what was its character, and was it a sequence or a hymn?) are discussed in the present author's *De oudste melodiek van Italië*, pp. 25–28, 70–71.

26 The oldest existing text of the Canticle of the Sun is in Codex 338 (f. 33 r. and v., 34 r.) in the city library of Assisi. This was written before 1255 (cf. Faloci-Pulignani in *Miscellanea franciscana*, VI, p. 44). The facsimile, which we have taken from Brancaloni, shows the three pages placed together to form a single text.

27 *Crestomazia*, p. 140: 'Proverbia super natura feminarum,' verse 29.

28 Bertoni, *Duecento*, p. 187.

29 *Il libro delle tre scritture di Fra Bonvesin da Riva*, ed. Biadene (Pisa 1902); cf. Bertoni, op. cit., p. 193.

30 Mussafia, 'Monumenti antichi di dialetti italiani', *Sitzungsbericht der Ks. Akademie der Wissenschaften, Philos.-hist. Klasse*, XLVI (Vienna 1864), pp. 140 ff.: *Jerusalem coelestis*, verses 151–2. The same notion appears north of the Alps in *Des Knaben Wunderhorn*: 'Der Himmel hängt voll Geigen . . .'

31 Cortona song book, Lauda 37 (ed. Liuzzi, I, p. 414).

32 Florence song book, Lauda 4 (MS Mgl. 2–I–122) (ed. Liuzzi, II, p. 21).

33 *Crestomazia*, p. 469; the whole *laude* has twenty-three verses.

34 The structure of the *laude* is that of the Italian *ballata* or the French *virelai*. The experts have disagreed about this *ballata* form, the Italians claiming it as native and the non-Italians maintaining it is an adaptation of the French *virelai*. The melodies of the *laudi* in Cortona MS 91 show the truth to lie midway: the

laude developed partly independently from the Latin hymn, but took over the refrain principle from northern France, where it was already usual. On musical grounds it is impossible to see the Latin sequence as the immediate predecessor of the *laude*, as Brancaloni (op. cit., with reference to the Canticle of the Sun) and Ippoliti (*Dalle Sequenze alle Laudi*, Osimo 1914) have done; cf. *De oudste melodiek van Italië*, pp. 70 f.

35 Cortona song book. Lauda 22; complete text in Liuzzi, I, 355 f.

36 MS Cortona 91 is in the first part, and MS Mgl. 2–I–122 from Florence is in the second part of Liuzzi's work, where Liuzzi's own introduction is full of musicological errors, and moreover his transcriptions are very unsatisfactory, though the facsimile reproductions are of indisputable value. Cf. *De oudste melodiek van Italië*, pp. 48–50.

37 Cortona song book, Lauda 1, refrain (Liuzzi, I, pp. 256 f.).

38 Ibid., Lauda 39, refrain (op. cit., I, pp. 434 f.).

39 Ed. Staaf, *Le Laudario di Pisa*.

40 The two songs are found in the Venice edition of Jacopone of 1617 (Lib. VII, 8 and VI, 37), but this is no evidence at all of their authenticity. Unlike the other *laudi* which we have taken from this collection, these two are doubtful, though Staaf never questions the authorship of Jacopone.

41 Pisa song book, Lauda 52 (ed. Staaf, pp. 140 f.).

42 Ibid., Lauda 19 (Staaf, p. 42).

43 Cf. E. Underhill, *Jacopone da Todi, poet and mystic* (London 1919); in many respects an excellent book.

44 Lauda 55, refrain (Ferri).

45 Lauda 76, verse 1 (Ferri).

46 Lauda 13, last verse (Ferri).

47 Lauda 25, verse 10 (Ferri).

48 Lauda *Non tardate o peccatori* (Tresatti).

49 Lauda *Nella mia mente* (Tresatti).

50 Lauda 81 (Ferri).

51 Lauda 75 (Ferri).

52 Lauda *En foco l'Amor mi mise* (Tresatti).

53 Lauda 90, end (Ferri).

54 Psychologically it seems unlikely that the *Stabat Mater* and the *Donna del Paradiso* (Ferri 93), though with similar themes, could be by the same man, or that Jacopone, the man of the people, should suddenly produce a Latin poem with so genteel a rhythm.

In the fourteenth century the author was believed to be John XXII (according to RIS, XVII, p. 1170), but for centuries a Roman tradition ascribed it to Jacopone's enemy Boniface VIII, according to Demattio, *Lettere in Italia prima di Dante* (Verona 1871), p. 178. In the nineteenth century the *Stabat Mater* was ascribed to Jacopone, together with seven other Latin poems, the authors of which for the most part we now know, according to Ozanam, *Les poètes franciscains en Italie au XIIIe siècle* (Paris 1870), pp. 213, 215. It seems probable, especially on account of its dramatic qualities hidden in the formal, balanced strophes, that the author nevertheless came from Franciscan circles, and Bonaventure might even be considered.

55 Cf. the Florentine MS Mgl. 2–I–122 in Liuzzi's edition.

56 There were Passion plays in Italy since 1243, but it is not known how far the vernacular was used. The oldest Italian *devozioni* belong to the fourteenth century.

57 D'Ancona, 'Due antiche Devozioni', *Rivista di Filologia romanza*, II, pp. 14 ff.

Bibliography

ACCAME, Paolo, 'Frammenti di Laudi sacre in dialette ligure antico', *Atti della Società ligure di storia patria*, XIX (1888), pp. 549 ff.

Acta Sanctorum, ed. J. Bollandus et socii (2nd ed., Paris 1854).

AEGERTER, E., *Joachim de Flore, l'Évangile éternel* (Paris 1928).

ALESSANDRI, E., and MAZZATINTI, G., *Inventario dei Manoscritti della Biblioteca del Convento di S. Francesco d'Assisi* (Forlì 1894).

AMARI, M., *Biblioteca arabo-sicula*, versione italiana (Turin 1880).

Altre narrazioni del vespro siciliano (Milan 1887).

ANCONA, Alessandro d', *Origini del Teatro in Italia*, 2 vols. (2nd ed. Turin 1891), vol. I.

La poesia popolare italiana (Leghorn 1878, 2nd ed. 1906).

'Due antiche Devozioni', *Rivista di Filologia romanza*, II, 2, pp. 1 ff.

Manuale della Letteratura italiana (Florence 1905–6; ed. of 1925), vol. I.

ANGELA DA FOLIGNO: *Le livre de la Bienheureuse Soeur Angèle de Foligno*, ed. Paul Doncœur (Latin text Toulouse 1925; French tr. Paris 1926).

Annales Placentini, ed. J. L. A. Huillard-Bréholles (Paris 1856).

ANTONII PATAVINI, S., *Sermones dominicales et in solemnitatibus*, ed. M. Locatelli (Padua 1895–1903).

Antonii de Padua, S., vitae duae, ed. L. de Kerval (Paris 1904).

ATTAL, S., *Frate Elia Compagno di S. Francesco* (Rome 1936).

BACCI, 'Juncta Pisanus Pictor', *Bolletino d'Arte del Ministero di pubblica istruzione* 1922, pp. 145 ff.

BARTHOLOMAEUS PISANUS, 'De conformitate vitae B. P. Francisci ad vitam D. N. Jesu Christi', *Anal. Franc.*, vols. IV and V (Quaracchi).

BATELLI, G., *Florilegio francescano di prose e poesie* (Turin 1923).

BENEDETTO, L. F., *Il Cantico di frate Sole* (Florence 1941).

BENNETT, R. F., *The early Dominicans* (Cambridge 1937).

BERTONI, G., *Il Laudario dei Battuti di Modena* (Halle 1909).

'Il Duecento', *Storia letteraria d'Italia*, vol. III (Milan 1910).

I Trovatori d'Italia (Modena 1915).

BETTAZZI, E., *Notizia di un Laudario del secolo XIII* (Arezzo 1890). 'Laudi di Borgo S. Sepolcro', *Giornale Storico* XVIII, 1891, p. 242.

BEVEGNATI, Fr. Giunta, *Antica leggenda della vita e de' miracoli di S. Margherita scritta dal Confessore di lei*, ed. E. Cirvelli (Siena 1897).

BIONDELLI, B., *Studi linguistici* (Milan 1856).

BOEHMER, Heinrich, *Analekten zur Geschichte des Franciscus von Assisi* (Tübingen 1904; 2nd ed. 1930).

BONAVENTURE, St, *Opera omnia* (Quaracchi 1898). In vol. VIII is included the *Legenda maior B. P. N. Francisci* (also in *Acta SS.*, Oct. II) and the *De triplici via* (which is also in the *Decem Opuscula*, Quaracchi 1896).

BONVESIN DA RIVA, *Varie Poesie*, ed. I. Bekker, in *Verhandlungen der Akademie der Wissenschaft zu Berlin* 1850, pp. 322, 379, 438; 1851, pp. 3, 90, 130.

Il libro delle tre scritture, ed. L. Biadene (Pisa 1902).

BORNE, F. van den, 'Die Anfänge des franziskanischen dritten Ordens', *Franzisk. Studien*, Beiheft 8 (Münster 1925).

'Antonius en Elias (Doctor Evangelicus)', *Collect. francisc. neerland.* VII (Den Bosch 1949).

BRANCALONI, L., *Il cantico di frate Sole* (2nd ed., Milan 1927).

BRACKMANN, A., 'Kaiser Friedrich II in "mythischer Schau"', *Hist. Zeitschrift* 1929, pp. 534 ff.

BROOKE, Rosalind, *Early Franciscan Government* (Cambridge 1959). [An essential book for the reassessment of Elias.—Tr.]

BRUNING, Eliseus, 'Giuliano da Spira e l'officio ritmico di S. Francesco', *Note d'Archivio*, IV, pp. 127 ff.

(ed.), v.s. Juliani a Spira.

CARDUCCI, G., 'Della lirica popollare italiana del secolo XIII e XIV', *Opere*, vol. XVIII, p. 65.

Intorno ad alcune rime dei secoli XIII e XIV, ibid., p. 109.

CASINI, T., *Forme metriche italiane* (Florence 1900).

CATALANO, M., 'Laudari ignoti di Disciplinati umbri', *Annuari dell'Istituto Bonghi* (Assisi 1925).

CECCONI, E., *Laudi di una Compagnia fiorentina* (Florence 1870).

CELANO, v.s. Thomas.

CESAREO, G. A., *Le origini della poesia lirica, e la poesia italiana sotto gli Svevi* (2nd ed. Milan 1924).

CHINI, *Canti popolari umbri* (Todi 1918).

CLOP DES SORINIÈRES, E., *Le chant dans l'ordre séraphique* (Solesmes 1900).

Les cantiques de St François et leurs mélodies (Rome 1909).

'La prose Dies Irae e l'Ordre des frères mineurs', *Revue du chant grégorien*, XVI, pp. 46 ff.

COHN, Willy, *Das Zeitalter der Hohenstaufen in Sizilien* (Breslau 1915).

COSMO, Umberto, *Con Madonna Povertà: studi francescani* (Bari (1940).

DANTE, *Convivio*.

Divina Commedia.

Epistolae.

la Vita Nuova.

de Vulgari Eloquentia.

DAVIDSOHN, R., *Geschichte von Florenz*, 4 vols. (Berlin 1896–1927), vols. I & II.

DE ANGELIS, *Capitoli dei Disciplinati di Siena* (Siena 1818).

DE BARTHOLOMAEIS, V., *Origini della poesia drammatica italiana* 2 vols. (Bologna N.D.).

DE JONG, Y., *Handboek der Kerkgeschiedenis*, vol. II (4th ed., Utrecht-Nijmegen 1947).

DELLA GIOVANNA, I., 'S. Francesco Giullare', *Giornale Storico*, XXV, 1895, pp. 1 ff.

DEMATTIO, F., *Lettere in Italia prima di Dante* (Verona 1871).

DEMUS, O. F., *The Mosaics of Norman Sicily* (London 1949).

DENIFLE, H., *Die Universitäten des Mittelalters bis* 1400 (Berlin 1885).

DIEZ, F., *Die Poesie der Troubadours* (Zwickau 1826).

DOMENICO DA PECCIOLI, 'Cronaca del Convento di S. Caterina di Pisa', *Arch. Stor. ital.*, VI, 2, pp. 399 ff.

EPPING, A., 'Antonius en zijn betekenis voor de Franciscaanse school', *Collect. franc. neerland*, VII (Den Bosch 1949).

ERBACH-FÜRSTENAU, Adalbert Graf zu, *Die Manfredbibel* (Leipzig 1910).

FABRIS, C., *Il più antico Laudario veneto* (Vicenza 1907).

FELDER, I., *Geschichte der wissenschaftlichen Studien im Franziskanerorden* (Freiburg i.B. 1904).

FERRARO, G., *Regola e Laudi dei Servi B.M.V. del 1281 a Bologna* (Livorno 1875).

Fioretti di San Francesco, I.

Fonti per la Storia d'Italia, pubblicate dall'Istituto storico italiano (Rome 1887 ff.).

FOSTER, K., *The Life of Saint Thomas Aquinas: biographical documents* (London 1959).

FRANCIS OF ASSISI, St, *Opuscula* (ed. Quaracchi 1904).

v.s. Bonaventure, *Fioretti, Legenda*, Thomas of Celano.

FREDERICK II, Emperor, *Liber Augustalis* (Constit. reg. utriusque Siciliae), ed. C. Carcani (Naples 1786).

Liber de Arte venandi cum avibus, ed. I G. Schneider (Leipzig 1788–9); modern ed. by K. A. Willemsen (Leipzig 1942).

GALLI, G., 'I Disciplinati dell'Umbria', *Giornale Storico*, suppl. IX (1906).

Laudi inedite dei Disciplinati umbri (Bergamo 1910).

GAMURRINI, G. F., *Gli statuti della pia fraternità di S. Maria d'Arezzo* (Florence 1870).

GASTOUÉ, A., 'Saint François, les frères mineurs et la musique', *Etudes franciscaines*, 1926, pp. 175 ff.

Sur les origines du Dies Irae, ibid., XX, p. 399.

GEBHART, E., *L'Italie mystique* (Paris 1890).

GEMELLI, A., *Il Franciscanesimo* (4th ed., Milan 1942).

GENNRICH, F., *Grundriss einer Formenlehre des mittelalterlichen Liedes* (Halle 1932).

GILSON, E., *Le Thomisme* (Paris 1923; Eng. Tr. E. Bullough, Cambridge 1924; 6th French ed. Paris 1948; Eng. Tr. L. Shook, London 1957).

L'Esprit de la Philosophie mediévale (Paris 1932; Eng. Tr. A. H. C. Downes, London 1936; 2nd French ed., Paris 1944).

La Philosophie de St Bonaventure (Paris 1924; Eng. Tr. I. Trethowan and F. J. Sheed, London 1938; 2nd French ed. Paris 1943).

St Thomas d'Aquin (Paris 1925).

GRABMANN, M., *Mittelalteriches Geistesleben*, 2 vols. (Munich 1926–36).

GRATIEN, Père, *Histoire de la Fondation et de l'Évolution de l'Ordre des Frères Mineurs au XIIIe siècle* (Paris 1928).

GREGOROVIUS, F., *Geschichte der Stadt Rom im Mittelalter*, 6 vols, esp. vol. V (Stuttgart 1878); Eng. Tr. A. Hamilton (London 1894).

GRIMALDI, G., and MONACI, E., 'Laudi dei Disciplinati di S. Croce in Urbino', *Studi romanzi* XII, 1915.

GRUNDMANN, H., *Studien uber Joachim von Floris* (Leipzig-Berlin 1927).

GUIRAUD, J. H., *Histoire de l'Inquisition au moyen âge*, 2 vols. (Paris 1935–8).

GÜTERBOCK, 'Eine Biographie Friedrichs des Zweiten', *Neues Archiv*, XXX, p. 66.

HAMPE, K., 'Kaiser Friedrich II', *Hist. Zeitschrift*, 1899, p. 1. *Das neueste Lebensbild Kaiser Friedrichs II*, ibid., 1932, p. 441.

HASELOFF, A. E. G., *Die Bauten der Hohenstaufen in Unteritalien* (Leipzig 1920).

HASKINS, C. H., *Studies in the History of medieval Science* (Cambridge, Mass., U.S.A. 1924).

HEFELE, K. J., *Die Bettelorden und das religiöse Volksleben Ober- und Mittelitaliens im 13. Jahrhundert* (Leipzig 1910).

HOLDER-EGGER, O., 'Italienische Profetien', *Neues Archiv*, XV, pp. 143 ff.

HUILLARD-BRÉHOLLES, J. L. A., *Historia diplomatica Friderici II*, 6 vols. (Paris 1852–61).

(ed.), *Annales Placentini* (Paris 1856).

HUIZINGA, J., *Geschonden wereld* (Haarlem 1945).

INNOCENT III, Pope, *De contemptu mundi*, in Migne PL 217, col. 701.

IPPOLITI, G., *Dalle Sequenze alle Laudi* (Osimo 1914).

JACOBUS A VITRIACO, *Historia Occidentalis* (Donai 1597).

JACOPONE DA TODI, *Le Laude, secondo la stampa fiorentina del 1490*, ed. G. Ferri (Bari 1915); later ed. (same numbering), *Laudi, Trattato e detti*, ed. F. Agene (Florence 1953).

Le Poesie spirituali, ed. F. Tresatti (Venice 1617).

Le più belle pagine di Fra Jacopone, ed. D. Giuliotti (Milan 1931).

JULIANI A SPIRA, *Officium ac Missa de festo S. P. N. Francisci*, ed. Eliseus Bruning (Rome 1926).

KANTOROWICZ, E., *Kaiser Friedrich II*, 2 vols (Berlin 1927); Eng. Tr. E. O. Lorimer (London 1931, 1957).

LAMPEN, W., 'Intorno al Dies Irae di fra Tommasso da Celano', *Studi francescani*, XIII, pp. 1 ff., 1927.

LANDINI, G., *Il codice aretino 180: Laudi antiche di Cortona* (Rome 1912).

LANZONI, F., *I primordi dell'ordine francescano in Faenza* (Faenza 1910).

Legenda antiqua B. P. N. Francisci, ed. Delorme, in *Arch. franc. hist.*, XV (1922).

Legenda major B. P. N. Francisci, v.s. Bonaventure.

Legenda trium sociorum, ed. Faloci-Pulignani (Foligno 1898).

LEHMANN, Paul, *Die Parodie im Mittelalter* (Munich 1922).

LEMPP, E. (ed.), *Frère Elie de Cortone* (Paris 1901).

LEPITRE, A., *Saint Antoine de Padoue* (6th ed. Paris 1917); Eng. Tr. of earlier ed. E. Guest (London 1902).

LEVI, Eugenia, *Lirica antica italiana* (Florence 1905; 2nd ed. 1908).

Liber censuum, Le, de l'Église romaine, ed. Faber and Duchesne (Paris 1889–1910).

LITTLE, A. G., *Guide to Franciscan Studies* (London 1920).

LIUZZI, Fernando, 'Profilo musicale di Jacopone', *Nuova Antologia,* Sept.–Oct. 1931, pp. 171 ff.

La Lauda e i primordi della melodia italiana, 2 vols. (Rome anno XIII E.F. 1934).

LUCHAIRE, Achille, *Innocent III,* 6 vols. (Paris 1904–8).

Les démocraties italiennes (Paris 1915).

MANCINI, Girolamo, *I manoscritti della libreria del Comune e dell'Accademia Etrusca* (Cortona 1884).

MANDONNET, P., *Dante Théologien* (Paris 1935).

and VICAIRE, M. H., *St Dominique, l'idée, l'homme, l'oeuvre* (2nd ed. Paris 1938); see also under 'Vicaire'.

MARGARET OF CORTONA, St, v.s. Bevegnati.

MARLE, Raimond van, *The Development of the Italian Schools of Painting,* 18 vols. (The Hague 1923), esp. vol. I.

Le Scuole della Pittura italiana (The Hague and Milan 1932), esp. vol. I.

MAZZATINTI, G., 'I Disciplinati di Gubbio et i loro uffici drammatici', *Giornale di filologia romanza* III pp. 85 ff.

'Laudi del Disciplinati di Gubbio', *Il Propugnatore,* II, 1, pp. 145 ff., 1888.

Canti popolari umbri (Bologna 1883).

MAZZONI, Guido, 'Laudi cortonesi del sec. XIII', *Il Propugnatore* II, 2, p. 210 and III 1, pp. 5 ff.

MONACI, E., *Crestomazia italiana dei primi secoli* (Città di Castello 1897); new and revised edition, ed. F. Arese (Città di Castello 1955).

'Uffici drammatici dei Disciplinati d'Umbria', *Rivista di filologia romanza,* I, p. 236.

MONTI, G. M., *Bibliografia della Lauda* (*Bibliofilia,* XXI–XXV).

Gli albori di musica e lirica religiosa italiana (Naples 1921).

Le confraternite medioevali dell'alta e media Italia, 2 vols. (Venice 1927).

Monumenta Germaniae Historica: Scriptores, ed. G. H. Pertz (Hanover 1826 ff.).

MORI, A., *Giullari di Dio* (Milan 1920).

MÜLLER, Eugen, 'Peter von Prezza', *Heidelberger Abhandlungen* 37 (Heidelberg 1913).

MULLER, H. C. A., *Voorlopers en navolgers van Marco Polo* (Leiden 1944).

MURATORI, L. A., *Dissertazioni sopra le antichità italiane* (Milan 1736–7).

Annali d'Italia (Milan 1738).

MUSSAFIA, Adolf, 'Monumenti antichi di dialetti italiani', *Sitzungsbericht der Ks. Akademie der Wissenschaften, Phil.-hist. Klasse XLVI* (Vienna 1864), pp. 140 ff.

NIESE, Hans, 'Zur Geschichte des geistigen Lebens am Hofe Kaiser Friedrichs II', *Hist. Zeitschrift*, 1912, pp. 473 ff.

NOLTHENIUS, H., *Serafijnse muzikanten* (Roeping Febr. 1946).

'Van monniken en minnestrelen in de lagelanden', *Mensch & Melodie*, III, 3, 1948.

'In de spiegel van de Waanzin', *Kroniek voor Kunst en Kultuur*, X, 11.

De oudste Melodiek van Italië: een studie over de muziek van het Duecento (Dissertation: Utrecht 1948).

Novellino, I.: le ciento novelle antike.

OZANAM, A. F., *Les poètes franciscains en Italie au XIIIe siècle* (Paris 1852); Eng. Tr. A. E. Nellen and N. C. Craig (London 1914).

PADOVAN, A., 'Gli uffici drammatici dei Disciplinati di Gubbio', *Arch. stor. per le Marche e per l'Umbria*, I, pp. 1 ff., 1884.

PELLEGRINI, F., 'Alcune forme metriche', *Studi di storia di letteratura italiana e straniera* (Livorno 1895).

PENNACCHI, 'Catalogo delle opere musicali . . . di Assisi', *Pubbl. dell'Assoc. dei Musicologi ital.*, ser. XI (Parma N.D.).

PÈRCOPO, Erasmo, 'Laudi e Devozioni della città di Aquila', *Giornale Storico*, VII, VIII, IX, XII, XV, XVIII, XX.

PERTILE, Antonio, *Storia del Diritto penale* (Turin 1892).

Storia del Diritto privato (Turin 1894).

Storia del Diritto pubblico (Turin 1896).

Storia della Procedura (Turin 1901).

POLO, Marco, *Travels*, ed. L. F. Benedetto, Eng. Tr. Aldo Ricci (London 1931).

POTTHAST, A., *Regesta pontificum Romanorum*, 2 vols (Berolini 1873–5).

RASHDALL, H., *The Universities of Europe in the Middle Ages*, new ed. F. M. Powicke and A. B. Emden, 3 vols (Oxford 1936).

'Registri d'Ugolino d'Ostia e Ottaviano degli Ubaldini', ed. G. Levi, *Fonti per la Storia d'Italia*, VIII (Rome 1900).

RENAN, E., *Averroës et l'Averroïsme* (Paris 1869).

RENIER, Rodolfo, 'Un codice antico di flagellanti della Biblioteca di Cortona', *Giornale Storico*, XI, 1888, pp. 109 ff.

Rerum Italicarum Scriptores, ed. L. A. Muratori (Milan 1723–51); new ed. Città di Castello 1900; quotations from the old edition.

ROCKINGER, L., 'Der Cedrus des Boncompagno', *Quellen zur bayerischen Geschichte*, IX, p. 123.

RONDONI, G., 'Laudi drammatici dei Disciplinati di Siena', *Giornale Storico*, II, 1883, p. 273.

Sacrum Commercium B. Francisci cum Domina Paupertate (Quaracchi 1929).

SALIMBENE DE ADAM OF PARMA, Fra, *Cronica*, in M. G. SS., XXXII. [A more accessible edition is that by F. Bernini (Bari 1942).— Tr.]

SALVATORELLI, L., 'L'Italia comunale', *Storia d'Italia*, vol. IV (Milan 1940).

SALZER, E., *Über di Anfänge der Signorie in Oberitalien* (Berlin 1900).

SANDERS, N., *De preken van Antonius*, in *Collect. franc. neerland.*, VII (Den Bosch 1949).

SASSEN, F., *Thomas van Aquino* (The Hague 1933).

SCARAMUZZI, *La figura intellettuale di S. Antonio di Padova* (Rome 1931).

SCHIFFER, Z., *Markgraf Hubert Pallavicini* (Leipzig 1910).

SCHMITT, Y., 'La metrica di Fra Jacopone', *Studi medievali*, I, 4, p. 513, 1905.

SCHNEEGANZ, H., *Die italienischen Geisslerlieder*, in Runge, *Lieder und Melodien der Geissler des Jahres 1349* (Leipzig 1900), pp. 45 ff.

SCHNÜRER, G., *Kirche und Kultur im Mittelalter*, 3 vols (2nd ed. Paderborn 1929).

SCHÜCK, 'Gedanken über die Zeit der ersten Benutzung des Kompasses', *Archiv für Geschichte der Naturwissenschaft* III [1910], pp. 138 f.

SCHULTZ, A., 'Die Lebensverhältnisse der italienischen Trobadors', *Zeitschrift für roman. Philologie*, VII, pp. 175 ff.

SCIPIONI, G. S., 'Tre laudi sacre pesaresi', *Giornale Storico*, VI, 1885, p. 212.

SESINI, U., *Le melodie trobadoriche nel canzoniere provenzale della Biblioteca Ambrosiana* (Turin 1942).

Speculum Perfectionis, ed. P. Sabatier (Paris 1898).

STAAF, E., *Le Laudario di Pisa du Ms. 8521 de la Bibliethèque de l'Arsénal de Paris* (Uppsala 1931).

STIEVE, F., *Ezzelino von Romano* (Leipzig 1909).

STRAUSS, 'Die Juden im Königreich Sizilien unter Normannen und Staufern', *Heidelberger Abhandlungen* 30 (Heidelberg 1910).

SUTTER, Karl, *Johann von Vicenza und die italienische Friedensbewegung* (Freiburg i.B. 1891).

SZOMBATHELY, de, *Re Enzo nella storia e nella leggenda* (Bologna 1912).

TARGIONI-TOZZETTI, O., Antologia di Poesia italiana (Leghorn 1885).

TENNERONI, A., *Lo Stabat Mater e la Donna del Paradiso* (Rome 1887).

Due antiche Laudi a S. Francesco (Rome 1901).

Inizii di antiche poesie religiose e morali (Florence 1909).

THODE, Henry, *Franz von Assisi und die Anfänge der Kunst der Renaissance in Italien* (Berlin 1885; Vienna 1936).

THOMAS AQUINAS, St, *Summa Theologica*.

THOMAS OF CANTIMPRÉ, *Liber Apum* (Douai 1597).

THOMAS OF CELANO, *S. Francisci Assisiensis Vita I* and *Vita II*, ed. U. d'Alençon (Rome 1906), ed. Quaracchi 1926–7, 1941.

TORRACA, F., *Studi sulla lirica italiana del Duecento* (Bologna 1902).

TOSCHI, P., *La poesia popolare religiosa in Italia* (Florence 1935).

UBERTINO a Casale, *Arbor Vitae Crucifixae Jesu* (Venice 1485).

UNDERHILL, E., *Jacopone da Todi, poet and mystic* (London 1919).

VICAIRE, M. H., *St Dominic and his Times* (London 1964). [The modern biography that has superseded all previous work.—Tr.]

VILLANI, *Istoria di Firenze*, in RIS, XIII.

VOLPE, N., *Movimenti religiosi e setti hereticali nella società medievale italiana* (Florence 1922).

WALSH, J., *The thirteenth, greatest of centuries* (New York 1924 and many eds to 1946).

WALZ, Angelus, *St Thomas Aquinas* (Eng. Tr. S. Bullough, Westminster, Maryland, U.S.A. 1951) [A standard modern biography.—Tr.]

WELY, van, 'De bronnen voor het leven van Antonius', *Collect. franc. neerland.*, VII (Den Bosch 1949).

WILLEMSEN, K. A., *Apulien, Land der Normannen, Land der Staufer* (4th ed., Leipzig 1944).

(ed.) *Liber de Arte venandi*, v.s. Frederick.

ZACCHETTI, *Laude sacre di Fontecolombo* (Oneglia 1898).

ZONTA, G., *Storia della letteratura italiana*, 3 vols (Turin 1928), esp. vol. I.

Acknowledgements

The photographs specially taken for this book are by Lala Aufsberg, of Sonthofen, Allgäu. No. 1 is reproduced through the kindness of the German Archaeological Institute in Rome. Nos 2, 6, 9, 10 and 20 are taken from the book of Hubert Graf Waldburg-Wolfegg, *Vom Südreich der Hofenstaufen* (photographs by Lala Aufsberg), by kind permission of the publishers Schnell und Steiner, Munich and Zurich. Nos 12, 24, 34, 44, 47, 48 are by Alinari, Florence. Nos 7, 33, 43, 45, and 46 were taken by the author and others.